Boswell's *Life of Johnson* is established as one of the foremost literary biographies in the English language. This collection of new essays, commemorating its bicentenary, investigates Boswell's achievements and limitations in both literary and personal contexts, and goes beyond the *Life* to examine the full range of Boswell's writings and interests (in legal, social, theological, political, and linguistic fields). Drawing Boswell out of Johnson's shadow, the volume places him in a wider context, juxtaposing Boswell with other contemporaries and compatriots in the Scottish enlightenment, such as Hume, Robertson, and Blair. In addition it investigates some of the critical and theoretical questions surrounding the notion of biographical representation in the *Life* itself. Boswell emerges as a writer engaged throughout his literary career in constructing a self or series of selves out of his divided Scottish identity.

This collection combines new archival research with fresh critical perspectives and constitutes a timely review of Boswell's current status in eighteenth-century literary studies.

NEW LIGHT ON BOSWELL

One of the first pages of the manuscript of Boswell's *Life of Johnson*. (The Beinecke Rare Book and Manuscript Library, Yale University)

NEW LIGHT
ON BOSWELL

CRITICAL AND
HISTORICAL ESSAYS ON THE
OCCASION OF THE BICENTENARY OF
THE LIFE OF JOHNSON

EDITED BY
GREG CLINGHAM

WITH AN INTRODUCTION BY
DAVID DAICHES

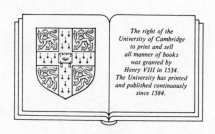

The right of the
University of Cambridge
to print and sell
all manner of books
was granted by
Henry VIII in 1534.
The University has printed
and published continuously
since 1584.

CAMBRIDGE UNIVERSITY PRESS

CAMBRIDGE

NEW YORK   PORT CHESTER   MELBOURNE   SYDNEY

Published by the Press Syndicate of the University of Cambridge
The Pitt Building, Trumpington Street, Cambridge CB2 1RP
40 West 20th Street, New York, NY 10011, USA
10 Stamford Road, Oakleigh, Melbourne 3166, Australia

First published 1991

Printed in Great Britain at the
University Press, Cambridge

British Library cataloguing in publication data

New light on Boswell: critical and historical essays on the
occasion of the bicentenary of the *Life of Johnson*.
1. Prose in English. Boswell, James, 1740–95
1. Clingham, Greg
828.608

Library of Congress cataloguing in publication data
New light on Boswell: critical and historical essays on the occasion
of the bicentenary of the *Life of Johnson* / edited by Greg Clingham;
with an introduction by David Daiches.
p. cm.
Includes index.
ISBN 0 521 38047 2 (hardback)
1. Boswell, James. 1740 – 1795. Life of Samuel Johnson.
2. Authors, English – 18th century – Biography – History and criticism.
3. Johnson, Samuel, 1709–1784 – Biography. 4. Biography (as a
literary form) 1. Clingham. Greg.
PR3533.B7N49 1991
828'.609—dc20 90-39992 CIP
ISBN 0 521 38047 2

CONTENTS

vii

NOTES ON CONTRIBUTORS

DAVID DAICHES has taught at universities on both sides of the Atlantic, including Edinburgh, Oxford, Chicago, Cornell, Cambridge, and Sussex. He has published some forty-five books, including *A Critical History of English Literature, The Novel and the Modern World, Critical Approaches to Literature, The Paradox of Scottish Culture, Robert Burns, James Boswell and His World,* and *God and the Poets,* which were the Gifford lectures for 1983. David Daiches was most recently Professor of English at Sussex University, and, from 1980–6, Director of the Institute for Advanced Studies in the Humanities at Edinburgh University. He is now retired.

THOMAS CRAWFORD is Honorary Reader in English at the University of Aberdeen, and the author of *Burns: A Study of the Poems and Songs* (1960), *Scott* (1965), *Society and the Lyric* (1979), and *Boswell, Burns, and the French Revolution* (1990). He is currently editing the correspondence between Boswell and W. J. Temple, and preparing a selection of Boswell's writings on Scotland. Thomas Crawford is Convener of the public board of the Association for Scottish Literary Studies, and is a member of the editorial committee of the Yale Edition of the Private Papers of James Boswell.

RICHARD B. SHER is Associate Dean of the College of Science and Liberal Arts and Associate Professor of History at New Jersey Institute of Technology. He is the author of *Church and University in the Scottish Enlightenment: The Moderate Literati of Edinburgh* (co-published by Princeton and Edinburgh University presses) as well as many articles and reviews on different aspects of eighteenth-century Scotland. Among his current projects is an interdisciplinary collection of essays on Scotland and America in the eighteenth century that will be co-edited by Jeffrey Smitten. Richard Sher is founder and Executive Secretary of the Eighteenth-Century Scottish Studies Society.

PAT ROGERS is DeBartolo Professor in the Liberal Arts, University of South Florida, at Tampa. Formerly President of the Johnson Society and of the British Society for Eighteenth-Century Studies, he has written widely on Johnson and Boswell, including the introduction to the World's Classics edition of Boswell's *Life of Johnson*. He is the editor of the *Oxford Illustrated History of English Literature* (1987, 1990), and an Advisory Editor of the *Blackwell Companion to the Enlightenment* (forthcoming). He has also recently published on Reynolds, Horace Walpole, Sarah Siddons, and Richardson.

JOAN H. PITTOCK is Senior Lecturer in English and Convener of the Cultural History degree at the University of Aberdeen. She is one of the founding editors of the *British Journal for Eighteenth-Century Studies* and was President of the Society in 1980–2. Joan Pittock has published books on seventeenth- and eighteenth-century literary history and co-edited collections of essays on cultural history. She is currently working on the history of the Oxford Chair of Poetry, and on literature and childhood.

THOMAS M. CURLEY is Professor of English at Bridgewater State College, Massachusetts. He has written extensively on the Age of Johnson, and has most recently edited a two-volume edition of Sir Robert Chambers's *A Course of Lectures on the English Law* (written with Samuel Johnson's assistance), and published by the University of Wisconsin Press and the Clarendon Press in 1986. He is currently at work on a biography, *Sir Robert Chambers, Law and Empire in the Age of Johnson*.

GORDON TURNBULL is an Assistant Professor of English at Yale University, where he is pursuing research on Boswell. Among his publications is the essay on Boswell for the *History of Scottish Literature*, II (1660–1800), ed. Andrew Hook (Aberdeen University Press, 1987).

RICHARD B. SCHWARTZ is the author of *Samuel Johnson and the New Science*, *Samuel Johnson and the Problem of Evil*, *Boswell's Johnson: A Preface to the "LIFE,"* and *Daily Life in Johnson's London*. He has edited *The Plays of Arthur Murphy* and *Theory and Tradition in Eighteenth-Century Studies*. He recently published a novel, *Frozen Stare*. Richard Schwartz is Professor of English and Dean of the Graduate School of Arts and Sciences at Georgetown University.

SUSAN MANNING is Assistant Lecturer in English, Cambridge University, and a Fellow of Newnham College. Her book *The Puritan–Provincial Vision*, a study of Scottish and American literature, was published by Cambridge University Press in 1990. She has also published articles on Hawthorne and Poe, on Hume and Scott, and is at present working on an edition of Scott's *Quentin Durward* and on a book on the art of pleasure in the eighteenth century.

JOHN J. BURKE, JR. is Professor of English and director of the English Honors Program at the University of Alabama in Tuscaloosa. He had chief responsibility for the volume *The Unknown Samuel Johnson* (1983). Since then he has published essays in *Boswell's "Life of Johnson": New Questions, New Answers* (1985); *Fresh Reflections on Samuel Johnson* (1987); and *The Age of Johnson*, II (1989). During 1990–1 he will be serving as president of SEASECS (Southeastern American Society for Eighteenth-Century Studies).

MARLIES K. DANZIGER is Professor of English at Hunter College and the Graduate School of the City University of New York. She is the editor, with Frank Brady, of *Boswell: The Great Biographer*, the recently-published last volume of the trade edition of Boswell's journals; her previous writings include *Goldsmith and Sheridan* and *Samuel Johnson on Literature*.

PAUL J. KORSHIN is Professor of English at the University of Pennsylvania. He recently edited *Johnson After Two Hundred Years* (1986) and is also the editor of *The Age of Johnson: A Scholarly Annual*. He is at work on a critical study of *The Rambler* that will be entitled *Samuel Johnson at Mid Century: A Study of "The Rambler."*

DONNA HEILAND is an Assistant Professor of English at Vassar College. She has done both editorial and critical work on Boswell, and is currently at work on a study entitled "Fictions of Empire: Eighteenth-Century Novels and the Question of Colonization."

GREG CLINGHAM taught English at Cambridge before moving to Fordham University, New York, where he is an Assistant Professor. He has published on Johnson, Dryden, Boswell, and other eighteenth-century figures in American, British, and French journals. His *Boswell: The Life of Johnson* is forthcoming in the Cambridge University Press Landmarks of World Literature series. He is currently completing a critical study of Johnson's *Lives of the Poets*.

PREFACE

James Boswell has been known as the author of one book, and that a very influential and, more recently, a very controversial one. After two hundred years Boswell's *Life of Johnson* (1791) is still widely read, and generates more debate as to its truth, its self-revelatory nature, and what it tells us about Johnson than it has at any time in the past. But whatever Boswell's strengths and shortcomings as a biographer, the portrait of Johnson that concludes the *Life* represents a summation of the biographer's efforts at grasping, understanding and passing on to posterity the essence of the man he revered so highly, and in relation to whom he expended much effort and ingenuity in defining himself. It is therefore fitting that this collection of essays, taking the occasion of the bicentenary of the *Life* to explore the relationship between Boswell's complex talents and his commitment to "writing the self," should be prefaced by the portrait of Johnson that concludes the *Life*. The following passage comes from *Boswell's Life of Johnson*, ed. G. B. Hill, revised and enlarged by L. F. Powell, 6 vols. (Oxford: Clarendon Press, 1934–64), IV, 425–30.

> His figure was large and well formed, and his countenance of the cast of an ancient statue; yet his appearance was rendered strange and somewhat uncouth, by convulsive cramps, by the scars of that distemper which it was once imagined the royal touch could cure, and by a slovenly mode of dress. He had the use only of one eye; yet so much does mind govern and even supply the deficiency of organs, that his visual perceptions, as far as they extended, were uncommonly quick and accurate. So morbid was his temperament, that he never knew the natural joy of a free and vigorous use of his limbs: when he walked, it was like the struggling gait of one in fetters; when he rode, he had no command or direction of his horse, but was carried as if in a balloon. That with his constitution and habits of life he should have lived seventy-five years, is a proof that an inherent *vivida vis* is a powerful preservative of the human frame.
>
> Man is, in general, made up of contradictory qualities; and these will ever shew themselves in strange succession, where a consistency in appearance at least, if not in reality, has not been attained by long habits of philosophical discipline. In proportion to the native vigour of the mind, the contradictory

qualities will be the more prominent, and more difficult to be adjusted; and, therefore, we are not to wonder, that Johnson exhibited an eminent example of this remark which I have made upon human nature. At different times, he seemed a different man, in some respects; not, however, in any great or essential article, upon which he had fully employed his mind, and settled certain principles of duty, but only in his manners, and in the display of argument and fancy in his talk. He was prone to superstition, but not to credulity. Though his imagination might incline him to a belief of the marvellous and the mysterious, his vigorous reason examined the evidence with jealousy. He was a sincere and zealous Christian, of high Church-of-England and monarchical principles, which he would not tamely suffer to be questioned; and had, perhaps, at an early period, narrowed his mind somewhat too much, both as to religion and politicks. His being impressed with the danger of extreme latitude in either, though he was of a very independent spirit, occasioned his appearing somewhat unfavourable to the prevalence of that noble freedom of sentiment which is the best possession of man. Nor can it be denied, that he had many prejudices; which, however, frequently suggested many of his pointed sayings, that rather shew a playfulness of fancy than any settled malignity. He was steady and inflexible in maintaining the obligations of religion and morality; both from a regard for the order of society, and from a veneration for the GREAT SOURCE of all order; correct, nay stern in his taste; hard to please, and easily offended; impetuous and irritable in his temper, but of a most humane and benevolent heart, which shewed itself not only in a most liberal charity, as far as his circumstances would allow, but in a thousand instances of active benevolence. He was afflicted with a bodily disease, which made him often restless and fretful; and with a constitutional melancholy, the clouds of which darkened the brightness of his fancy, and gave a gloomy cast to his whole course of thinking: we, therefore, ought not to wonder at his sallies of impatience and passion at any time; especially when provoked by obtrusive ignorance, or presuming petulance; and allowance must be made for his uttering hasty and satirical sallies, even against his best friends. And, surely, when it is considered, that, "amidst sickness and sorrow," he exerted his faculties in so many works for the benefit of mankind, and particularly that he atchieved the great and admirable DICTIONARY of our language, we must be astonished at his resolution. The solemn text, "of him to whom much is given, much will be required," seems to have been ever present to his mind, in a rigorous sense, and to have made him dissatisfied with his labours and acts of goodness, however comparatively great; so that the unavoidable consciousness of his superiority was, in that respect, a cause of disquiet. He suffered so much from this, and from the gloom which perpetually haunted him, and made solitude frightful, that it may be said of him, "If in this life only he had hope, he was of all men most miserable." He loved praise, when it was brought to him; but was too proud to seek for it. He was somewhat susceptible of flattery. As he was general and unconfined in his studies, he cannot be considered as master of any one particular science; but he had accumulated a vast and various collection of learning and knowledge, which was so arranged in his mind, as to be ever in readiness to be brought forth. But his superiority over other learned men consisted chiefly in what may be called the art of thinking, the art of using his mind; a certain continual power of seizing the useful substance of all that he knew, and exhibiting it in a clear and forcible manner; so that knowledge, which we often see to be no better than lumber in men of dull understanding, was, in him, true, evident, and actual wisdom. His moral precepts are practical; for they are drawn from an intimate acquaintance with human nature. His maxims carry conviction; for they are founded on the basis of common sense, and a very attentive and minute survey of real life. His mind was so full of imagery, that he might have been perpetually a poet; yet it is remarkable, that, however rich his prose is in this respect, his poetical pieces, in general, have not much of that splendour, but are rather distinguished by strong sentiment, and acute observation, conveyed in harmonious and energetick verse, particularly in heroick couplets. Though usually grave, and even aweful, in his deportment, he possessed uncommon and peculiar powers of wit and humour; he frequently indulged himself in colloquial pleasantry; and the heartiest merriment was often enjoyed in his company; with this great advantage, that as it was entirely free from any poisonous tincture of vice or impiety, it was salutary to those who shared in it. He had accustomed himself to such accuracy in his common conversation, that he at all times expressed his thoughts with great force, and an elegant choice of language, the effect of which was aided by his having a loud voice, and a slow deliberate utterance. In him were united a most logical head with a most fertile imagination, which gave him an extraordinary advantage in arguing: for he could reason close or wide, as he saw best for the moment. Exulting in his intellectual strength and dexterity, he could, when he pleased, be the greatest sophist that ever contended in the lists of declamation; and, from a spirit of contradiction, and a delight in shewing his powers, he would often maintain the wrong side with equal warmth and ingenuity; so that, when there was an audience, his real opinions could seldom be gathered from his talk; though when he was in company with a single friend, he would discuss a subject with genuine fairness: but he was too conscientious to make errour permanent and pernicious, by deliberately writing it; and, in all his numerous works, he earnestly inculcated what appeared to him to be the truth; his piety being constant, and the ruling principle of all his conduct.

Such was SAMUEL JOHNSON, a man whose talents, acquirements, and virtues, were so extraordinary, that the more his character is considered, the more he will be regarded by the present age, and by posterity, with admiration and reverence.

ACKNOWLEDGEMENTS

I wish to thank Fordham University and the National Endowment for the Humanities for financial assistance in preparing this collection. Howard Erskine-Hill helped to get this project off the ground and supported it throughout. The interest and acumen of Kevin Taylor, my editor at Cambridge, strengthened this book and facilitated its production. I would also like to thank the contributors, who made this book possible; and my students at Fordham, who listened to my talking about Boswell with a kindly skepticism and exemplary good humor.

ABBREVIATIONS

Life	James Boswell, *The Life of Samuel Johnson, LL.D.*, *with a Journal of a Tour to the Hebrides*, ed. G. B. Hill, rev. L. F. Powell, 6 vols. (Oxford: Clarendon Press, 1934–64).
Letters Erskine	*Letters between the Honourable Andrew Erskine and James Boswell, Esq.* (London, 1763).
Account of Corsica	James Boswell, *An Account of Corsica, The Journal of a Tour to that Island; and Memoirs of Pascal Paoli* (Glasgow and London, 1768).
Letters	*The Letters of James Boswell*, ed. C. B. Tinker, 2 vols. (Oxford: Clarendon Press, 1924).
Hypochondriack	*The Hypochondriack* (James Boswell's essays appearing in the *London Magazine*, November 1777 to August 1783), ed. Margery Bailey, 2 vols. (Stanford: Stanford University Press, 1928).

THE YALE EDITIONS OF THE PRIVATE PAPERS OF JAMES BOSWELL

"Trade" edition

London Journal	*Boswell's London Journal, 1762–1763*, ed. Frederick A. Pottle (New York: McGraw-Hill, 1950; London: Heinemann, 1951).
Boswell in Holland	*Boswell in Holland, 1763–1764*, ed. Frederick A. Pottle (New York: McGraw-Hill and London: Heinemann, 1952).
Grand Tour I	*Boswell on the Grand Tour: Germany and Switzerland, 1764*, ed. Frederick A. Pottle (New York: McGraw-Hill and London: Heinemann, 1953).
In Search of a Wife	*Boswell in Search of a Wife, 1766–1769*, ed. Frank Brady and Frederick A. Pottle (New York: McGraw-Hill, 1956; London: Heinemann, 1957).

Defence   *Boswell for the Defence, 1769–1774*, ed.
                           William K. Wimsatt, Jr. and Frederick A.
                           Pottle (New York: McGraw-Hill, 1959;
                           London: Heinemann, 1960).

Ominous Years   *Boswell: The Ominous Years, 1774–1776*, ed.
                           Charles Ryskamp and Frederick A. Pottle
                           (New York: McGraw-Hill and London:
                           Heinemann, 1963).

Boswell in Extremes   *Boswell in Extremes, 1776–1778*, ed. C. M.
                           Weiss and Frederick A. Pottle (New York:
                           McGraw-Hill, 1970).

Laird   *Boswell: Laird of Auchinleck, 1778–1782*, ed.
                           Joseph W. Reed and Frederick A. Pottle (New
                           York: McGraw-Hill, 1977).

Applause   *Boswell: The Applause of the Jury, 1782–1785*,
                           ed. Irma S. Lustig (New York, Toronto, and
                           London: McGraw-Hill, 1981).

English Experiment   *Boswell: The English Experiment, 1785–1789*,
                           ed. Irma S. Lustig and Frederick A. Pottle
                           (New York, Toronto, and London: Heine-
                           mann, 1986).

Great Biographer   *Boswell: The Great Biographer*, ed. Marlies K.
                           Danziger and Frank Brady (New York and
                           Toronto: McGraw-Hill and London: Heine-
                           mann, 1989).

Research edition
Corr: Grange   *The Correspondence of James Boswell and John
                           Johnston of Grange*, ed. R. S. Walker (New
                           York: McGraw-Hill and London: Heinemann,
                           1966).

Corr: Life   *The Correspondence and Other Papers of James
                           Boswell Relating to the Making of the "Life of
                           Johnson,"* ed. Marshall Waingrow (New York:
                           McGraw-Hill and London: Heinemann,
                           1969).

Corr: Garrick, Burke, Malone   *The Correspondence of James Boswell with David
                           Garrick, Edmund Burke, and Edmund Malone*,
                           ed. (Burke) Thomas W. Copeland, Peter S.
                           Baker, Rachel McClellan, Robert Mankin,
                           and Mark Wollaeger; (Garrick) George M.
                           Kahrl and Rachel McClellan; and (Malone)
                           James M. Osborn and Peter S. Baker (New
                           York: McGraw-Hill and London: Heinemann,
                           1986).

Earlier Years   Frederick A. Pottle, *James Boswell: The Earlier Years, 1740–1769* (New York: McGraw-Hill, 1966).

Later Years   Frank Brady, *James Boswell: The Later Years, 1769–1795* (New York: McGraw-Hill, 1984).

New Questions, New Answers   John A. Vance (ed.), *Boswell's "Life of Johnson": New Questions, New Answers* (Athens, Ga: University of Georgia Press, 1985).

INTRODUCTION: BOSWELL'S AMBIGUITIES

David Daiches

James Boswell remains one of the most fascinating and puzzling figures in literary history. Regarded at one time as a shallow egoist who succeeded by some kind of naive mimetic ability in producing one of the greatest of biographies, thus becoming an accidental genius, he is now visible to us as a much more complex and artful person whose inner tensions and contradictions are bound up with remarkable talents. The massive Boswell repository now at Yale, with its diaries, letters, notes, drafts, and other manuscripts, has yielded and continues to yield multiple new insights into Boswell's mind and art. No fully agreed synthesis has emerged. As the following pages show, it is possible to explain and evaluate Boswell and his work in many different ways and to interpret the relation between his life and character on the one hand and his literary output on the other very diversely. There is no dispute, however, about his *interestingness* or, in spite of the various ways in which his sensibility can be related to moods and fashions of his age, about his originality.

Before the publication of his journals, Boswell's fame rested almost entirely on his *Life of Johnson*, though his *Journal of a Tour to the Hebrides with Samuel Johnson LL.D.* and, to a lesser extent, his *Journal of a Tour to Corsica* were also admired. But his diaries and the other papers now at Yale have enlarged the whole context of our awareness of the man and his complexities and enabled us to read the familiar works with new eyes. We can see him as just as brilliant in laying out his own character as he is in presenting that of another. We can see him as the great interviewer. We can see in his remarkable counterpointing of his own personality with that of others a balancing of subject and object that yields unique results. We can see him as the inveterate role-taker. We can see in his shifting moods and changing ambitions both the sensibility of his age and the special qualities of his own character. And we can see in the continuing alternation between the proud Scottish laird vaunting his high Scottish pedigree and the past glories of his native country and the passionate Londoner who relished what he called the "English juiciness of mind" as opposed to what he considered the narrow

provincialism of Edinburgh (even the Edinburgh of the Scottish Enlightenment) an illustration of the cultural schizophrenia that had been developing
in Scotland ever since the Union of 1707. We can thus look at history
through Boswell or at Boswell through history. Whichever way we do it,
Boswell acts as an illuminator.

The paradoxes abound. Boswell the egoist continually fascinated by his
own states of mind is also, as Gordon Turnbull reminds us, Boswell the
lawyer who virtually destroyed his chances of promotion in the Scottish bar
by his passionate identification with his clients and his inability to separate
his role as legal representative from that of sympathizer and rescuer. Boswell
the self-proclaimed genius could belittle or even ridicule himself in order to
set off the character of a man he hero-worshiped, and he could also use his
hero as fuel for his own self-esteem. Boswell the writer of the greatest
biography in English is also the biographer who is incapable of real empathy
with his subject but, as Greg Clingham's essay suggests, shows him off
rather than enters in loving comprehension into the inwardness of his life
and work. Boswell the conservative lover of Catholic and Anglican ritual is
also, as Richard Sher points out, Boswell the Scottish defender of populist
theology against the conservative Moderates. Boswell the spontaneous
correspondent is also, as Thomas Crawford shows, the skillful manipulator
of different epistolary styles that reflect not only different moods but also
different orders of friendship. The list is endless. He tells us of his sexual
fantasies and plannings while in a mood of pious devotion in church. We can
set his perpetual worrying about the nature of God and the reality of a future
state against his compulsive whoring and drinking bouts. Above all, there is
the contrast between the Boswell who is at the mercy of his moods and
appetites with the artist in superb control of his material who constructs,
organizes, patterns, arranges, balances.

There is thus no other writer in the English language who cries out for
examination by different readers from different points of view to the degree
that Boswell does. His chameleon quality demands that he be looked at from
different angles. Johnson himself seems to have been able to see Boswell
from many points of view simultaneously. He understood his moods of
melancholy, he understood the tensions in his relations with his father, he
understood and encouraged and enjoyed his activities as a diarist, he
relished Boswell's moods of gaiety and extrovert exuberance, he appreciated
(probably more profoundly than he ever told Boswell) his religious doubts
and difficulties, he was aware of Boswell's search for a father-figure and was
prepared to play that role for him, he sympathized with and encouraged
Boswell's feelings as a Scottish landowner with position and responsibilities,
he was well aware of Boswell's manipulation of him in order to provide
memorable scenes and sayings (and sometimes protested about it). In fact –
and this is another paradox – the subject understood the biographer more

profoundly than the biographer understood the subject. It was part of Boswell's genius that he was able to reveal this without being fully aware of what he was revealing.

"By a Genius" was the phrase put on the title page of an otherwise anonymous pamphlet published by Boswell in 1760, when he had just turned twenty years of age. This was partly self-mockery and partly serious. Boswell from an early age thought himself destined to greatness, though he kept changing his mind about the kind of greatness he aimed at. In February 1763 he protested in a lively letter to Lord Eglinton that he was a genius and wrote his hoped-for obituary describing James Boswell as an amiable man who improved and beautified his ancestral estate of Auchinleck, distinguished himself in Parliament, commanded a regiment of Foot Guards, "and was one of the brightest wits in the court of George the Third." Thus he looked forward to economic, political, military, and social success but, unless the notion of writer is included in "wit," not specifically as a man of letters. Yet he began writing at an early age – verses, newspaper articles, pamphlets, not to mention his journals – and maintained strong literary interests all his life. It took him a long time, though, to concede that his main role in life was to be literary. A few months before his death he wrote to his son James, "I cannot be contented with merely literary fame, and social enjoyments. I must still hope for some credible employment." He meant employment in law or politics in England. Yet he took pride in the acclaim with which his *Life of Johnson* was received. His journals, of course, remained unpublished and unknown (apart from those of his journey to Corsica and to the Hebrides with Johnson) until the present century. For all his enormous vanity, it can be said that Boswell hid his true light under a bushel.

There is something oddly dispassionate in Boswell's awareness of himself. His egotism and ambition were not ruthless forces driving him on to pursue success in a chosen career; they were products of a curiosity about himself of the same kind as his curiosity about other people. He is fully aware of the chameleon element in his own character, of his need to model himself now on this man and now on that, and he positively relishes the contradictions that he observes in his own nature. He sees himself as an actor, sometimes also as a producer, and even occasionally as author or part-author of the play in which he and his friends and associates are taking part. His passion for the stage manifested itself at an early age and, as Susan Manning makes clear in her essay, is an important clue to his character. An actor is supposed to be able to get out of himself and enter into the personality of the character he is acting. In a sense this is what Boswell often did – seeing himself as Rousseau or Voltaire before presenting himself to each of them so that he could know what aspect of him they would be most likely to respond to. When he sought Rousseau's advice or pressed Voltaire to tell him what he really believed about religion he was speaking, as it were, in each case from within the other person's consciousness, having prepared himself by studying it and imaginatively entering into it. At the same time we can hear the note of personal anxiety in Boswell's attempt to push Voltaire into confessing to more than he believed. This emerges more clearly and more consistently in his relation to Johnson. From Johnson he wanted approval and reassurance; he would have liked (but consistently failed to receive) Johnson's approval of "patriarchal" sexual practices and he sought and obtained qualified reassurance with respect to Christianity and an afterlife. But he also tried in a way to *become* Johnson before engaging in conversation with him so that he could know to what aspects of his mind and emotions he could most successfully appeal. Yet, as more than one of the writers here argue, he never entered the totality of Johnson's self. Donna Heiland, Greg Clingham, and Marlies Danziger each illuminate in a different way some aspect of the difference between subject and object in Boswell's great biography. Some gap is of course inevitable. If A writes about B, A must clearly be distinguished from B if the account is to have any significance. Biography is not autobiography. But a biographer (or interviewer or character-sketcher) who is aware of the contradictory facets of his *own* character can make an attempt to angle those facets most consonant with the character of his subject and so be a different person, as it were, in writing about Johnson from the person he is when writing about Rousseau or Wilkes or Paoli. Consider, as Richard Schwartz does, Boswell's relation to Hume. Here there was no facet of Boswell's character other than the purely social and convivial that he could wheel into position when confronting Hume so as to penetrate the reality of Hume's character and beliefs. The dream he had in later life that told him that Hume had been only joking when professing skepticism is the measure of the gap between the two characters. Among his many selves, of which he was so conscious, Boswell did not have a self that could mesh with that of Hume. And if it can be argued that he did not have a self that could mesh with that of Johnson either, that he venerated rather than loved Johnson and showed him off rather than entered into his very self, one can only reply that here is a question of degree. In some ways – limited certainly, but real – there was a Johnsonian Boswell and it could be brought into play by Boswell for his own purpose. It cannot be said that there was in any way a Humean Boswell.

It might perhaps be said that Boswell's role vis-à-vis the characters he interviewed or wrote about was the very reverse of that of the "impartial spectator" that Adam Smith, whose lectures Boswell had heard in Glasgow, postulated as the theoretical arbiter of moral approval. Boswell aimed to be the *partial* spectator, not in the sense that he imposed his own interests on those of his subject but that he wanted to take his subject's part, to enter into him. And if even with Johnson he could not wholly succeed in this aim, it was nevertheless what he hoped and tried to do. Of course in a sense all human

relations are of this kind. There are few of us who do not in some degree
attempt to angle ourselves towards the person with whom we are trying to
relate: aggressive self-assertion is very much the exception in social intercourse. Dr. Johnson in his social relationships might appear to have been
aggressively self-assertive, yet there is ample evidence that this was a superficial overlay and underneath he often was, as he showed in his *Lives of the
Poets*, a man of surprisingly widely accommodating sympathies.

Boswell's procedure as a writer is far removed from that recommended by
Stephen Dedalus in Joyce's *Portrait of the Artist as a Young Man*, where the
ideal artist is described as being "like the God of creation, [remaining] within
or behind or beyond or above his handiwork." His is the supreme example of
a refusal to withdraw from his handiwork, and it is that refusal that justifies
our concern to probe the relation between self and literary achievement in
his life and work. Shakespeare has invited many more critics than Boswell
has done, but inquiries into Shakespeare the man, though not uncommon at
one time, represent an eccentric and even unreal aspect of the Shakespearean critical tradition: overwhelmingly critics have concerned themselves
with the meaning of the text or with the bibliographical questions involved in
establishing the text of the plays. Boswell invites questioning in a special way.
If he is not our greatest writer, he is one of our most fascinating.

There remains the question of Boswell's uniqueness. As we read his
journals it sometimes appears that he is like the rest of us, only more so. His
varying moods, his combination of sensuality and moral earnestness, his
curiosity about himself and others, his vanity and self-doubts, his role-
modelling, are all recognizable aspects of the human condition. Is it his
frankness about all this that is so exceptional? Is it the abandon with which he
moves from one aspect of his nature to another that is so remarkable? There
are few readers of the journals who cannot help feeling at some point and in
some sense *de te fabula*, that the story is about themselves. But how does this
relate to his consummate ability as an interviewer and a biographer? The
quality of his ability to angle different aspects of his character towards
different subjects, which I have discussed, is surely highly unusual. One
might say that it is not Boswell's character that is so unusual, but the way he
displays it and exploits it.

It would be misleading, however, to regard this as in any way dishonest.
The aspects of his character that he revolves for his own contemplation and
as an aid to invoking the character of others really did exist and were not
distorted in the exposure. The counterpointing of exhibitionism and
sympathy is both remarkable and genuine. It was this that attracted people to
Boswell. "Give me your hand. I have taken a liking to you." This famous
declaration of Johnson's is only one, if the most memorable, of many
instances of Boswell's capacity to attract affection. We know that his cousin
Margaret loved him long before he proposed to her and that she retained

that love in spite of Boswell's regular desertions to London and of his frequent bouts of drunkenness and whoring. She could have had no more illusions about him than the modern reader of his devastatingly frank journals can have. And the modern reader of the journals is also aware of Boswell's attractiveness. We may feel distaste, disapproval, even at times revulsion, but this posturing exhibitionist, this compulsive self-examiner, this inquisitive contemplator of other people's natures, subject to periodic bouts of disabling melancholy and subject also to an almost ludicrous degree to virtually all the weaknesses of the flesh, retains – indeed compels – our sympathy.

How far is dependence on the self a trustworthy road to literary excellence in biography and autobiography? Boswell's dependence was far from consistent or naive; as Marlies Danziger shows, in his *Life of Johnson* he counterpoints self-display and self-restraint and can in various ways and for various purposes subsume personal feeling in abstract generalization. It can also be argued, as Joan Pittock suggests, that Boswell's volatile egotistic vision cuts across eighteenth-century critical conventions and strikes a curiously modern note. Part of the answer to my question lies in the fact that Boswell was not in fact crudely dependent on his own egotistical responses, but selected, organized, manipulated and, in the *Life of Johnson*, even suppressed them. The self was a tool at the writer's disposal. This may seem very like the Romantic view of literature as personal confession, with its dependence on individual sensitivity and its tendency to view literature as the record of those "spots of time" (in Wordsworth's phrase) in which the writer's awareness is suddenly enlarged. But Boswell's practice was really very different. To see the self as the writer's tool rather than the writer's guide is very much an eighteenth-century view, one associated principally with Sterne, who of course had considerable influence on Boswell's writing. Further, the self – as much modern criticism holds – can be a critical and exegetical device for interrogating the literary text and extracting new meanings from it: it is, one might almost say, the essential tool of de-constructionalism, enabling the critic to extract new meanings from old texts and allowing him to proclaim the endless diversity of potential interpretations. In this sense the "death of the author," that by now hackneyed phrase of modern criticism, is the birth of the dominating critical self. The integrity of the literary text dissolves before individual scrutiny into whatever meanings the mind and sensibilities of the scrutineer can, in the light of his own mental and emotional history, discover in it. The self has really come into its own.

But this is hardly Boswell's critical method. He was enough a man of his age to believe in objective critical standards, and for all his relish of the individual and the eccentric there is no evidence that as a literary critic he disagreed with Johnson's view that "just representation of general nature" was the object of literary fictions. Further, though he loved to record the specific and the individual, Boswell, well grounded as he was in the Latin classics and in the view that they were indeed classics, never questioned the notion of a literary canon or entertained the belief that the meaning of great literary works was infinitely variable – or even that there could be any serious doubt about what truly great literary works were. Nor did he regard literature, as he seems to have regarded music, as simply a mood-inducing device. So, although he may evoke special sympathies among adherents of recent critical fashions, Boswell can hardly be regarded as one of their founding fathers.

Nevertheless Boswell does sound an especially sympathetic chord among modern readers. Now that we know him so well, and can see how he used his self both in autobiographical and biographical writing, we can see that in spite of his eighteenth-century habits and standards, he does stand somewhat outside the spirit of the age. For the self that he exhibits exceeds its function as a writer's tool and reaches out beyond the limits of the consciousness of any given age to make contact with very different consciousnesses.

There is one way, however, in which he speaks very much for his own time and place: that is as a Scotsman of the generations immediately after the Union of 1707. There is no need to rehearse again Boswell's ambivalence about Scotland, his mixture of pride and shame at being Scots, his anxiety to speak in standard southern English, and all the other apparent inconsistencies and contradictions in his attitude to his native country and his own people. This, however, is less unique than some critics have realized. The national trauma with which the Scottish people faced the fact that their own Parliament had voted itself out of existence in an "incorporating union" with England and the complex of attitudes that it bred can be documented in innumerable instances. David Hume, who regarded the Scots that he spoke (but did not write) as a "very corrupt dialect" of English, was nevertheless a proud Scot who manifested his patriotism in many ways, not least by settling in Edinburgh during the latter part of his life. Robert Burns both wrote anti-Union songs and defended the Union, he voiced both Jacobite and Hanoverian sympathies, and at different times expressed anti-English Scottish nationalism and British loyalty. The accommodation of British loyalty and Scottish feeling, now known as "concentric loyalty," went on apace throughout eighteenth-century Scotland, to culminate in Walter Scott's combination of passion for the Scottish past and commitment to British progress and modernity. It could be argued that the ambivalence reflected in these attitudes represented more than the consequences of the Union of 1707 and that, as Gregory Smith argued long ago and as the modern Scottish poet Hugh MacDiarmid enthusiastically reaffirmed, the Scot throughout history has always had a divided self, and as a result from the beginning manifested the "Caledonian Antisyzygy," a yoking of opposite extremes, "the sudden jostling of contraries." Boswell, it might be thought, is too individual a case to be diagnosed as an example of this characteristically Scottish psychological phenomenon, which in any case is not explained simply by being defined and named. Further, there was mental disturbance in Boswell's heredity: his own brother John had to be confined for long periods of his life, and Boswell himself admitted that his family were either "all crack-brained" or were "remarkable for genius and worth" but afflicted with a cast of melancholy of the kind that often accompanies genius. It is however worth remembering that in the multiple self that Boswell drew on so remarkably in both autobiography and biography there was something akin to what has often been observed as characteristic of the Scottish personality. It was a Scot, James Hogg, who in his *Confessions of a Justified Sinner* first explored the phenomenon of the divided self, and it was another Scot, Robert Louis Stevenson, who gave it its most popular expression in his account of Dr. Jekyll and Mr. Hyde. Boswell meditating sexual adventures while in a mood of pious devotion in church could perhaps be seen as a prime example of the Jekyll-and-Hyde syndrome.

With reference to Boswell's feelings of Scottish patriotism, it should be noted that his interest in freedom for Corsica was connected in his mind with a sense of Scotland's wars of independence against the English kings Edward I and II. It is remarkable that he should have used as epigraph to his *Account of Corsica* the most ringing sentence from the Declaration of Arbroath, the famous letter sent to the Pope by the Scots barons in 1320 containing a classic statement of the case for Scottish independence. The statement, so often quoted by Scottish historians and politicians today, was not well known in Boswell's time, but Boswell ferreted it out and displayed it proudly. His mixture of feelings with respect to Corsica, Scotland, and England was an early indication of his inner complexities. It is perhaps worth noting that the phrase "mixture of feelings" was used by Walter Scott to describe his own emotions in presenting his *Minstrelsy of the Scottish Border* to the public. Boswell's many-faceted self can thus be ranged historically with other examples of divided Scottish characters.

However we look at Boswell, we are left with a set of paradoxes. It is perhaps for the psychologist to attempt a real explanation of those paradoxes, but the biographer, the social and cultural historian, the literary researcher, and the literary critic can help to show what it is that has to be explained and what value-judgements seem in the end to be indicated. But in fact there is no end: questions answered bring new questions to the fore, and Boswell remains, as he would have liked to remain, a compulsive object of curiosity.

Part I

BOSWELL AND EIGHTEENTH-CENTURY
SCOTTISH CULTURE

2

BOSWELL AND THE RHETORIC OF FRIENDSHIP

Thomas Crawford

In an important essay Bruce Redford touches on one of the most intriguing aspects of the Boswell problem: "the question of literary alchemy – life into art, art into life, a life in art – and the nature of Boswell's own trans-formational powers. In the hands of a master, the familiar letter creates an autonomous verbal universe, a true literary system that achieves, both formally and ontologically, the status of *poetic* reality – at once internally consistent, vital, and self-supporting." Such mastery entails rhetoric of an essentially *literary* kind, deployed to foster an illusion of talking, whose effect is to create letters which are at one and the same time counters in an exchange and units in whole correspondences which are *romans fleuves*. It implies the art of the miniaturist, who cultivates "Jane Austen's one small square of ivory" and takes infinite pains on a limited scale.[1] But for Boswell, life came first; his aim as a writer was to reflect and heighten events which had spontaneously happened in life, or which he had originated or stage-managed in life. This is as true of his letters as of any other part of his *œuvre*. In this essay I shall not be concerned, in the main, with Boswell's correspondence with heroes and great men, but with his letters to three friends who were more or less his equals and contemporaries – the Hon. Andrew Erskine, John Johnston of Grange, and William Johnson Temple.

THE ERSKINE CORRESPONDENCE

Boswell's letters to Erskine employ on the whole a more self-consciously "literary" rhetoric than those he wrote to Temple and Grange, and yet they fit in perfectly with the reality of their relationship as it comes out in the *London Journal*.

> We were in a luscious flow of spirits and vastly merry. "How we do chase a thought," said Erskine, "when once it is started. Let it run as it pleases over hill and dale and take numberless windings, still we are at it. It has a greyhound at its heels every turn." (*London Journal*, February 14, 1763, p. 189)

Their connection grew out of a Bassanio–Gratiano relationship between George Dempster (eight years older than Boswell, he had been elected MP for Perth Burghs in April 1761) and Erskine (the third son of the Jacobite fifth Earl of Kellie and Boswell's exact contemporary; he was a lieutenant in the Seventy-first Regiment of Foot and a minor poet of some skill). When Boswell made it a threesome in mid-May 1761, it very soon broadened into a foursome to include Alexander Donaldson, publisher of *A Collection of Original Poems, by the Rev. Mr. Blacklock and other Scotch Gentlemen*. The first volume had appeared in 1760; the second (1762) was in preparation when Boswell first met Erskine. Erskine's poems are prominent in the miscellany; Dempster had some pieces in it; and Boswell contributed no less than thirty to the second volume.[2]

Although the contrary is sometimes assumed, the letters to and from Erskine were not originally intended for publication. They were "genuine" in the sense that they were sent through the post, and amidst all their fooling they contained information of interest to both men, such as travel plans and proposals to meet. Apart from such factual matter, they were as Lord Auchinleck described them in his horrified response:

> When I went on my Circuit to Jedburgh, I received a fresh mortification. The news [i.e. the newspaper] were brought to me, and therein was contained an account of the publishing some letters of yours; and one of them was insert as a specimen. I read it, and found that though it might pass between two intimate young lads in the same way that people over a bottle will be vastly entertained with one another's rant, it was extremely odd to send such a piece to the press to be perused by all and sundry. (*London Journal*, May 30, 1763, p. 338)

It nevertheless seems that not even Boswell had thought of publication until fairly late on, and when he "proposed the scheme to Erskine" the latter "at first opposed it much. But at last the inclination seized him and he became as fond of it as I" (Journal, April 12, 1763 – the very day the *Letters* were published in London). Some of the forty letters printed were amended or "improved" from the texts as originally written; indeed, even the dates of some were altered.

The letters show Boswell to be highly conscious of questions of rhetoric and style, as one might expect from the young man who had attended Adam Smith's course on Rhetoric at Glasgow only two years before the correspondence began. Thus his letter of January 11, 1762 is full of literary allusion: "I shall not follow the formal and orderly method of Bishop Latimer, in his Sermons before King Edward the Sixth; but, on the contrary, shall adopt the easy, desultory stile of one whom at present I shall not venture to name." But a clue is given in the next paragraph, where *Tristram Shandy* is mentioned (*Letters Erskine*, pp. 64–5). On February 11, 1762, in a letter not in the published volume, Boswell's preoccupation with style and spontaneity leads him to the primitivist observation that the speech of ordinary people – folk speech, which in this case would be in vernacular Scots – can be more poetic than the language of high art.[3] Yet as befits the general tone of the correspondence it is expressed facetiously:

> I received your last this morning by the hands of Roy the handsom Grenadier. Our maids are all fallen in love with him. They are raving in heroics with such vociferation that my ears are quite stunned and my senses quite stupified.
>
> It is astonishing to think what effects the amorous fury is attended with. With what inconceivable radiance it illumines the darkest minds. Here now is a parcel of uncultivated Girls who upon my word are venting the boldest flights of fancy, the most exuberant sallies of Genius arrayed in the richest language I have ever heard. I begin realy to entertain an inferior idea of Poetry from what I used to do. And how can it be otherwise, when I hear and see a common culinary dirty Damsel soaring every bit as high as either Shakespeare Milton Captain Erskine or Myself? (MS Yale L 514)

Few rhetoricians are mentioned by name, though there is enthusiastic praise of Lord Kames's *Elements of Criticism* on two occasions. Throughout the correspondence there is deliberate use of common tropes and figures to create and express their relationship. Thus on January 22, 1762 Boswell writes in these terms about the printing of Donaldson's collection:

> [Donaldson] is a loadstone of prodigious power, and attracts all my poetic needles ... D——'s encomiums have rendered my humility still prouder; they are indeed superb, and worthy of an opposer of the German War. I suppose they have not lost a bit of beef by their long journey, and I should imagine that the Highland air has agreed well with them, and that they have agreed well with the Highland air. They occasioned much laughter in my heart, and much heart in my laughter. (*Letters Erskine*, pp. 71–2)

The allusive comparison is between Donaldson's encomiums and highland cattle on the drove-roads: Erskine was at that time at New Tarbet on the western shore of Loch Lomond.

Boswell sometimes achieves an effect of exuberant energy by piling up parallel phrases, as when he embroiders on Erskine's brother's hyperbolical praise of London (*Letters Erskine*, p. 78), or by an ascending series of rhetorical questions (pp. 84–5). On one occasion (May 8, 1762; pp. 103–4) he presses a Sternian satire on pedantry into an expanded comment on Lady Jenny Macfarlane's fondness for Scots folk music, whose ironical effect depends on knowing that the old song "Eppie McNab" had bawdy words.[4] The foolery concerns the music only, but one must assume that both correspondents were aware of some "indelicate" version, even if Lady Jenny may only have known the title of the tune. Boswell's allusive rhetorical embroidery reflects the indefinable ambience of an intimate group that also included women, and conveys the young men's sly awareness of their foibles.

Thus the letter that mentions "Eppie McNab" also comments on an adventure of another female member of the circle, Lady Betty Macfarlane, whose encounter with a turkey-cock Boswell was later to make the subject of a burlesque ode. Such passages, and the exchange of verses, form the very staple of this correspondence.

A fairly late letter in the series, but which is not among those printed, begins as a technical exercise in the figure of alliteration – a ploy, Boswell claims, to purge his melancholy. He starts off with Erskine's nickname:

> Dear Dash, Memento mori is my momentous Motto. I am as melancholy as a Mauretanian Miller's Motherly Mare with much Milk plunging for a misty Month in the Middle of a miserable moorish Mire. You may see how low I am by My thus M-ing, or as they pronounce it in Aberdeenshire, *aiming* at Wit. Alas! alas! is it come to this. (September 3, 1762, MS Yale L 527)

Boswell drew a line beneath his M-ing, and began again: "My Dear Friend, I realy can write none I am so dull; but I assure you, I love you better than ever. I long to hear of you, and more to see you." The expressions and intonation patterns are now those of ordinary conversational English, and when he comes to the business part of the letter, proposing a meeting, he does so in repeated, insistent, vigorous questions ("Will I be kindly entertained? Will you be glad to see me?...") that stress how he has had a renewal of friendly feelings towards Erskine after a period of separation.

The very last letter in the published volume shifts from questions – this time more fantastical – to an excited but still somewhat literary and essayistic rendering of "the amazing bustle of existence" which is London, only to move yet again to the plain statements of everyday friendship: "I don't know what to say to you about myself: if I can get into the guards, it will please me much; if not, I can't help it." He ends with a sentence which perfectly illustrates the claim that the thrust of all Boswell's personal letters is "to establish the identity of 'that favourite subject, Myself' as a recognizable and recognized Great Person":[5]

> What a fine animated prospect of life now spreads before me! Be assured, that my genius will be highly improved, and please yourself with the hopes of receiving letters still more entertaining. (November 20, 1762; *Letters Erskine*, pp. 155–6)

But any such hopes were not to be realized. Erskine was himself in London during almost the whole period of the *London Journal*, and their frequent meetings meant there was no need for long letters. Their last meeting before Boswell's continental travels seems to have been on July 7, 1763, when "Erskine said we ought to write now and then to each other a letter of good amusing facts, which I agreed to" (*London Journal*, p. 297). Boswell wrote one such letter, from July 5 to 22, 1763, detailing the events of these days in a style half-way between his brief impressionistic diary "notes" and that of the fully written Journal. The letter as effervescent impromptu has been replaced by the journal as *fleuve*; letter and journal have *fused* (MS Yale L 529). Three further letters from Boswell to Erskine have survived: a trifle of July 26, 1763; an apology on August 25, 1768 because he lacked the wherewithal to help Erskine "purchase a company" (MS Yale L 530), and, twenty-five years later, on March 6, 1793, a reply to one from Erskine commending the *Life of Johnson* (MS Yale L 531).

THE CORRESPONDENCE WITH GRANGE

Two months before he began to edit their letters for the printer, Boswell had come to the conclusion that there was a qualitative difference between his feelings for Dempster and Erskine on the one hand, and those he had for Johnston, Temple, and McQuhae on the other. The latter were "true friends," whereas the Boswell–Dempster–Erskine triumvirate were "in the style of companions. It is only fancy that cements us. It is only because we are entertaining to one another that we are so much together" (*London Journal*, February 16, 1763, p. 191). He returned to the topic six months later, this time omitting McQuhae:

> A companion loves some agreeable qualities which a man may possess, but a friend loves the man himself...I joked and said that if I was going to be married, Temple and Johnston would be the men whom I would have in my room, with the door locked, a piece of cheese, two moulded candles, and a bottle of claret upon the mahogany table, round which we would sit in quiet attention consulting and examining the settlements. But that when the wedding was over and festivity was going on, then I would send for Dempster and Erskine, and we would be jolly and hearty and laugh and talk and make sport. (*London Journal*, July 7, 1763, pp. 296–7).

True friends were those with whom Boswell would willingly share his journal; thus the *London Journal* was written for Grange, while the lost journal of his stay in Holland was intended to be read by Temple before going to Grange (September 23, 1763); and at various times from early 1766 onwards he had shown later journals to Temple.[6] John Johnston of Grange had been a somewhat elderly undergraduate at Edinburgh at the same time as the fifteen-year-old Boswell. During their student days Grange was leader, stirring Boswell's imagination with nostalgic dreams of Scotland's heroic past; but soon after the correspondence began their roles reversed. Grange was now the passive receiver, with Boswell the distant provider of "romance" (pp. xvii–xix). The "truth" of friendship is strikingly revealed in the middle part of their correspondence when Johnston, disappointed in love, told Boswell on April 18, 1772 that he would carry his sympathetic letter into the country "to peruse when I am Solitary and thoughtfull" (p. 279). It comes out too in the later part, when Boswell asked Burke, Dundas, and even Pitt to find some pension or office for his friend (p. xxxvi); and much earlier, on August 29, 1770, when the Boswells' first child died shortly after birth:

> My Dear Friend: It was not kind in you to leave me alone yesterday. I had a terrible day. My Wife after much trouble and danger was at last delivered of a son. But the poor child lived but a very short while. Pray come to me directly. Yours J. B. (pp. 263–4)

This is the rhetoric of true friendship in everyday life, barely differing from the language of thousands of people with no literary pretensions whatsoever, and miles away from any attempt by Boswell to build himself into a Great Person. This intimate salutation contrasts with the more usual "Dear Johnston," "My Dear Johnston," "My Dear Sir," or even plain "Dear Sir." Because of his choice of noun his first sentence is like a lover's reproach, and the absolute simplicity of the remainder testifies to the eloquence of the plainest words. One is reminded of Lear's "Pray you, undo this button."

More than half of the surviving Boswell–Grange letters are youthful ones, dating from Boswell's twentieth to his twenty-sixth year. Like his other compulsive routines on the Grand Tour – the Journal in all its forms, French and Dutch themes, ten lines of verse a day – the correspondence with Grange was essential to his "soul-making." In the thirty-six days before leaving for Holland he wrote to him no less than eighteen times, and during his stay on the continent a regular letter to Grange took on ceremonial significance, with the Journal itself a term in a ritualistic transaction. "I indulge you with liberty to read my letters," he wrote on January 20, 1764, "but let the Journal be reserved till I am sitting at your fire-side" (p. 120). After Boswell left Holland, a change took place in the pattern. During his nineteen months in Germany, Switzerland, Italy, Corsica, and France, Grange received only three letters; yet Boswell wrote no fewer than fifty-five. The majority were addressed and sealed, but never posted, to be read only after his return – an extraordinary dislocation of the normal letter-writing transaction. Johnston's pleasure as lone recipient was to be postponed so that it could form part of a new and *mutual* pleasure: writer and reader united with speaker and hearer. At first Boswell decided to write to Grange from every court and city where he stayed for more than three days (*Journal*, October 1, 1764), then at a later point from every town in which he dined or supped or slept (*Corr: Grange*, December 15, 1765). Even the address was a rhetorical act; writing to Grange, or anyone else, from a place with historical and literary associations was both language as gesture and gesture as language. Furthermore, to call up memories of past happiness is an almost instinctive part of the rhetoric of friendship. The "auld lang syne" that Boswell recreated in some of his letters to Grange was in the first instance purely personal, but it also referred to the imagined glories of Scotland's past, when she was an independent kingdom (letters to Grange, February 15 and July 19, 1763).

Boswell, when writing to a "true" friend, often employed the very same techniques and devices which he used in his letters to a "superficial" friend like Erskine. As he self-critically noted to Grange on December 9, 1765: "I set out with a play of alliteration which has no meaning but carrys with it the sagacious air of a maxim" (p. 193). Sometimes he utters the clichés of friendship embroidered with artificial "thous and thees," sometimes he coins an epical tag for his correspondent. Both are found in this sentence: "Congratulate with me Thou old and faithfull freind of Boswell thou firm Borderer who hast allways stood by him in fair weather and foul" (October 6, 1764, p. 137). Twenty years later such emotions have to be read between the lines: "I am not *so well* here [i.e. at Auchinleck, pining for London] this year as I was the last. You understand me; and therefore I need say no more" (August 23, 1783, p. 302). True friends, like lovers, may have their own private vocabulary, or use familiar words in new senses to render communication more intimate. Thus Boswell and Grange continually use "antiquity" and "antique" to mean "melancholia" and "melancholic," but I have noticed only one occurrence in the Journal (the *London Journal*, intended in any case for Grange), and none at all in the correspondence with Temple. And on one occasion (February 12, 1765) he employs "romanise" in a sense subtly different from any cited by the *OED*, but one perfectly in keeping with their private communings – namely, to "feel into" Roman remains in such a way as to recreate within oneself what was reputed to be Roman *amor patriae*, and then fuse that emotion with love for one's *own* country (presumably, since Grange was the correspondent, with love for Scotland).

Just as in the Erskine correspondence, Boswell sometimes drops into the essayistic style when writing to Grange ("The Materials of which Man is made in france cannot make a true Coachman," January 9, 1766, p. 207). Sometimes he imitates the monologues and soliloquies of novelists and dramatists ("Good God! what distracted horrors did I now endure," September 23, 1763, p. 113), or the style of novelistic narrative with its faculty psychology and personification of emotions ("a very warm letter, in which anger, anxiety and affection were mingled," September 10, 1764, p. 131). Or again, writing with some irony, he can apply to himself sophisticated formulae which stereotype the decadent roles of civil society: "last winter, I was the ardent votary of pleasure, a gay sceptic who never looked beyond the present hour, a heroe and Philosopher in Dissipation and Vice" (January 20, 1764, p. 119). These expressions are parallel to the "firm Borderer" already quoted, calling up images of Grange's frontier ancestors and reflecting a propensity to group people into psychological types according to their ancestry, nationality, and social or cultural position. One letter burlesques the biblical style of a Presbyterian divine for most of its length (July 14, 1763), while another derives its structure from the counterposing of two opposite styles – those of facetious irony and extended comparison (February 15, 1763) – a rhetoric which would not have been out of place in writing to Erskine.

Boswell's letter to Grange of December 5, 1764, after his first visit to Rousseau, is a miniature masterpiece:

> My Dear Johnston: Art thou alive o! my freind? or has thy spirit quitted it's earthly habitation. To hear of thy death would not now distress me. I would glory to think of thy exaltation.
>
> Johnston I am in the Village which contains Rousseau. These three days I have visited that Sublime Sage. He has enlightened my mind. He has kindled my Soul. Yes, we are Immortal. Yes. Jesus has given us a Revelation. I feel an enthusiasm beyond expression. Good Heaven am I so elevated? Where is Gloom? Where is Discontent? Where are all the little vexations of the World? O Johnston! Wert thou but here! I am in a beautifull wild Valley surrounded by immense mountains. I am just setting out for Neufchatel. But I return to Rousseau. I am to be alone on Horseback in a dark Winter night, while the earth is covered with Snow. My present Sentiments give me a force and a vigour like the Lion in the desart. Farwell My Dear Freind. (pp. 147–8)

The initial paragraph, so outrageous in its sentimental wit as to hit us with almost the grotesque force of a metaphysical conceit, leads on to one whose short, gasping statements, questions and exclamations catch all the exultation of the moment, at the same time as it expertly distills his impressionistic anticipation of the wild ride from Neufchâtel to Môtiers, "the village which contains Rousseau." An exquisitely worked square of ivory may not be the appropriate comparison, but the letter is still perfect. Another excellent letter, that of July 24, 1765, does, however, show more signs of working, in Lytton Strachey's and Redford's sense. It modulates beautifully from an essayistic quotation from Addison in the first sentence, "Brescia is famous for its iron works," by means of Sternian association ("iron has run in my head since ever I arrived...This is the country where assassination is most frequent and Men and Women go often armed") to his decision to buy a gun:

> So young is still this fancifull head of mine that I had no sooner bought my Gun than the ideas returned which used to stir my blood at Auchinleck when I was eager to be a Soldier; I brandished my Gun (if the sword will permit me for once that expression) I slung it carelessly over my left arm like a handsom fowler or a Captain of a marching Regiment and I must own that I even shoulder'd my firelock like any bold Brother Soldier in his Majesty King George's service; all these motions I performed to an English march which I

whistled and upon the honour of a Man who is not ashamed to discover the simplicity of his sentiments at times I do declare I was as happy as I could wish and giving my broad gold-lac'd hat a gracefull turn to one side of my head I thought myself a very great Man. My Dear Johnston I give you leave to smile. But let me tell you that in whatever way we can enjoy an innocent happiness in this sad world let us not disdain to enjoy it. The illustrious Johnson once cured me of haughty pride which despised small amusements. He told me "Sir, nothing is too little for so little a creature as man." We are all little at periods of our lives and if we were all as candid Philosophers as I am would just march as I have done. (pp. 178–9)

In their maturity, the friendship between Boswell and Grange was conducted largely apart from letters. From 1766 to 1785 Edinburgh was the centre of Boswell's professional and family life, as it was of Johnston's. During these twenty years the *Journal* mentions repeated conversations, dinners, teas, meetings in taverns and at Leith Races, and consultations about legal and other business on over two hundred occasions, but there were comparatively few letters. Only three survive from the last two years of the correspondence, 1785–6: two from Boswell and one from Grange, whose health had broken down in the spring of 1785. He died in July 1786.

THE BOSWELL–TEMPLE CORRESPONDENCE

If Grange was Boswell's "oldest" friend in the strictly literal sense that he had got to know him before he met Temple, nevertheless it was Temple with whom he was "most intimate": "my old and most intimate friend" is his favourite formula for Temple in the *Life of Johnson* and elsewhere (II, 316). There seems no doubt that Temple's Englishness (even if it was no more than the Englishness of the most northerly part of Northumbria) was part of his original attraction for Boswell when they were students together in 1755–7. While Grange stimulated what Boswell termed Scottish "ideas," Temple appealed to the anti-Scot in him. "Boswell seems to have thought of his friends as like the two sides of his nature, antipathetic to each other – at any rate he appears to have done nothing during his university days to bring them together, class-fellows as they were" (*Corr: Grange*, p. xviii). In 1758 Temple left Edinburgh for Trinity Hall, Cambridge, to lay the academic foundations for what he hoped would be a career at the English Bar. By 1763 he had chambers in Inner Temple Lane, and the friends met frequently during the period of the first London journal. It was shortly after this that Temple began his painful progress towards a clerical career, ending up as a simple country clergyman in the west of England.

Boswell's commonest salutations to Temple are "My dear Temple" and "My dear Friend"; but whereas we have only one letter in which he addresses Grange in the superlative, he uses the phrase "My Dearest

Friend" to Temple on at least six occasions. "My Sad Friend" and "My Worthy Friend" begin two letters to Grange, but none to Temple – though Temple was often sad, and he is sometimes called "worthy" in the main body of the letter; neither is there a parallel to the almost Burnsian "My Honest Johnston." Expressions of mutual friendship in the middle of a letter are more fulsome in the earlier years, and there is one letter in which Boswell says he feels "love" for Temple "from my soul" (September 2, 1775; I, 240).[7] If there are no words or senses private to Boswell and Temple alone, like the connotations of "antiquity" in the Grange correspondence, there are other marks of intimacy such as allusions to literary works each knew the other loved. Reminiscences of shared experience are triggered off by the mere mention of words of geographical provenance ("Arthur's Seat"), those denoting culture-heroes ("Voltaire! Rousseau! immortal names" [May 3–8, 1779; II, 283–7]) or the dialectal vocabulary and pronunciation of their old Greek professor ("Would it not *torture* you to be again at Professor Hunter's, eating *jeel* [jelly]," April 2, 1791; II, 432). And epistolary intimacy may be heightened by recalling times of intense communion, such as a conversation in the garden of the Inner Temple in 1763 which featured "the true disinterested celestial" nature of their friendship (April 17, 1764; MS Yale L 1219), or Boswell's promise of sobriety under the solemn yew at Mamhead (August 12, 1775; I, 236–40).

Both correspondents refer to their letters as a form of talking. When Boswell is at his most conversational, short sentences predominate; the tone of colloquial exchange is often assured by a formula like "Only think of that, Temple!" after he has reported some extraordinary or paradoxical event; and the exclamations can be simplified to the mere rendition of laughter, as in the following extract, from the years of his search for a wife, where all the compressed allusions refer to persons and events with which Temple was thoroughly familiar from previous letters:

> Temple, will you allow me to marry a Scots lass? ha! ha! ha! What shall I tell you? Zélide has been in London this winter. I never hear from her. She is a strange creature...But I am well rid of her...I have broke the trammels of business and am roving unconfined with my worthy Temple. (February 1–March 8, 1767; I, 104)

Boswell, in his "talking" to Temple, can be highly conscious of style. "I have not words to express my feelings. I fear not to write to you in the strong incorrect manner. My heart speaks. O my freind!" (April 17, 1764; MS Yale L 1219). As in the Journal, Boswell the subject can stand back and contemplate himself as object, as well as the external world as object; but in these letters to Temple he is not a dispassionate but an excited observer, imaginatively putting himself in the position of the dull, plodding many – the cits, the "warldly race" – then impishly inviting Temple to marvel at his excesses and inconsistencies, so that three points of view can interfuse – that of the "unco guid," what Boswell imagines Temple's will be, and Boswell's own. This two-way relationship with a correspondent enables him to project a different emotional tone and type of self-observation from his practice in the Journal, and it is made possible because one of Boswell's many selves desperately wanted to act prudently and succeed in a worldly sense. As a rule, this special variant of the Boswellian subject–object dialectic forms only part of a letter, and Temple's response may be twofold: a vicarious, voyeuristic pleasure in his friend's excesses, and a brother-confessor's adjuration to pull himself together. After Temple had fully embarked on the clerical life, steadying advice prevailed.

There is one letter from Boswell, however, which was entirely given over to a delirious exhibitionism, that of April 28, 1766 (MS Yale L 1234), in which he recounts his passion for Euphemia Bruce, the gardener's daughter at Auchinleck, and his overwhelming impulse to marry her and get a wife with whom he would live "just as with a Mistress, without the disgrace and remorse." It is surely one of the best pieces of sentimentalist writing – and feeling – in the whole Boswell canon:

> My friend, give me your hand. Lead me away from what is probably a delusion that would make me give up with the world and sink into a mere animal. And yet is it not being singularly happy that after the gloom I have endured, the dreary speculations I have formed, and the vast variety of all sorts of adventures that I have run through, my mind should not be a bit corrupted, and I should feel the elegant passion with all the pure simplicity and tender agitations of youth? Surely I have the genuine soul of love. When dusting the rooms with my charmer, am I not like Agamemnon amongst the Thracian girls? All this may do for a summer. But is it possible that I could imagine the dear delirium would last for life? I will rouse my philosophic spirit, and fly from this fascination.

All the circumstances surrounding this letter bordered on the rhetoric of living rather than of writing, the manipulation of events so that he could either write about them or at the very least respond to them in a literary way. He began it "while the delirium was really existing," but strongly suspected even at the time that it would not last. Before three weeks were up, the "madness" had left him:

> I can now send you with a good grace what would certainly have alarmed you, but will now be truly amusing. Romantic as I am, it was so strange a scene in the play of my life that I myself was quite astonished at it. I give you my word of honour it was literally true. There are few people who could give credit to it. But you, who have traced me since ever I fairly entered upon the stage, will not doubt of it. It is a little humbling, to be sure. It was the effect of great force and great weakness of mind. I am certainly a most various composition. (Letter to Temple, May 17, 1766; Ms Yale L 1235)

Boswell's comments are diametrically opposite to the "free association" remarks on Zélide quoted above. He is almost dispassionately aware of two contrasting possible responses in his correspondent; stands outside his role-playing like a *spectator* in the theatre; is naively proud that the humdrum many would not believe such acts and feelings possible, at the same time as he is himself astonished at the contradictions in his behaviour – that he can show strength and weakness simultaneously.

As might be expected from his friend's bookish interests, Boswell employs an essayistic style to Temple more often than to Erskine and Grange. He even uses philosophical terms when reporting that his own venereal disease may have put his mistress and their unborn child in danger: "Will you forgive me, Temple, for exclaiming that all this evil is too much for the offence of my getting drunk, because I would drink Miss Blair's health, every round, in a large bumper? But general laws often seem hard in particular cases" (July 29, 1767; I, 117). One of the shortest letters seems the merest bagatelle, yet its combination of absolute simplicity and unassuming intimacy conveys the whole spirit of their friendship at mid-career:

> I was lately troubled a good deal, as formerly, about human liberty, and God's prescience. I had recourse to the great Montesquieu, in one of his *Lettres Persannes*, and had the subject made clear to me, as I once had by that letter, when I was at Mamhead, I forget whether by chance or by your directing me to it. Are you ever disturbed with abstract doubts? (January 3, 1775; I, 206–7)

Once the excitement of youth was over, the rhetoric of Boswell's letters to Temple becomes less exuberant and more homely. They evince even more strikingly than before what W. K. Wimsatt called his "native and perhaps hardly conscious talent for saying things straight," and F. A. Pottle his "plate-glass style."[8] But in the later Temple correspondence that style is not always, indeed not generally, "unmodulated," nor does it always "hold both subject and reader at a distance," as Redford claims is the norm for Boswell's letters (p. 51). Consider how Boswell announces the birth of his son, Sandy, writing from Edinburgh on October 10, 1775:

> I am really uneasy that I have been so long of hearing from you. I wrote to you in August, I think, from this place; and in September from Auchinleck. But, instead of complaining of your silence, I feel a kind of exaltation in thus being superiour to you in the duties of friendship. – However, to put an end to uninteresting reflections, let me inform you that last night my wife was safely delivered of a SON. You know, my dearest friend, of what importance this is to me; of what importance it is to the Family of Auchinleck which, you may be well convinced, is my supreme object in this world. My wife was very ill in her labour; but is in a good way; and the child appears to be as well as we could wish. My kind compliments to Mrs. Temple. I am hurried and cannot expatiate on this happy event. I hope you will find time to do it with your elegant pen, thou characteriser of Gray! (I, 241–2)

The sentence saying he is "superiour" in the duties of friendship is not naively bumptious, as a careless reading might suggest; on the contrary, it carries a gently humorous, sentimental irony which is taken up again in the slightly heavier "uninteresting reflections," while the sonorous rhythm of the final apostrophe completes an unobtrusively *beautiful* sentence whose solemn tone is qualified by that same gentle humour. That apostrophe, moreover, is an epic label for a *literatus*, as "thou firm Borderer" was for Johnston, the descendant of moss-troopers and reivers.

In the tragic crisis of Boswell's life, when he was hanging on in London as his wife lay dying at Auchinleck, Temple as always gave him commonsense advice, and Boswell replied with a direct, simple demand for more: "Whatever then I at times may *feel*, my *reason* acquits me from any blame in this separation. Comfort and encourage me, my dear freind. You do it better than any body...you have poured balm upon my sore mind" (March 5, 1789; II, 359). When he summarizes his feelings three months before Margaret's death he uses the rhetoric of cliché, transformed by one brilliant phrase of extreme compression, "a just upbraiding gloom":

> we cannot be ignorant that each repeated attack makes her less able to recover; and supposing that *now* the disease should increase, and, as sometimes happens, should take a rapid course, she may be carried off while I am four hundred miles from her. The alternative is dreadful, and though she with admirable generosity bids me not be in a haste to leave London (knowing my extreme fondness for it), I should have a heart as hard as a stone were I to remain here; and should the fatal event happen in my absence, I should have a just upbraiding gloom upon my mind for the rest of my life. (March 31, 1789; II, 364)

This is ordinary prose, but harmoniously cadenced, as are the measured parallels and symmetries of the following summary of his condition, climaxed appropriately by a hackneyed quotation:

> What a state is my present – full of ambition and projects to attain wealth and eminence, yet embarrassed in my circumstances and depressed with family distress, which at times makes every thing in life seem indifferent. I often repeat Johnson's lines in his *Vanity of Human Wishes*,
>
> > Shall helpless man, in ignorance sedate,
> > Roll darkling down the torrent of his fate?   (May 22, 1789; II, 371)

Boswell's reply of July 3, 1789 to Temple's letter of condolence on Margaret's death shows him instinctively falling into the rhythms and cadences of sermon literature, not now burlesqued as they had been in some early letters to Grange: "O my friend, this is affliction indeed," to be immediately followed by the stark bare facts of the wild ride north, and the clichés of "fatal stroke" and "dismal event," which do not in the least seem marks of bad writing because they are held in suspension by the vividness of the surrounding impressions:

> My two boys and I posted from London to Auchinleck, night and day, in 64 hours 1/4. But alas! our haste was all in vain. The fatal stroke had taken place before we set out. It was very strange that we had no intelligence whatever upon the road, not even in our own parish, nor till my second daughter came running out from our house, and announced to us the dismal event in a burst of tears. (II, 373)

Though he did not see Margaret's body till four days after her death, his reaction was the universal one of Lear with Cordelia dead in his arms:

> But alas to see my excellent wife, and the mother of my children, and that most sensible lively woman, lying cold and pale and insensible was very shocking to me. I could not help doubting it was a deception. I could hardly bring myself to agree that the body should be removed, for it was still a consolation to me to go and kneel by it, and talk to my dear dear Peggie. (II, 374)

Nearly five months later the language of abstract philosophy enabled him to sum up his mental state with a kind of solemn wit:

> Such is the gloomy *ground* of my mind, that any agreable perceptions have an uncommon though but a momentary brightness. But alas, my friend, be the *accidents* as they may, how is the *substance*? How am *I*? With a pious submission to GOD, but at the same time a kind of obstinate feeling towards men, I walk about upon the earth with inward discontent, though I may appear the most cheerful man you meet. I may have many *gratifications*; but the *comfort* of life is at an end. (November 28, 1789; II, 382)

Only seventeen letters to Temple survive between November 1789 and Boswell's death in May 1795, though he wrote many more which are now missing. But of one thing at least we can be certain: had they survived, they would have given further proof of Boswell's mastery of the plate-glass style and the rhetoric of everyday life.

One aspect of that rhetoric, found especially in the Erskine correspondence, was the rhetoric of *bonhomie* – an extension of Boswell's extraordinary ability to establish immediate intimacy with strangers.[9] An early *coup* of this "sportsman whose game was difficult men,"[10] the first interview with Rousseau, was preceded by an epistolary masterpiece whose short simple sentences, insistent imperatives, and cunning pastiche of Rousseauistic feeling-tone made capitulation almost inevitable:

> I have much to tell you. Though I am only a young man, I have experienced a variety of existence that will amaze you. I find myself in serious and delicate circumstances concerning which I sincerely hope to have the counsel of the author of the *Nouvelle Héloïse*. If you are the charitable man I believe you to be, you cannot hesitate to grant it to me. Open your door, then, Sir, to a man who

dares to tell you that he deserves to enter it. Place your confidence in a stranger who is different. You will not regret it. (*Grand Tour I*, p. 215)

Perhaps "rhetoric of insinuation" is a better term for this performance. Boswell followed his first interview with the "Ébauche de ma Vie,"[11] which displays the same naiveté, real and assumed, as the letter – a cunning green-goose brashness calculated to make the philosopher disposed to counsel him on his most pressing personal problems; its rhetoric uses many phrases and sentiments intended to convince Rousseau that they were both on the same wavelength. The result was a draw: the sportsman brought down his game, while the philosopher had the satisfaction of giving moralistic advice *de haut en bas*. When his association with the great was as deep and prolonged as it was with Johnson, Boswell could speak of his love for him; as he wrote on February 23, 1777, "I do not believe that a more perfect attachment ever existed in the history of mankind" (*Life*, III, 105). Though the plate-glass style dominates his letters to Johnson, there are occasions (paralleling the letters to Rousseau) when his style is tinged with his correspondent's own (e.g. the remarks on David Hume and Dr. Dodd in the letter of June 9, 1777; *Life*, III, 119). He can express a humorous delight in the simultaneous equality of their relationship by recalling "Your angry voice at Ashbourne... still sounds aweful 'in my mind's ears,'" using onomatopoeia, alliteration and literary allusion to render the big bow-wow (February 28, 1778; *Life*, III, 221). In contrast, he can snobbishly abase himself in letters to Lord Pembroke: as Redford puts it, "Even an epistolary friendship, fostered by verbal artifice, cannot take root when one of the partners insists upon reminding the other (and himself) of their discrepancy in rank."[12]

The tone of Boswell's letters to Lord Hailes sometimes hovers between flattery and abasement, particularly after an unfortunate quarrel in 1771; what comes through is a faintly unctuous variant of the rhetoric of insinuation:

> Your readiness as a writer is wonderfull. I never knew any one so quick... You dispell the *clouds* of historical errour. When you put questions to me that require the accurate research of an antiquarian I feel myself a child. But I shall do what I can. I doubt not but I shall get you some account of Percy's lands in Ayrshire and the Charter of *King's Case*. (April 19, 1777; MS Yale L 604)

There is one correspondence only whose rhetoric, in Bruce Redford's opinion, equals that of the greatest masters of "the converse of the pen" – that with Wilkes. Their rapport was indeed extraordinary, but it was like that between Boswell, Erskine, and Dempster in the early 1760s rather than that of "true celestial friendship." Boswell recognized this from the beginning: "As the gay John Wilkes you are most pleasing to me, and I shall be glad to hear from you often. Let serious matters be out of the question, and you and I perfectly harmonise" (June 15, 1765; MS Yale L 1285). Even the exuberant and allusive *jeu d'esprit* which Redford quotes as one of the best of all Boswell's letters is in the last resort superficial.[13] It raises the froth of the letter to Erskine about Lady Jenny Macfarlane and Eppie McNab to the plane of mature wit – but it is still froth. And there is surely a faint trace of insinuation, of Boswell putting himself on a footing to which he feels, at the back of his mind, he may not really be entitled:

> We must contrive to meet oftener than we did last spring, and to drink something more animating than Chocolade; though indeed you and I have such spirits that we scarcely require any thing to increase our vivacity. (February 27, 1779; MS Yale L 1293).

Examination of Boswell's letters to Erskine, Grange, and Temple suggests qualification of the general view of Boswell as correspondent. There are probably more individual masterpieces and superlative passages embedded in long "sprawling" letters than critics like Redford seem prepared to admit. The plate-glass style is not merely a matter of short simple sentences, or longer loose ones structured by co-ordinate rather than subordinate clauses; there is more variation in sentence-structure and prose rhythm than one would think at first glance; and, as Reiberg pointed out long ago: "he has in stock a good many trite phrases, allusions, echoes, and images from the classics, the novel and the drama which, along with his use of exclamation, apostrophe, and rhetorical question, help to project a sense of the dramatic, even the theatrical."[14] Sentimentalism is a major influence, operating through novels, plays, essays, and sermons. This holds good not just for the early letters to Erskine and Grange: as we have seen, he employed sentimental rhetoric to Temple when rendering his deepest emotions during his last decade.

Boswell's developing selfhood and search for identity led him on the one hand to join and sometimes create a whole network of relations between persons, which inevitably entailed connections with a series of interlocking *social* networks (Ayrshire and Edinburgh landowning and legal families, the theatre, the *literati*, the Faculty of Advocates, various groupings in London society, the Club, the newspaper and publishing world, and many others). His soul-making is revealed in the creation, even manufacture, of significant moments in life, involving the projection of his ego into a group, or on to significant individuals. This last process was analogous to scientific experiment as much as to dramatic performance, and led to his forging links between the moments and links between the networks, with the aim of making not merely his life a Whole, but life plus networks into a totality. Of course this was just an aim, and he did not succeed. Each relationship, each network, was part of the vast *roman fleuve* which was Boswell's life, and each correspondence reflected and overlapped with it, while rendering only some of its currents. One set of letters, those to Johnson, are especially significant for their part in another entity, with its own unique and separate relation to life: the Great Biography.

NOTES

1 Bruce B. Redford, "Boswell as Correspondent; Boswell as Letter-Writer," *Yale University Library Gazette*, 56 (1982), 40–52 (pp. 48 and 49 quoted).

2 F. A. Pottle, *The Literary Career of James Boswell, Esq.* (Oxford: Clarendon Press, 1929), pp. 13–14.

3 Unpublished letters between Boswell and Erskine are identified parenthetically by their manuscript numbers in the Yale Boswell Catalogue, and are quoted by kind permission of Yale University. Citations from the relevant volumes of the McGraw-Hill/Heinemann trade edition of Boswell's Journal are quoted by kind permission of the publishers and Yale University.

4 A bawdy text is quoted in the notes to *Poems and Songs of Robert Burns*, ed. James Kinsley, 3 vols. (Oxford: Clarendon Press, 1968), III, 1392.

5 See Rufus Reiberg, "James Boswell's Personal Correspondence: the Dramatized Quest for Identity," in *The Familiar Letter in the Eighteenth Century*, ed. Howard Anderson, Philip B. Daghlian, and Irvin Ehrenpreis (Laurence, Kansas: University of Kansas Press, 1966), pp. 244–68 (p. 246 quoted).

6 In this section parenthetical citation is to *Corr: Grange* unless otherwise stated.

7 Letters to W. J. Temple are quoted from *Letters* and page numbers and dates are cited in the text. Unpublished letters to Temple are identified parenthetically by the number of the manuscript in the Yale Boswell Catalogue, and quoted by kind permission of Yale University.

8 Both cited in Redford, "Boswell as Correspondent," p. 50.

9 Brady, *Later Years*, pp. 181, 184.

10 Pottle, *Earlier Years*, p. 163.

11 A translation of the autobiographical sketch Boswell gave Rousseau forms chapter 1 of *Earlier Years*, pp. 1–6.

12 Bruce Redford, *The Converse of the Pen: Acts of Intimacy in the Eighteenth-Century Familiar Letter* (Chicago: University of Chicago Press, 1987), p. 187.

13 *Converse of the Pen*, pp. 203–4.

14 Reiberg, "James Boswell's Personal Correspondence," p. 264.

3

SCOTTISH DIVINES AND LEGAL LAIRDS:
BOSWELL'S SCOTS
PRESBYTERIAN IDENTITY

Richard B. Sher

In the autumn of 1762, when James Boswell made the famous London jaunt that led to his initial meeting with Samuel Johnson, William Robertson took office as Principal of Edinburgh University. The appointment was a momentous one not only for the university but also for the Church of Scotland and the Scottish Enlightenment. As the leader of the Moderate party in the kirk and author of an acclaimed history of Scotland published in 1759, Robertson, then forty-one years old, was the personification of a new breed of Scots Presbyterian clergymen, the "Moderate literati," who stood for religious moderation and toleration, polite learning and polite preaching, and other Enlightenment principles, as well as for socially and politically conservative values that endeared them to the landed classes.[1] Robertson's appointment as Principal represented a critical step in the institutionalization of those principles and values. The three decades of "Dr. Robertson's *administration*," as Dugald Stewart termed it, saw the heyday of the Scottish Enlightenment. The University of Edinburgh gained international acclaim as a leading center of learning, and the Church of Scotland exchanged its reputation as a hotbed of Presbyterian fanaticism for one as a "hot-bed of genius."[2] Robertson's Edinburgh was a place to which Scotland's most notorious sceptic and infidel, David Hume, could return late in life without fear of persecution.

Boswell's attitude towards these developments was no simple matter. Attracted to certain aspects of the "enlightened" program of Robertson and the Moderates, he was strongly repulsed by others, to the point of attacking them savagely in anonymous articles in the *London Magazine*. How can such articles be explained? This essay seeks to answer this question by exposing a side of Boswell's personality that has not been fully appreciated by scholars: his identity as a Scots Presbyterian lawyer and laird, as well-off landowners in Scotland were called. The focus here is not on Boswell's well-known relationships with his real and surrogate fathers, Lord Auchinleck and Samuel Johnson (though the former's role in helping to forge this aspect of

28

his son's personality was obviously great), but rather on his relationships with three forgotten men whose authority was less obvious: his boyhood tutor and lifelong country pastor John Dun and the Edinburgh advocates Andrew Crosbie and John Maclaurin.

I

In the same year that Robertson became Principal, his Moderate colleague Hugh Blair obtained a Regius professorship of rhetoric and belles lettres at Edinburgh University. The following April the forty-five-year-old professor turned to Boswell, then half his age, as he prepared for his first extensive visit to London. Confessing that he expected to feel out of place in the metropolis, Blair was grateful for Boswell's offer of guidance.[3] He had good reasons for concern. The 1760s was the decade when anti-Scottish feeling, often posing as political opposition to the nominally Scottish Earl of Bute, reached new heights in London. Moreover, Blair, like Robertson, spoke English with a strong Scottish accent and regarded England almost as a foreign land. It did not belong to their generation of Scottish literati to feel fully at home in England. As Boswell put the matter in 1774, "Hume, Robertson, and other greater geniuses than I am prefer Scotland. But they have neither that peculiar and permanent love of London and all its circumstances which I have; nor are they so much in unison with the English as I am" (*Defence*, p. 216).

And so young Boswell took Blair under his wing. As the two Scots wandered together through the streets of London, Boswell took special delight in guiding his "learned and ingenious" clerical friend under the windows of his "first London lady of the town" (*London Journal*, pp. 234–6). It was a typical Boswellian gesture, juxtaposing the priggish and the lewd, the public and the private, the moral and the immoral. On another occasion a depressed Boswell sank further into the doldrums after hearing Blair preach at the Scots Presbyterian meeting house in Monkwell Street: "Blair's New Kirk delivery[4] and the Dissenters roaring out the Psalms sitting on their backsides, together with the extempore prayers, and in short the whole vulgar idea of the Presbyterian worship, made me very gloomy." He therefore hastened to catch the end of the serivce at St. Paul's, where "I... had my mind set right again" (*London Journal*, p. 259). In still another episode, Boswell took Blair to the theatre and, in what he termed "a wild freak of youthful extravagance," entertained the audience with animal noises; when the crowd expressed appreciation for the cow only, Blair, "with an air of the utmost gravity and earnestness," told his friend: "My dear sir, I would *confine* myself to the *cow*!"[5]

These incidents reveal a great deal about Boswell's attitudes towards Scotland, England, and their leading cities. On the one hand, London represented pomp and politeness, symbolized by the grand Anglican service at St. Paul's. On the other hand, London meant liberation and dissipation, the chance to cavort more readily with ladies of the night and imitate cows as much as he pleased. From the latter point of view Edinburgh represented the formal and the proper, London the very opposite. London was intoxicating, Edinburgh suffocating.[6] Seen in this way, these incidents serve to remind us of the vast space betwixt the poles of Boswell's personality. If Boswell was attracted by London's infinite opportunities for experiencing both low and high life, he was less comfortable with the middle ground between.[7] And that middle ground was precisely the territory occupied by the Robertson–Blair circle of Scots Presbyterian clergymen of letters. After returning to Scotland in the spring of 1763, Blair advised Boswell to achieve respectability by studying law in Scotland. "You will not find it so grievous to put on the fetters of Custom, & to live like other men, when once you have formed a resolution to do it," he observed, with apparent reference to conversations the two men had held in London. "In the midst of the common jog trot of Life, you will always find many little amusements & pleasures; and may safely leave the high road a little, provided you do not go off it so far that people don't know where to find you."[8] Here was a formula for Presbyterian propriety with a liberal twist: Lord Auchinleck's medicine with a sugar coating, but Auchinleck's medicine nonetheless.

Even the Club was in its way a symbol of English politeness and superiority. Once again Boswell provided the appropriate Scottish contrast in his youthful *London Journal*, where he criticized the Edinburgh Poker Club, founded by the William Robertson circle in order to stir up support for a Scots militia, for "doing all that they can to destroy politeness. They would abolish all respect due to rank and external circumstances, and they would live like a kind of literary barbarians. For my own share, I own I would rather want their instructive conversation than be hurt by their rudeness" (*London Journal*, p. 300). Robertson, Hume, and the other Poker members were not always like that, he was quick to add, and they were least like that when a stranger was present. But all in all the Edinburgh literati were in Boswell's eyes "literary barbarians" when compared with the London men of letters whose company he preferred and whose respect he craved.[9]

Another Moderate clergyman, Alexander Carlyle, confirmed Boswell's assertion that "the Militia or the Poker Club" broke down class barriers, since it "not only Included the Literati, But many Noblemen and Gentlemen of Fortune and of the Liberal Professions, who mixd together with all the Freedom of Convivial Meetings once a week During 6 months in the Year." But Carlyle gave these facts a positive slant by arguing that the Poker contributed to "Forming and polishing the Manners which are Suitable to Civilis'd Society. For they Banish'd Pedantry from the Conversation of Scholars, and exalted the Ideas and Enlarg'd the Views of the Gentry: and

Created in the several Orders a New Interest in each other, which had not Taken place before in this Country."[10] It would seem, then, that what Boswell objected to about the Poker was the intimate mixing not, as one might expect from his own account, of high and low (the Poker's membership list contained none of the latter) but of high and middle. A laird's son who had associated on the most familiar terms with socially disreputable theatre people when a student at Edinburgh in the late 1750s (and with members of an even less respectable profession on many occasions), Boswell never reproached *himself* with helping to "destroy politeness." For politeness had nothing to do with actors and prostitutes. But when gentlemen of his class and country drank, plotted and joked in too familiar a manner with clergymen and scholars, Boswell grew uneasy and protested.

In their quest for a middle ground between enthusiasm and propriety, the Moderates of Blair's generation pursued a polite Presbyterian ideal that was not always to Boswell's liking. When in Edinburgh he often heard Blair preach in the New Kirk, where legal gentry like the Boswells had their family seats, and at times he was touched by his words. In regard to doctrine he had few complaints, at one point agreeing with Blair that "my religion is of the same cast with yours" (*Boswell in Extremes*, p. 358). Yet Boswell was never completely comfortable with the Moderates' social philosophy or with the Scottish Presbyterian mode of worship generally. He always "regretted that we had not the decency of the Church of England in this country," as he put it after taking communion at the New Kirk on November 12, 1780 (*Laird*, p. 269). For him, Moderate Presbyterianism represented at best a fragile compromise between his conflicting religious impulses.

There were, in any event, other factors that carried Boswell away from the Moderates. One of the most important was family ties.[11] Boswell's mother was an "extremely pious" Presbyterian whose vision of hell and damnation made her son "shudder."[12] Her sister Mary was married to Alexander Webster, an eminent evangelical preacher in Edinburgh and a major figure in the anti-Moderate or Popular party. Boswell's journals are filled with Sunday dinners, suppers and drinks with Webster, whose conversation may sometimes have undone the effect of Hugh Blair's Moderate preaching earlier in the day. On the other side of the family, the two previous lairds of Auchinleck – Boswell's father Alexander and especially his grandfather James – distinguished themselves as opponents of both the Moderates (or their forerunners) and, at the opposite extreme, of the radical Calvinists who chose to secede from the established church rather than submit to what seemed to them a corrupt or Erastian church polity. Both men were active in ecclesiastical affairs and often represented their presbyteries as ruling elders in the annual general assembly: assembly registers in the Scottish Record Office, for example, reveal that Boswell's own father was a ruling elder every year from 1755 through 1762. And both men served, in their turn, as sole patrons of Auchinleck, possessing the right, in effect, to fill vacancies in the parish church with any formally qualified clergyman of their choosing. In eighteenth-century Scotland that right was a matter of considerable controversy, and in opposing ecclesiastical patronage Popular party lairds sometimes found themselves in the peculiar position of acting – or at least arguing – against their own political interest.

In practice, parish patrons tended to use their authority at least partly for their own ends whether they supported the Moderate or Popular party. Thus, Boswell's father presented to the church at Auchinleck in 1752 his family chaplain and son's tutor, John Dun (1724–92), who was more memorable in young James's mind for cowardly deference to the laird than for evangelical piety. In the biographical sketch he prepared for Rousseau, Boswell credited Dun with introducing him to the *Spectator*, the Roman poets and a very mild species of religion that contrasted noticeably with the austere Calvinism of his mother:

> My governor sometimes spoke to me of religion, but in a simple and pleasing way. He told me that if I behaved well during my life, I should be happy in the other world. There I should hear beautiful music. There I should acquire the sublime knowledge that God will grant to the righteous; and there I should meet all the great men of whom I had read, and all the dear friends I had known. At last my governor put me in love with heaven, and some hope entered into my religion.[13]

In an earlier draft of the sketch he criticized the obsequiousness of Dun and his successor, both of whom seemed to be "men without manners, men of the meanest sort of education. They were like my father's servants. They ate at table, but they hardly dared open their mouths. I saw them treated with contempt."[14] Here is another neglected clue in the mystery of Boswell: he generally considered Scots Presbyterian clergymen to be well beneath him socially and therefore unworthy of the air of greatness that some of them (such as William Robertson) came to assume.

Frederick Pottle admonished Boswell for his lack of generosity towards Dun and acknowledged the great debt owed to the man who provided Boswell's first exposure to the English and Latin classics and to rational religion. Yet Pottle based this assessment on nothing more than Boswell's own accounts, and he qualified his praise of Dun in order to emphasize his subject's genius: "Judging from Dun's own style (we have several of his letters) he could not himself have been of much help to his pupil by way of example. But Boswell was an apt pupil, for he had a literary gift. Once embarked on the reading of English classics, he became his own teacher."[15] Pottle would have gained a fuller appreciation of Dun if he had consulted not merely his few remaining letters but also his two volumes of *Sermons*, published by subscription at Kilmarnock in Ayrshire in 1790. He would perhaps have gained more respect for Dun's prose style, and he would certainly have discovered a versatile man of letters and teacher whose commitment to liberal Christian principles had not waned over the years and whose influence on young Boswell must have been considerable. It is a sign of his continued respect for his former tutor that Boswell led the subscribers to Dun's *Sermons* by purchasing six sets of the work. When Boswell heard the news of Dun's death in 1792 he was deeply grieved (*Great Biographer*, p. 189).

In the preface to his *Sermons* Dun considered how one could say something interesting about subjects that had been discussed repeatedly by so many distinguished writers "for eighteen hundred years." His solution was to acknowledge that "all I can do is, to give old but precious and golden wares a new brush. The end in view is answered, if curiosity shall lead some persons, *Zaccheus-like*, to read what may be useful to them" (I, iv). This clue about Dun's teaching methodology was followed by an attack on writers who "put on the cloak of reserve" because "they don't trust us" and "don't let us into *real life*. An author should risk – despise his enemies when instructing or amusing his friends" (I, v). These were lessons Boswell learned well. We may infer that when studying the classics young Boswell was required to get "some of the best passages by heart," since Dun speaks admiringly of that method in this own case (I, vi).[16] But Dun's emphasis in regard to education is clearly on the need for excitement and vitality rather than rote learning, as in this critical passage: "It is not from want of knowledge, but want of attention, that men in this age do err. Instruction and admonition often repeated, becomes tiresome and nauseous; but if put into a new dress, has the appearance of novelty, attracts notice, and gives pleasure" (I, v).

True to his word, Dun produces an extraordinarily diverse pot-pourri. There is nothing exceptionable about the sermons themselves, which address subjects such as providence, consolation about death, the duty of ministers and people, miracles, the immortality of the righteous (preached on the occasion of Lord Auchinleck's death) and the Glorious Revolution in a manner consistent with Moderate Scottish Presbyterianism. There are, however, only fourteen sermons in his two published volumes. The remainder of the work is filled with odes to liberty, a hymn to providence, lectures on God's omnipresence and on the parable of the virgins, epistles on affliction, two substantial discourses entirely in Latin, an address to communicants, a Scots poem replying to Burns's "Address to the Deil," historical documents, anecdotes, declarations, moral tales, and lengthy notes on everything from Scots Presbyterian religious and social practices (which are favorably contrasted with English ones) to witches, India, and the reading of novels. In the conclusion to his volumes, Dun observes: "I early saw an objection to them, that it would be said, there is too great a *mixture* in one book." After noting that John Knox had also mixed various religious genres with "merry tales," he reveals his real aim:

> And now I must let my reader into the secret, that my original wish, in attempting this publication, was, that, by something not gloomy, but, if in my power, pleasant, natural, and neat, I might lead the lively genius, and man of taste, into serious thoughts: and I shall think all my toil... well bestowed and rewarded, if one single soul is made serious unto salvation. (II, 285–6)

Long before this publication, it would seem, Dun had done a great deal to lead his most famous pupil "into serious thoughts" and perhaps even "unto salvation." He may also have had a greater hand than has previously been thought in stimulating Boswell's appreciation for multiple literary genres and willingness to shed "the cloak of reserve" in his writings.

What of Dun's influence on Boswell's Scots Presbyterian identity? The *Sermons* of 1790 confirm the gentleness and moderation of Dun's religious teachings, which had evidently remained consistent since Boswell experienced them at mid-century. This commitment to polite Presbyterianism probably explains the presence on the subscription list of the Moderate ministers Hugh Blair and Alexander Carlyle. Yet John Dun was no Moderate in a party sense; on the contrary, his views on church politics were those of the Popular party. Just one year after his presentation to the parish of Auchinleck he took part in a bitter controversy in the general assembly. The assembly of 1752 had deposed the evangelical minister Thomas Gillespie as part of a concerted effort by the Moderates to assert the authority of the general assembly in presentation or patronage disputes as well as the authority of their own party within the general assembly. In 1753 the Popular party made an all-out effort to undo the defeat of the previous year by pressing to reinstate or "repone" Gillespie. Boswell's uncle Alexander Webster was elected Moderator of the general assembly that year, and Dun was a member representing the Presbytery of Ayr. After a warm debate the effort to repone Gillespie came up short by three votes. Dun, who was of the generation of William Robertson, was among the many ministers who signed their names to a dissent against the assembly's subsequent resolution on the matter.[17] In the 1760s Dun is thought to have written an anonymous *Address to Procure a Repeal of the Patronage Act*; and when the Popular party made the century's last major effort to achieve that end in 1784, he delivered a supportive speech in the general assembly that was later published.[18] In notes to his *Sermons* Dun repeatedly expresses concern for the people and attacks the law of patronage as "expressly contrary I say to the solemn treaty of the UNION in 1707, betwixt England and Scotland" (I, 256).

John Dun, then, was that rare bird in late eighteenth-century Scotland: a theological, educational, and literary moderate who was at the same time a strong advocate of Popular party views on the most important issue separating the two ecclesiastical parties, church patronage. He combined a deep faith in the essential truths of Christianity with consistently liberal attitudes towards both theological and political issues in the kirk, and he found no contradiction (as many Popular party clergymen did) between polite literature and Christain faith. It can hardly be a coincidence that James Boswell adopted a similar outlook. Though Boswell's attraction to Anglican and Roman Catholic forms of worship took him in directions utterly foreign to Dun, his dominant religious personality remained that of a Scots Presbyterian in the mould of his childhood tutor.

II

Another force driving Boswell away from the Moderates was his friendship with fellow gentlemen advocates Andrew Crosbie of Holm (1736–85) and John Maclaurin of Dreghorn (1734–96). They were among the colleagues with whom Boswell associated and identified for much of his professional life in Edinburgh, and Boswell scholars have not fully grasped their importance in shaping and nurturing Boswell's personality. Both were a few years older than Boswell, and both were active in the struggle against church patronage and the Moderate party. In 1766 – the year in which Boswell finally settled down to an Edinburgh legal career – Maclaurin published (anonymously) *Thoughts on the Right of Patronage*, which took a radical stance by Popular party standards. Three years later Crosbie published (also anonymously) *Thoughts of a Layman concerning Patronage and Presentations*, which was circulated throughout Scotland by the hundreds as part of a Popular party offensive against the law of patronage.[19] Crosbie, in fact, was the lay leader of the Popular party and attended the general assembly as an elder almost every year from the late 1750s to the mid-1780s. He was also related to Boswell through a common uncle eminent in the legal profession and in Scottish politics: Charles Erskine, Lord Tinwald.[20] Maclaurin, whose uncle John was one of the leading evangelical ministers in the west of Scotland, was also an elder in the general assembly on occasion but apparently proved more useful as an advocate of Popular party causes (according to his biographer, he accepted no other kind) at the bar of the assembly.[21]

Since relatively little has been written about these Popular party lawyers, several points are worth noting in the context of Boswell's Edinburgh world. First, these were clubbable, poetry-loving wits who embraced Boswell and made the life of a Scots Presbyterian legal laird more bearable to him. Some of this comes across in Maclaurin's playful "Song Inscribed to James Boswell, Esq. on His First Appearance as a Lawyer before the general assembly of the Church of Scotland" (1770), which concludes:

> Therefore, Boswell, 'tis clear,
> You had better appear
> The elders' *unruly* among;
> Be sure you stick close by
> Our friend, Andrew Crosby,
> Or else you'll be damnably wrong,[22]

Other light-hearted poems reprinted in Maclaurin's *Works* bore titles such as "On Johnson's Dictionary" and "Of Dr. Johnson's Style" (no doubt these two bits of wit were intended specially for Boswell), "A Birth-Day Ode in Honour of the Late Mr Andrew Crosby," and "An Epistle to the Rev. Dr Thos. Blacklock." The last of these poems paid tribute to the blind Popular party minister and poet named in *A Collection of Original Poems by the Rev. Mr. Blacklock and Other Scotch Gentlemen* (Edinburgh, 1760), which also included several pieces by Boswell's Jacobite friend Andrew Erskine and "a great many" by Maclaurin.[23] In 1776 Maclaurin, Crosbie, and Boswell collaborated on a raucous satire of Scottish judicial life, "The Justiciary Opera," which reflects the drunken state of its authors at least as much as their wit. In fact, heavy drinking and revelry at pubs like the Crown Tavern and the Star and Garter constituted a vital component of this legal subculture.[24]

As with Boswell, however, the outward appearance of light-hearted fun shielded deeper concerns. Despite their roistering, Maclaurin and Crosbie were serious about the imporance of literature and polite learning. In the case of Maclaurin, who wrote enough material to fill two posthumous volumes, this point is perhaps obvious. But it is equally true of Crosbie, who was considered a learned man by Boswell and others even though he published little. His election to the Select Society in 1758 (Boswell also became a member in 1761) and his role as a founding member and fellow of the Society of Antiquaries in Scotland provide some support for this assessment, as does the impressive library he left behind.[25] Assuming there is truth in the widely held assumption that Crosbie was the model for Sir Walter Scott's advocate Pleydell in *Guy Mannering*, the following description of Pleydell's library is revealing: "It was a well-proportioned room...surrounded with books, the best editions of the best authors, and in particular, an admirable collection of classics. 'These,' said Pleydell, 'are my tools of trade. A lawyer without history or literature is a mechanic, a mere working mason; if he possesses some knowledge of these, he may venture to call himself an architect.'"[26] Yet for all his learning, or pretensions to it, Crosbie never made a name for himself in the republic of letters. Neither, for that matter, did Maclaurin, and even Boswell remained a marginal figure in the intellectual life of the Scottish Enlightenment. At a time when other Scottish literary men, including clergymen who were their social inferiors, were achieving considerable fame, wealth, and status as a reward for their intellectual accomplishments, a certain amount of frustration and resentment was perhaps inevitable among these legal men of letters.

High-spirited tippling and light-hearted wit also helped mask serious psychological problems. Melancholia was a constant concern. Maclaurin especially could be moody, and his poem "Ennui,"[27] with its evocation of foul weather and gloomy spirits, expressed an underlying motif common to his legal friends. Another common motif appears in Maclaurin's birthday ode to Crosbie, whose fate is foretold at birth by the gods:

> In bustle, and in strife,
> He wrestle must thro' life:
> I hear him plead,
> Tho' all unfee'd,
> With utmost energy of soul,
> For litigants on the poor's roll:
> Most causes his arguments carry,
> While eager he raves,
> For all sorts of knaves
> Before the Grand Justiciary.
> Against fix'd Fate don't obstinately draw,
> This fav'rite child devoted is to Law.

In the concluding stanza Jove proclaims that law will not be the only ingredient in Crosbie's "strange cup of life":

> 'Tis order'd, boy, Law, Love, and Wine,
> Shall thy strange cup of life compose;
> But tho' the three are all divine,
> The last shall be thy darling doze.

This was but a poetic way of saying that Crosbie would drink himself to death at age forty-nine. When Maclaurin described himself, in the poetic preface to his *Essays in Verse*, he captured yet another aspect of his circle's group sensibility:

> If in these pages, sometimes there be found,
> A line unpolish'd, or discordant sound,
> Shou'd now and then your acc'rate ear detect,
> False language, or provincial dialect,
> Do not severely criticise the flaw,
> His country, Scotland, his profession, Law.
> The first invidious, labour'd as he sung,
> To mar the graces, of the English tongue;
> The niggard last, denied sufficient time,
> To smooth each verse, and modulate each rhime.

Poetry and polite learning, wit, heavy drinking, periodic bouts of melancholia, sexual "romping," uncertainty about Scotland's "provincial dialect" when set against English standards and the constant "bustle" and "strife" of their "niggard" profession – these classic Boswellian traits were part of a broader lifestyle that Crosbie and Maclaurin shared and to some extent nurtured.

Another point that deserves mention is the radicalism of these men. Maclaurin was said to be a warm "friend and lover of liberty; and wherever he found oppression, he was an advocate against it" (*Works*, I, xvii). His writings certainly bear out this remark, for his published poems and essays are filled with radical ideas on topics such as the American Revolution, the French Revolution and subsequent French wars, emigration, liberty of the press, the rights of colliers, the slave trade, and even the rights of animals. For his opinions on the French Revolution in particular, he was branded "a Republican, a Democrat; and it was even insinuated that he wished for a revolution in this country" (I, xx). During the 1790s he became a recluse, afraid to trust outsiders at a time when his political ideas were viewed with so much suspicion. Until then, however, his radicalism was no barrier to a successful legal career that culminated in his appointment to a judgeship as Lord Dreghorn in 1788. Crosbie's career was similar, in that he also espoused liberal and radical ideas, even breaking with the Popular party in the late 1770s over the issue of Roman Catholic relief (for which the "No Popery" mob tried to burn down his house). And he, too, had a brilliant legal career that brought wealth, a fine house in the New Town, and the likelihood of promotion to the bench – until the severe financial crisis of the early 1780s left him destitute and (along with heavy drinking) hastened his premature death in February 1785 (*Applause*, p. 54).

In light of their radicalism, Crosbie's and especially Maclaurin's anti-patronage pamphlets of the 1760s acquire special significance. Noting that the Scottish people were deprived of any opportunity for political participation in the civil sphere, Crosbie went on to argue that the Church of Scotland represented the one place where Scottish liberty had been preserved. "The whole system of Presbyterian church-government tends to excite ideas of liberty, and to animate men with an affection for it," he stated in *Thoughts of a Layman* (p. 28). Crosbie's alternative to filling vacant parish churches by means of patronage was a complex representative system that divided authority among the local heritors or landowners, the kirk session or elders of the vacant parish, the parishioners, and perhaps even the patron (pp. 49–50). This plan was somewhat more radical than the standard Popular party position of the day, which recommended a return to the system – instituted in 1690 but overturned by the Patronage Act of 1712 – of selection solely by local heritors and elders.[28]

Yet Crosbie's views seem tame compared to what Maclaurin had to say in *Thoughts on the Right of Patronage*. Besides putting forward a variety of arguments against the hated Patronage Act, Maclaurin found the Act of 1690 nearly as objectionable because it gave too much power to landowners at the expense of the people. Just as the patron's true end is not the "comfort and instruction of the common people" but rather "the provision of a friend or dependent," so "the rich, who are commonly understood to be the

Heritors" would not be likely to make their selections with the "comfort and instruction" of "the poor, that is the tenants, labouring people, etc." foremost in their minds.[29] If the law of patronage could not be repealed, patrons – being "gentlemen of fortune, who live in affluence and ease, while the common people struggle with labour and want"–had a responsibility to act compassionately towards the people, and "to sweeten for them the bitter cup of life as much as possible." This responsibility was rooted in "the good of the country, and common humanity" and applied even if they were not personally religious (or Presbyterian, he might have added).[30] This message was addressed to the patrons and future patrons of Scotland, and there is every reason to believe that at least one of the latter took it to heart. When James Boswell assumed the duties of laird and patron of Auchinleck in the latter part of his life, he seems to have been genuinely concerned about the wishes and needs of the parishioners; after the death of John Dun in 1792 he took his responsibilities as patron very seriously (*Great Biographer*, pp. 189–90).

In a more general sense the radicalism of Crosbie and Maclaurin seems to have influenced Boswell during the late 1760s and 1770s. Their influence was probably greatest in the arena of ecclesiastical politics, where Boswell's prejudices in favor of the Popular party on the basis of family ties and other factors received powerful ideological reinforcement. But secular political matters were also affected. The issue of Corsican liberty, Boswell's primary political passion during this period, was the sort of cause his radical legal friends would have applauded, just as it was a cause that Johnson considered a waste of time (even if he appreciated Boswell's accomplishment from a purely literary point of view) (*Life*, II, 22, 58, 70). We know that in the summer of 1768 Crosbie was actively involved with Boswell in conducting a Scottish subscription to buy guns for Paoli, and that he put up a considerable amount of his own money to underwrite the enterprise while the funds were being raised.[31] In all probability Crosbie and his circle had been providing, since 1766 at the latest, encouragement and support for the Corsican project that could not be found elsewhere; it is perhaps not too much to say that Boswell's love of liberty was fired by the radical Edinburgh milieu in which he flourished after his return from the continent. Boswell's sympathy for the American Revolution can be explained in the same way. In that instance his liberal views placed him in opposition both to Johnson and to the Moderates, who saw eye to eye on such topics as political order and social subordination. Towards the end of 1776 Boswell grew so angry with Hugh Blair for praying against the Americans on a fast day appointed by the King for that very purpose that he began to "shun" the New Kirk whenever Blair preached and finally communicated his criticisms and concerns in a letter to his pastor (*Boswell in Extremes*, pp. 56, 88, 359–60). In protest against the fast day Boswell not only "paid no regard to it" but also spoke out forcefully against it in polite company; significantly, "Maclaurin agreed with me" (*Boswell in Extremes*, p. 65). It is unlikely that Boswell would have expressed himself so forcefully in the company of Johnson, where his words would have been sure to provoke a hostile rather than a sympathetic response.

The radicalism of Crosbie, Maclaurin and Boswell should be seen within the context of the British tradition of "country" or "civic humanist" idiom and ideology. As J. G. A. Pocock has shown, that tradition could be either Whig or Tory but was always, in its purest form, elitist because it rested on the notion of independent, virtuous, liberty-loving, landowning "citizens" acting for the good of the nation, often by checking the power of the monarch or central government.[32] In Scotland the fountainhead of this paradigm was the thought of Andrew Fletcher of Saltoun. Later in the century it was invoked by Moderate agitators for a Scots militia as well as by the radical Whig Earls of Selkirk, Buchan, and Lauderdale.[33] Considering Nicholas Phillipson's demonstration of the quasi-aristocratic standing of the legal profession in eighteenth-century Scotland, where every judge was styled "lord" and where advocates (barristers) tended to descend from and buy or marry into the gentry,[34] it is not surprising to find legal men like Boswell and his friends drawing upon this tradition. In a letter of February 13, 1762, for example, Crosbie (an active member of the Poker Club) used classic "country" rhetoric to describe the Scots militia scheme as "the only Constitutional Ballance against the Immense power that is thrown into the hands of the Crown by the present State of the Standing Army, and which, should we ever be cursed with an Ambitious Prince, the Nation may severely feel the effects of."[35] Boswell's own enthusiasm for the Scots militia during the 1770s rested in part on similar principles, for he associated the militia cause with "a noble Tory interest" that represented a challenge to the existing system of centralized political management (*Ominous Years*, p. 268).[36]

The critical point is that Boswell's radical ideology must not be considered that of an isolated or confused figure, black sheep or rebel against his social class. On the contrary, Boswell's ideology was grounded both in a long-standing "country" tradition and in a contemporary circle of friends who saw the world much the way he did, and both were decidedly aristocratic. Far from representing rebellion against his social standing, Boswell's adoption of "country" radicalism during the 1760s and 1770s may actually have constituted a premature assertion of his standing as an independent laird.

A final way in which Crosbie and Maclaurin may have influenced Boswell concerns their manner of attacking the Moderates and the "enlightened" culture the Moderates represented. During the 1750s and early 1760s Maclaurin in particular produced several anonymous pamphlets and broadsides that ridiculed the Moderates and their vision of enlightenment. The most famous of these writings, the *Apology for the Writers against the*

Tragedy of Douglas and *The Philosopher's Opera*, appeared during the 1757 pamphlet war over John Home's controversial play *Douglas* but also lampooned David Hume and the Select Society to which the Moderate circle belonged. Other anonymous performances by the young Maclaurin, such as the *Keekiad: A Poem* (London, 1760), were downright obscene. Though the attributions of such works to Maclaurin are not always grounded in hard evidence, he was the acknowledged master of witty, scurrilous, anti-Moderate verse. Sometimes Maclaurin's irreverence went too far, for he also made light of Scripture, Christian views on immortality, and other subjects that Boswell took very seriously.[37] Crosbie's skeptical religious beliefs also troubled him.[38] Yet Maclaurin and Crosbie's serious writings on the patronage issue adopted a self-righteous, pious tone and criticized the Moderates for their alleged failings as men of God. Thus, Maclaurin's *Thoughts on the Right of Patronage* noted "the great change in the style, manners, sentiments, and sermons of the [Scottish] clergy. They are, no doubt, now more learned, more philosophic, and more celebrated in the republic of letters, than they were half a century ago; but it does not therefore follow, that they will give more comfort and instruction to the common people" (pp. 250–1). On the contrary, Maclaurin charged, they are less inclined to preach on popular subjects and in a popular style, or to live the sort of austere lives the people expect of their pastors. Crosbie's *Thoughts of a Layman* went further, arguing that politeness and refinement were at best irrelevant and at worst serious liabilities for Scottish clergymen.[39]

III

It is now possible to begin to comprehend Boswell's anonymous articles on the Scottish kirk in the *London Magazine*. The "Sketch of the Constitution of the Church of Scotland" of 1772 and its 1773 sequel, "Debates in the General Assembly of the Church of Scotland" may be constructively viewed as a single, coherent literary work, comprising four distinct parts.[40] In part one (April 1772) Boswell presented a brief outline of the structure of the Church of Scotland, its two ecclesiastical parties and its annual general assembly, which he declared "an excellent school for eloquence" and perhaps "the most learned assembly of men that now meet for deliberation as a court, or tribunal, or legislative body" (pp. 182–3). He criticized William Robertson, praised his own Popular party friends and stated the article's paradoxical thesis, which he restated more concisely thirteen years later when supposedly quoting this article: "'The popular party has most eloquence; Dr. Robertson's [Moderate party] most influence.'"[41]

Part two, which takes up the last part of the April 1772 installment and the whole of the one published in May, consists of highlights from a particular debate in the general assembly of 1771, the "Cause of St. Ninians." This was a classic patronage case, in which the assembly had to decide whether a clergyman who had been presented to fill the vacant church at St. Ninians by the lawful patron of that parish should be inducted there, even though he was thoroughly unacceptable to the congregation. After warm arguments on both sides the Moderate party carried the day by two votes, despite "many protests" and even insinuations that the assembly clerk (the Moderate George Wishart) had cheated when counting the votes. Boswell added passages from the written case of the people of St. Ninians by the "ingenious young barrister" who would become the foremost Popular party lawyer and radical Whig in late eighteenth-century Scotland, Henry Erskine, as well as a "repartee" between Robertson and "the great champion of the popular party," Rev. John Freebairn of Dunbarton. The 1772 article concluded with a long note pointing out that "the above specimens of oratory…evidently shew the present state of speaking in the *Church of Scotland* to be very different from what has been published as Presbyterian Eloquence" (alluding presumably to an old anti-Presbyterian pamphlet of the troubled 1690s, *Scotch Presbyterian Eloquence*) and raised expectations for further specimens of Scottish ecclesiastical oratory in subsequent issues.

Those further specimens began appearing in April 1773, in what may be considered the third part of Boswell's essay. Once again he focused on a particular general assembly debate, this one concerning a case of alleged nepotism in the parish of Marykirk in Aberdeenshire, where an innkeeper called John Brymer had purchased the right of patronage from the faculty at King's College and subsequently presented his own son to the church. And once again the point was to show that, even though the Popular party got the better of the argument, the Moderate party won the contest, for the general assembly had supported the presentation of young Brymer without a vote. This debate had occurred in the assembly of 1772, though the date was never mentioned by Boswell. The fourth and last part of the work appeared in August 1773. It consisted of a long speech by one of the leading clerical voices in the Popular party, Charles Nisbet of Montrose, on a parish annexation dispute in the general assembly of 1771. Nisbet's speech concluded with a paragraph from the *Rambler* (no. 145, condemning oppression by legal authority), by "'a celebrated author, who is an ornament to the present age.'" To this passage was appended a single sentence that gave the piece a happy ending: "Though Principal Robertson, John Home, and several more of the court luminaries, spoke warmly in favour of the annexation, the general assembly, by a great majority, *reversed* the sentence of which Mr. Nisbet complained; and *for once the force of oratory was visibly exemplified*" (p. 401, latter emphasis added).

With this sentence Boswell neatly tied up the loose ends in his series of articles on the kirk. Having examined two causes in which Popular party eloquence was apparently thwarted by Moderate political management, he finished by turning his own thesis on its head. By skillfully reporting on selected debates from past general assembly meetings, and by cleverly manipulating the reports to create the illusion of change over time, he left the reader with three distinct impressions: that the general assembly of the Church of Scotland was a great and noble scene of eloquence; that the Popular party consistently outdebated the Moderates in the assembly; and that, though the Popular party had previously been unable to translate its superior eloquence into political advantage, this situation was now beginning to change. Each of these impressions was in fact questionable. We have seen that Boswell could be highly critical of Presbyterianism in general, and we know further that he actually detested the general assembly (*"that vulgar and rascally* court," he called it in his journal entry of May 26, 1777) and dreaded having to prostitute his services there (*Boswell in Extremes*, p. 128).[42] And Boswell's is the only contemporary account that gives the oratorical edge to the Popular party in the general assembly, which continued to be dominated by the Moderates throughout the eighteenth century.

The "Sketch" of 1772 and "Debates" of 1773 constituted effective pieces of ecclesiastical journalism in the service of the Popular party. The timing of these publications – each beginning its periodical run in the month of April – was not unrelated to this purpose, for it was common practice to publish material designed to stir up support for one's ecclesiastical party just before the general assembly convened in late May.[43] Boswell was also using these publications to promote kirk and country, by informing English readers about the organization of Scotland's national church and by showing them in particular that its annual general assembly was a distinguished institution. In addition, Boswell used these ecclesiastical writings to promote his friends and kin. Here is the evidence he presented in the "Sketch" to support his contention that the Popular party was oratorically superior to the Moderates:

> We may mention, in particular, two gentlemen of the law, Messieurs Crosbie and Mac Laurin, Advocates. Both are masters of the subject; and both speak in a manner that would do them honour in any assembly. Mr. Crosbie harangues with a firmness, a boldness, and a warmth, that have gained him the title of *Serjeant Crosbie* in the civil courts, and *Saint Crosbie* in the ecclesiastical. Mr. Mac Laurin, who is son to the celebrated Professor Colin Mac Laurin, and who gave so great a proof of his abilities in his defence of *Mungo Campbell*,[44] argues warmly too, but with more precision, and at the same time more fancy. He has written several essays in verse; and his speeches are always seasoned with wit and humour. When he was younger, he dealt them out more liberally. He is now more sparing of them. It was observed, by a lively friend of his, distinguished for the originality of his comparisons, "Mac Laurin has as much wit and humour as ever he had; but, fearing to overseason the dish, he has clapped the lid upon the castor, and instead of throwing out those qualities copiously as formerly, he sprinkles them with more address." (p. 184)

Thus did Boswell pay tribute to his friends and, in the process, publicize Maclaurin's renunciation of the childish productions of his youth (an act with which Boswell of all people could fully identify). He also managed to acknowledge the contributions of "The Rev. Dr. *Webster*, at *Edinburgh*, celebrated for his copious eloquence, for his quickness of repartee, and for his abilities in calculation" (p. 185).

Above all, Boswell's *London Magazine* writings on the Church of Scotland promoted Boswell himself and helped him to define his complex identity. If Boswell was compelled by circumstances to be a Presbyterian lawyer in Edinburgh, it must have soothed his ego to have English readers see this career in the best possible light. If he had to earn guineas pleading causes at the bar of the general assembly, it was surely helpful to have that body portrayed as an exceedingly dignified scene of ecclesiastical eloquence. More specifically, Boswell himself appears as a character in the ecclesiastical dramas he depicted. In the St. Ninians debate he was one of the counsels for the patron (a reminder that he did not enjoy the luxury of defending only Popular party causes, as Crosbie and Maclaurin apparently did). He delivered a very brief statement, laced with military metaphors and Latin allusions, and actually set himself up for a rebuke by Freebairn which concluded with the observation that, upon entering this general assembly, "I did not expect, that a people struggling for liberty would be attacked by the friend of Paoli" (p. 185). It may at first seem strange that Boswell would allow himself to be so used in one of his own publications, but then Boswell liked publicity in general and particularly liked publicity about his role as the champion of Corsican liberty.[45]

Moreover, the "Sketch" served as an advertisement for Boswell's ability as an ecclesiastical lawyer (after all, the patron of St. Ninians had won his cause), while at the same time showing where his real allegiance lay. In the Marykirk simony case at the next general assembly, Boswell was sole counsel for the parishioners, and his four-page speech occupied nearly the entire opening installment of his 1773 "Debates." It was a good speech, clear and to the point, on behalf of a cause that Boswell obviously supported wholeheartedly. Though it did not carry the day, this was no disgrace, for Boswell's "Sketch" had already established that Popular party eloquence was vulnerable to Moderate machinations.[46] At the very least these publications publicized Boswell's own role by portraying him as a featured player in the general assembly's distinguished cast. They may also have won favour with Boswell's father by taking an active part on the Popular party side. Finally, they served to redefine Boswell's identity as a Popular party lawyer in the Crosbie-Maclaurin mould – an identity that helped Boswell in his struggle to come to terms with his place as a Scots Presbyterian legal laird.

In the course of establishing that identity, Boswell attacked the leader of the rival Moderate party, William Robertson, with a savageness that might astonish readers of the *Life* and Hebrides *Tour*. In those works Robertson appears almost exclusively as an eminent historian and man of letters, respected in varying degrees by both Boswell and Johnson. There are occasional criticisms, but they are generally mild and immediately rendered inoffensive by Boswell. On two different occasions, for example, Johnson is either implicitly or explicitly critical of Robertson in the context of his ongoing debate with Boswell on the merits of Scottish literature. On the first occasion (spring 1768) Johnson refuses to be lured into Boswell's trap, saying that he loves Robertson and won't talk of his *History of Scotland*. Boswell then remarks: "It is but justice both to him and Dr. Robertson to add, that though he indulged himself in this sally of wit, he had too good taste not to be fully sensible of the merits of that admirable work." On the second occasion (April 20, 1773) Boswell brings Johnson out with the question: "Will you not admit the superiority of Robertson, in whose History we find such penetration – such painting?" When Johnson replies that Robertson's work should be viewed as "romance" – "History it is not," he states, because it contains too little substance and prose that is too ornamental – Boswell observes that his friend probably criticized "Dr. Robertson's excellent historical works" merely in order to win the "contest" with Boswell himself, for his real opinions would probably not "so widely differ from the rest of the literary world" (*Life*, II, 53, 237–8).[47]

This assessment rings true as far as Johnson is concerned. He occasionally referred to Robertson or Blair as "the dog," but then this was his way. If he would not hear them preach in Scotland, his refusal was nothing personal: Johnson was single-handedly responsible for getting Blair's celebrated sermons published ("though the dog is a Scotchman, and a Presbyterian, and every thing he should not be"); besides, he was quite willing to hear Robertson preach if it were from "a tree" rather than the pulpit of a dreaded Presbyterian church (*Life*, IV, 98, V, 121). Ossian was a testier point of contention, but Robertson was not a prime target of Johnson's scorn on that particular issue. For all their differences, and for all his prejudices against Scotland, Johnson shared with these Moderate divines one common ground in social and political conservatism and another in love of literature, learning, and virtue. He was therefore "much pleased" at hearing that Robertson was looking forward to seeing him in Scotland (*Life*, II, 232), and he seems to have enjoyed being taken on a tour of Edinburgh and its university by the Principal and Adam Ferguson. Walking home from an Edinburgh supper at which Robertson and Blair had "talked well upon subordination and government," Johnson was heard to say: "'Sir, these two doctors are good men, and wise men.'"[48]

With Boswell himself the matter is different. There are hints in the journals and notes that he was being considerably less than truthful when he praised Robertson's histories so strongly in the *Life*. On April 18, 1775 he stated in the company of Johnson and others that Robertson was "just a PACKER," meaning one who simply packed information into his books; "'All history in an Almanack'."[49] But readers of the *Life* never heard about this conversation. Instead they encountered Johnson's opposite criticism – that Robertson had not put enough substance into his book – and discovered Boswell defending the Principal in the manner discussed above. At the time of the Hebrides *Tour* we know that Boswell was concerned about offending Robertson (*Corr: Garrick, Burke, Malone*, p. 284), but the *Life* appeared two years after Robertson's death. Even then, apparently, Boswell was reluctant to treat the leading figure of the Scottish Presbyterian Enlightenment too harshly in a work known to be his.

No such fears held him back in his anonymous periodical publications on the kirk. In the "Sketch" he attacked Robertson without mercy:

> Dr. Robertson, author of the histories of Scotland of Charles V. may be called the leader of the court party. He is a member of the Assembly every year, and shews an ambition to be at the head of the *Kirk of Scotland* that seems hardly compatible with a mind accustomed to the contemplation of great and extensive objects. He sits like a Prime Minister upon the treasury-bench, and has his chosen supporters. *It would be indecent to suppose that he can have his prepared and determined voters*. He speaks as he writes. He has much address; and having, or being believed to have, interest with those in power in the state, there is no wonder that he should be followed by many; for all objects of ambition are comparatively important. Each country clergyman expects a better living, a benefice in a town, a chair in the university, or perhaps aspires to royal favour. (p. 184)

This was exceptionally nasty stuff, and Boswell's italicizing served to underline his sarcasm. Robertson was reduced to a mere politician: power-hungry, ambitious, and wholly without principle. The very name that Boswell gave to the Moderates – "the court party" – suggested political subservience and unscrupulous place-hunting. Boswell's obvious motive was to score points for the Popular party by denigrating the Moderates' leader. Other, more subtle factors may also have been at work. The day before Boswell stayed up all night to write this installment of the "Sketch," he had been delighted to hear Garrick blast Robertson for "persecuting [James] Beattie for having attacked Hume"; "It was really pretty to hear Mr. Garrick talk thus" (*Defence*, pp. 124–6, 141). Like Garrick, Boswell obviously resented the fact that Robertson and his circle of Moderate literati had rallied to Hume's defence in response to the hostile attacks on Humean skepticism in Beattie's *Essay on Truth* (1770).

But Boswell's resentment towards Robertson ran deeper still. The critique in the "Sketch" betrays a tone of social snobbery, as if Robertson had overstepped his bounds by aspiring to have and be more than a Scottish

Presbyterian clergyman should. The only comparable case in past Scottish history was that of William Carstares during and after the age of William III, and it is perhaps not coincidental that when Boswell read Joseph McCormick's biography of Carstares in late August 1774 (borrowing his copy from Crosbie, who warned him that "there was nothing in it"), he concluded with disdain that the subject of the work was "just an artful sagacious Presbyterian divine" (*Defence*, p. 283).[50] Robertson's lucrative offices and fees from his books had brought him not only great fame but also considerable material wealth–an issue on which Boswell was particularly sensitive at this time in his life. Along with Blair, Robertson was said to be the first Scots Presbyterian clergyman to keep a private carriage. Lurking just beneath the surface of Boswell's account are strong feelings of resentment that a poor "country clergyman" (for so Robertson was until his translation to an Edinburgh church in 1756) had risen so high while landed gentlemen like him had to struggle to make ends meet.[51]

By the time readers of the April 1772 number of the *London Magazine* got to Boswell's "Sketch," they would already have learned from the front-page article by Robert Liston, entitled "Character of Dr. Robertson," that Robertson had risen from humble origins "to greater dignities and emoluments than have ever been enjoyed by any Presbyterian clergyman, since the time of the Reformation" (p. 279). That article was as big a puff as any Moderate could have desired for his chief. Among other things, it stated that Robertson had been called to an Edinburgh church "by a popular election" (true, but the election had been carefully managed from above); that his *History of Scotland* had been called "the best history in the English Language"; that his numerous offices had been bestowed upon him "unsolicited and unexpected"; and that his *Charles V* had earned its author the highest amount of any book ever published and had lived up to expectations. "In a word," the "Character" concluded, "he may be pronounced to be one of the most perfect characters of the age; and his name will be a lasting honour to the island that gave him birth" (pp. 279–80). Since Boswell was on good terms with the editor of the *London Magazine*, Edward Dilly, it is just possible that he knew about Liston's puff in advance and wrote the April installment of his "Sketch" to counteract it. The two pieces made a neatly balanced pair, and it is therefore not surprising that the *Scots Magazine* reprinted them together in its April issue. But Boswell may have felt that his "Sketch" was not enough, for the June number of the *London Magazine* contained a more focused response that Pottle attributed to him: "Sceptical Observations *upon a late Character* of Dr. Robertson."[52] That article began by noting that the "fond idea of embellishing one of our *living literati*...has not escaped without animadversion in North Britain." It pointed out that the "Character" of Robertson had "no doubt, been given in the London Magazine for the evident purpose of extending, or reviving the Doctor's reputation, in all the corners of the British empire." Then it proceeded to refute the specific compliments that the "Character" had so generously bestowed. First, it printed some "waggish" verses that mocked Robertson's celebrated ecclesiastical eloquence in language reminiscent of the young John Maclaurin:

> The torrents of your eloquence should now
> Rush out, and carry every thing before 'em.
> By a religious *copia verorum*;
> Checking all poor *fanatics* in their way,
> And spreading patronage from sea to sea:
> 'Twere else unnatural upon my soul;
> The proverb justly says, *long fair, long foul*.[53]

After justly disputing the claim that Robertson's "plurality of good offices" had been bestowed "unsolicited and unexpected," the article challenged Robertson's credentials as a historian for his unfair treatment of Mary Queen of Scots and his general inferiority to Hume, Clarendon, and Lyttleton.[54] Then came a paragraph on Robertson's dealings with booksellers, which suggested that in negotiating the sale of his *History of Scotland* he had ill-used the Edinburgh bookseller Alexander Kincaid in order to squeeze a better offer from the London bookseller Andrew Millar, and which implied (erroneously, it would seem) that sales of *Charles V* had not justified the high price paid for it. The final paragraph echoed the "Sketches," as well as the anti-patronage pamphlets of Maclaurin and Crosbie, in its hostility to Robertson as Moderate party leader and man of letters:

> As to what is said of Dr. Robertson's having spent his life as the leader of a church party, and consequently in regulating the passions, the interests, the prejudices of a numerous faction, we cannot, for our parts, admire the character of a *Reverend Party-man*; especially, if the party led on by him is a destroying party to any regular body of Christians. We, for our parts, esteem and reverence a clergyman, whose life is principally devoted to his great and important duty.

As set forth in the concluding quotation by Freebairn, a clergyman's "great and important duty" was defined as concerning himself with his pastoral responsibilities without regard to "any sordid views of temporal gain, or even to the applause of men which literary performances may acquire."

In her pioneering article on Boswell and the Church of Scotland, Mary Margaret Stewart pointed out that Boswell applied a different and much stricter standard of conduct to the clergy than to himself. More generally, she showed that he usually took the side of the Popular party against the Moderates, even though certain aspects of his personality and taste seemed more conducive to the opposite position.[55] Although Stewart noted the role of family connections in shaping this aspect of Boswell's ever-contradictory self, we have seen that other factors, including above all the influence and example of the Popular party clergyman John Dun and the Popular party lawyers Andrew Crosbie and John Maclaurin, must also be taken into consideration. From Dun he gained an appreciation for moderate Christianity, as well as for polite Latin and English literary models; from Crosbie and Maclaurin he learned the use of ridicule and invective against get-ahead Moderates like William Robertson and John Home and discovered how to play the role of a committed, witty, intelligent, outspoken, eccentric, hard-drinking, boisterous, sexually promiscuous, periodically melancholy Edinburgh advocate; from all three men he acquired a strong sense of social and ecclesiastical justice for the "people" and a deep ideological commitment to the political principles of the Popular party in the Church of Scotland, especially animosity towards seemingly authoritarian Moderate policies with regard to church patronage. Particularly in regard to Crosbie and Maclaurin, the model here is not the familiar one of a son struggling to satisfy or defy his (real or adopted) father but rather that of a young professional man associating with, and learning from, his slightly older and more accomplished colleagues and friends. If a family metaphor is required, it is one of younger and older brothers rather than of parent and child.

The contradictory ways in which Boswell treated William Robertson reflect the divisions within Boswell's own identity. As a self-conscious London man of letters, Boswell treated Robertson graciously. In the *Life* he showed respect for his company as well as for his ability as a historian, even if he privately considered Robertson's entire Edinburgh literary circle crude and uninspiring. In his capacity as a pupil and parishioner of John Dun and a member of the brotherhood of radical Scots Presbyterian legal lairds, however, his judgement was completely reversed, and Robertson became the target of Boswell's most scurrilous wrath. He and his kind were deemed too staid and pompous, too politically and ecclesiastically conservative, too quick to acquire a level of wealth and social status unsuited to their profession and their relatively low social rank. Even Robertson's character as a man and ability as a historian were subjected to hostile invective. If Boswell's identity as a Johnsonian man of letters was chiefly a product of London rather than of Auchinleck and Edinburgh, his long-neglected identity as a Scots Presbyterian legal laird was largely shaped by three little-known Scotsmen who provided him with professional, religious, literary, and ideological guidance during some of the most impressionable periods of his life.

NOTES

The author is grateful to Jeffrey Smitten and Gordon Turnbull for helpful comments on this essay, a version of which was presented at the Columbia University Seminar on Eighteenth-Century Culture in September 1989.

1 Richard B. Sher, *Church and University in the Scottish Enlightenment: The Moderate Literati of Edinburgh* (Princeton: Princeton University Press, and Edinburgh: Edinburgh University Press, 1985).

2 This term is applied to Edinburgh generally in Smollett's *Humphry Clinker* (1771), but with the local clergy chiefly in mind.

3 "I am sensible I make this Excursion rather too late in Life. You will find me awkward & stiff, & not so fit for mixing in new Circles in Company; but I shall at least have the pleasure of going about to gaze & stare at a great many new & amusing objects; and to have you sometimes for my guide will give me great pleasure" (Blair to Boswell, February 19, 1763, C156, Boswell Papers, Yale University Library). I am grateful to Yale University for permission to cite portions of the Blair–Boswell correspondence, which will eventually appear in a volume of Boswell's correspondence with the Scots literati that I am editing for the Yale Editions of the Private Papers of James Boswell.

4 The New Kirk in St. Giles Cathedral was Blair's Edinburgh church, the most prestigious in Scotland.

5 James Boswell, *Journal of a Tour to the Hebrides with Samuel Johnson, LL.D.*, ed. Frederick A. Pottle and Charles H. Bennett (New York: McGraw-Hill, 1961), p. 387, n. 3. Boswell worried about Blair's reaction to publication of this anecdote and was relieved to report to Malone that "he even takes the *Cow* pleasantly" (*Corr: Garrick, Burke, Malone*, p. 284).

6 Boswell used precisely this metaphor in comparing Edinburgh's effect on him to that of "*Grotta del Cane*," an Italian site known for its suffocating vapours (*Laird*, p. 379). See the suggestive discussions of this tension in Gordon Turnbull, "James Boswell: Biography and the Union," in *The History of Scottish Literature, 1660–1880*, ed. Andrew Hook (Aberdeen: Aberdeen University Press, 1987), pp. 157–74, and Andrew Noble, "James Boswell: Scotland's Prodigal Son," in *Improvement and Enlightenment*, ed. T. M. Devine (Edinburgh: John Donald, 1989). pp. 22–42. See also the brilliant chapter on the contradictory and chameleonic tendencies in Boswell's personality in Kenneth Simpson, *The Protean Scot: The Crisis of Identity in Eighteenth-Century Scottish Literature* (Aberdeen: Aberdeen University Press, 1988), Chapter 5, which reached me after this essay had been written.

7 On March 30, 1783 Boswell remarked of a happy social evening: "I had a deliberate enjoyment of that species of life which the middle ranks have in London" (*Applause*, p. 89). Though the remark is generally positive, its tone (particularly the distancing words "deliberate" and "species") serves to underscore just how alien such a lifestyle remained for Boswell.

8 Blair to Boswell, July 16, 1763, C157, Boswell Papers, Yale University Library.

9 On October 20, 1778, after expressing his disgust for Blair's "vanity, burring pronunciation, and drawling manner with the Lothian tone," Boswell added: "Perhaps I have written too strongly of my dissatisfaction with Dr. Blair. But the truth is that the conversation which I enjoy in London has made me very difficult to be pleased" (*Laird*, pp. 31–2).

10 Alexander Carlyle, "A Comparison of Two Eminent Characters Attempted after the Manner of Plutarch," in *Anecdotes and Characters of the Times*, ed. James Kinsley (London: Oxford University Press, 1973), p. 282.

11 See Mary Margaret Stewart, "James Boswell and the National Church of Scotland," *Huntington Library Quarterly*, 30 (1967), 374–7.

12 "Sketch of the Early Life of James Boswell, Written by Himself for Jean Jacques Rousseau" (1764), in *Earlier Years*, p. 2.

13 *Earlier Years*, p. 3.

14 Quoted in *Earlier Years*, p. 18.

15 *Earlier Years*, pp. 18, 24, 28, quoting p. 28.

16 To this may be added Boswell's own complaint that "I was badly brought up" because, for all his memorizing of phrases, grammatical rules, and stories, "I was not trained to think about what I was reading" (*Boswell in Holland*, p. 125).

17 *Annals of the General Assembly of the Church of Scotland* (*1739–66*), ed. Nathaniel Morren, 2 vols. (Edinburgh, 1838–40), I, 21–3.

18 *Scots Magazine*, 29 (1767), 12; John Dun, *The Law of Patronage in Scotland an Unjust Law, as Contrary to Faith Solemnly Pledged to that Nation* (Edinburgh, [1784]).

19 See Richard Sher and Alexander Murdoch, "Patronage and Party in the Church of Scotland, 1750–1800," in *Church, Politics and Society: Scotland 1408–1929*, ed. Norman Macdougall (Edinburgh: John Donald, 1983), pp. 209–11.

20 Frank Miller, *Andrew Crosbie: A Reputed Original of Paulus Pleydell in "Guy Mannering,"* 2nd ed. (Annan: Cuthberton & Laidlaw, 1925), p. 7. Tinwald was the husband of Crosbie's mother's sister as well as the brother of Boswell's mother's father.

21 My chief source of information about Maclaurin's life is the anonymous biographical sketch in the posthumous *Works of the Late John Maclaurin, Esq. of Dreghorn*, 2 vols. (Edinburgh, 1798), I, v–xxii.

22 Maclaurin, *Works*, I, 36–7. See the reference to an earlier (1770) draft of this poem with a different title in *Defence*, p. 7.

23 Boswell and Erskine subsequently became the leading contributors to the second volume of the *Collection*, published in 1762 (*Earlier Years*, pp. 64, 70–1). The publisher of both collections was Alexander Donaldson, whom Boswell and Maclaurin successfully defended in the famous copyright case of 1773–4. Boswell's pamphlet in that case is well known (*Defence*, p. 205), but see also Maclaurin's *Considerations on the Nature and Origin of Literary Property* (Edinburgh, 1767), reprinted in his *Works*, II, 73–136.

24 Miller, *Andrew Crosbie*, p. 13.

25 *Andrew Crosbie*, p. 19; Roger L. Emerson, "The Social Composition of Enlightened Scotland: The Select Society of Edinburgh, 1754–1764," *Studies on Voltaire and the Eighteenth Century*, 114 (1973), 291–329; *Catalogue of a Valuable Collection of Books, which Belonged to the Late Andrew Crosbie, Esq.* (Edinburgh, 1785).

26 Sir Walter Scott, *Guy Mannering*, Chapter 37. The parallel between Crosbie and Pleydell was certainly not complete, however, for Pleydell describes himself as "a member of the suffering and Episcopal church of Scotland."

27 The poem first appeared in Maclaurin's *Essays in Verse* (1769) and was reprinted in his *Works*, I, 24–8.

28 For a fuller discussion, see Sher and Murdoch, "Patronage and Party," pp. 197–220.

29 Maclaurin, *Works*, II, 247, 268.

30 *Works*, II, pp. 269–70.

31 *Earlier Years*, p. 390. Crosbie's library contained two different editions of Boswell's *Account of Corsica*.

32 See, for example, J. G. A. Pocock, *The Machiavellian Moment: Florentine Political Thought and the Atlantic Republican Tradition* (Princeton: Princeton University Press, 1975).

33 On the former, see Sher, *Church and University*, Chapter 6, and John Robertson, *The Scottish Enlightenment and the Militia Issue* (Edinburgh: John Donald, 1985); on the latter, see Bruce P. Lenman, "Aristocratic 'Country' Whiggery in Scotland and the American Revolution," in *Scotland and America in the Age of the Enlightenment*, ed. Richard B. Sher and Jeffrey R. Smitten (Edinburgh: Edinburgh University Press, and Princeton: Princeton Universtiy Press, 1990), pp. 180–92.

34 Nicholas Phillipson, "Lawyers, Landowners, and the Civic Leadership of Post-Union Scotland," in *Lawyers in Their Social Setting*, ed. D. N. MacCormick (Edinburgh: Green, 1976), pp. 171–94.

35 Quoted in Miller, *Andrew Crosbie*, p. 23.

36 See also Robertson, *Scottish Enlightenment*, pp. 130–2.

37 See, for example, the following comments in the appropriate volumes of Boswell's published journals: Maclaurin "offended me by a kind of profaneness in quoting Scripture" (September 16, 1774); "his head turned when he thought of a Supreme Being" (December 27, 1780); "I only regretted that he had not religion" (March 3, 1781); "It was unpleasing to hear Maclaurin express his infidelity" (July 13, 1781); "I only regretted his infidelity. It hurt me" (November 5, 1781); "His Infidelity disagreeable" (March 27, 1782).

38 In spring 1778 Boswell wrote in his journal: "I regretted that Crosbie was not a Christian. I found from his conversation upon Christianity, which was decent and showed he had read a good deal though not enough, that he believed the great circumstances of Gospel history. But thought Christ only a very able and a very good Man, who taught amiable precepts, and in order to have influence upon a most superstitious people, pretended to have supernatural powers" (*Boswell in Extremes*, p. 219). It is certainly ironic that the lay leader of the Popular or Orthodox party in the kirk was apparently guilty of the very socinian heresy that the Moderates were sometimes accused – with considerably less justification – of espousing. Perhaps this paradox gave rise to one Moderate's charge that Crosbie was just "playing a game" in ecclesiastical politics in order to gain popularity and employment. See *The Autobiography of Dr. Alexander Carlyle of Inveresk, 1722–1805*, ed. John Hill Burton, new ed. (London and Edinburgh: T. N. Foulis, 1910), pp. 453, 468.

39 For example: "Refinement and elegance often rises, not only beyond the ideas or conception of the vulgar, but so far above that style of language which they are accustomed to receive all their ideas in, that they do not easily comprehend the meaning of it, and it conveys to their minds the same imperfections and indistinctness, as a preacher who uses a foreign tongue would do, to an audience who had been taught to read and understand the language, that he uses, but who had never been in use to speak it themselves, or to converse with those that spoke

it" (Crosbie, *Thoughts of a Layman*, pp. 34–5). The issue was considered important enough to provoke an indignant reply from the Moderate minister Henry Grieve, who defended "polite literature" and "decorum of manners" as useful attributes for clergymen in *Observations on the Overture concerning Patronage, with Remarks on a Late Pamphlet, entitled, Thoughts of a Layman concerning Patronage and Presentations* (Edinburgh, 1769), pp. 9–14.

40 "A Sketch of the Constitution of the Church of *Scotland*, and the State of Parties in it at present; with Specimens of the Oratory of some of the most distinguished Members of that Church now living," *London Magazine*, 41 (April and May 1772), 181–7, 237–42 – cited hereafter as "Sketch"; "Debates in the General Assembly of the Church of Scotland," *London Magazine*, 42 (April–August 1773), 188–91, 227–9, 296–9, 340–4, 396–401 – cited hereafter as "Debates." Both articles are attributed to Boswell in Frederick A. Pottle, *The Literary Career of James Boswell, Esq.* (Oxford: Oxford University Press, 1929), p. 223. Parenthetical citations to these essays below refer to pages in the *London Magazine*.

41 Boswell, *Tour*, p. 171. See also "Sketch," p. 184.

42 In a particularly revealing letter to William Temple, dated June 3, 1775, Boswell observed: "There is *de facto* something low and coarse in such employment, though *upon paper*, it is a *Supreme Judicatore*. But guineas must be had. . ." He went on to explain that this day would require "more than ordinary spirit" because he was to face in debate "Dr. Robertson, John Home, and a good many more of them" (*Letters*, I, 229).

43 The "Sketch" was reprinted, with some changes, in the *Scots Magazine* for April and May 1772 (34, pp. 187–92, 225–32), where it would have been still more useful as a piece of ecclesiastical propaganda. In 1779 Boswell followed the same pattern by publishing "Speeches in the General Assembly of the Church of Scotland" in the May through September numbers of the *Scots Magazine*.

44 See John Maclaurin, *Information for Mungo Campbell* ([Edinburgh], 1770). Campbell was an excise officer at Saltcoats who had been charged with the murder of the Earl of Eglinton.

45 Maclaurin's *Song Inscribed to James Boswell* had already played on the same theme:

> Sure great was the folly
> In him whom Paoli
> His friendship permitted to share;
> To go for a Guinea,
> Dear Boswell, what mean ye
> To plead at so humble a bar?
>
> Zounds, the whole shire of Ayr
> Quite asonish'd will stare.
> And thus will indignant exclaim: –
> Shall he make orations
> To aid presentations!
> The blockhead is greatly to blame.
>
> The Lords of the Session
> Will fall in a passion,

And that is too easily done;
While your friends at Auchinleck,
With their hearts like to break
Will call you unnatural son. (*Works*, I, 37–8)

46 In later years this interpretation enabled Boswell to gain satisfaction from his performances as a general assembly lawyer even though his arguments on behalf of "the people" did not carry the day. See, for example, his comments on the Biggar and Fenwick patronage cases at the general assembly of 1780 in *Laird*, pp. 218–19.

47 John A. Vance, "The Laughing Johnson and the Shaping of Boswell's *Life*," in *New Questions, New Answers*, p. 213, points out that although Johnson was only "talking for victory" on these occasions, his criticisms of Robertson tend to stick in the reader's mind more than Boswell's "more truthful addenda."

48 Boswell, *Tour*, p. 388. For his part, Robertson praised Johnson (in Boswell's company, at any rate) for always being "gentle and good-humoured, and courteous with me" (*Life*, III, 332).

49 *The Private Papers of James Boswell from Malahide Castle*, ed. Geoffrey Scott and F. A. Pottle, 18 vols. (New York, 1928–34), VI, 45.

50 McCormick was a leading Moderate clergyman who owed his position as principal of St. Andrews University to the patronage of Robertson, among others. As I have argued elsewhere, McCormick's life of Carstares, which was prefixed to his *State-Papers and Letters Addressed to William Carstares* (Edinburgh, 1774), portrayed Carstares as if he were a late eighteenth-century Moderate much like William Robertson (Sher and Murdoch, "Patronage and Party," pp. 197–220).

51 The most Boswell could hope to make during this period was about £600 a year, but to do that he had to scramble for £300 in legal fees and receive from his father the full £300 allowance that was due him – neither of which were certain. He also had considerable debts. Even after becoming laird of Auchinleck in 1782, Boswell could count on only about £500 a year (*Later Years*, pp. 13, 109, 116–18, 231–2). By contrast, Robertson's academic, ecclesiastical, and government offices provided £600 a year plus a house and orchard, and his *History of Charles V* (1769) alone brought him the staggering sum of £3,500 (and an additional £500–£1,000 for later editions).

52 Pottle, *Literary Career*, p. 223; *Defence*, p. 141. Pottle's attribution of the "Sceptical Observations" to Boswell seems to have rested on two bits of evidence: that some of the strictures on Robertson paralleled those in the "Sketch," and that the closing quotation from Freebairn is lifted straight out of the second installment of the "Sketch." Though this evidence is too weak to be considered conclusive, Boswell's authorship of this piece seems likely.

53 See "Elegy to Patronage" in Maclaurin, *Works*, I, 43–4.

54 "We will in this instance pit the infidel against the divine, and lay our money on the head of the former; for we will venture to say, that there is a much greater store of both philosophical observation, and brilliancy of sentiment, in the one than in the other." But, he continues, Clarendon and Lyttleton are even better historians than Hume. On Mary, the article praises Tytler's *Enquiry into the Evidence against Mary Queen of Scots* as an "unerring" refutation of both Robertson

and Hume. If this "Sketch" was indeed by Boswell, his assessment of Robertson's treatment of Mary had undergone a radical change since first reading Robertson's *History of Scotland*, when he wrote to John Johnston: "I have read Robertson's *History* [of Scotland] for the first time, which has carried me back in Imagination to the ancient days of Scottish Grandeur; has filled my mind with generous ideas of the valour of our Ancestors, and made me feel, a pleasing sympathy for the beautifull accomplished Mary" (letter of September 13, 1762 in *Corr: Grange*, p. 15).

55 Stewart, "Boswell and the Church," esp. pp. 382–5.

4

BOSWELL AND THE SCOTTICISM

Pat Rogers

A well-known passage in *Humphry Clinker* (1771) serves to focus linguistic issues which bear on the Scottish Enlightenment, and which help to illuminate Boswell's attitudes in relation to the dominant intellectual movement of his time. At Durham, Smollett's party of travellers have encountered the eccentric, indeed consciously Quixotic, figure of Lismahagow. Soon afterwards, on July 13, Jery Melford writes to his friend Sir Watkin Phillips of the first major contretemps involving Lismahagow, when the grizzled lieutenant sets out a paradoxical case:

> He proceeded to set out his assertion that the English language was spoken with greater propriety at Edinburgh than in London. – He said, what we generally called the Scottish dialect was, in fact, true, genuine old English, with a mixture of some French terms and idioms, adopted in a long intercourse betwixt the French and Scots nations; that the modern English, from affectation and false refinement, had weakened, and even corrupted their language, by throwing out the guttural sounds, altering the pronunciation and the quantity, and disusing many words and terms of great significance. In consequence of the these innovations, the works of our best poets, such as Chaucer, Spenser, and even Shakespeare, were become, in many parts, unintelligible to the natives of South-Britain, whereas the Scots, who retain the ancient language, understand them without the help of a glossary.

Lismahagow goes on to give a number of detailed instances in support of his claim, arguing that the "energy" of southern English had been "impaired" by the false refinements mentioned, and that an overall vowel-shift had made the language unlike any other European tongue, and thus difficult for foreigners to acquire.

Naturally the belligerent Matthew Bramble is impelled to offer some corrective of this view, but Lismahagow is undaunted, and the check serves "only to agitate his humour for disputation":

> He said, if every nation had its own recitative or music the Scots had theirs, and the Scotchman who had not yet acquired the cadence of the English, would naturally use his own in speaking their language; therefore, if he was

56

better understood than the native, his recitative must be more intelligible than that of the English; of consequence, the dialect of the Scots had an advantage over their fellow subjects, and this was another strong presumption that the modern English had corrupted their language in the article of pronunciation.[1]

The argument dissolves into a wider set of paradoxical assertions, and then peters out. But there are several expressions here which point up a major debate of the time. The phrase "the dialect of the Scots" hints at a broad aspect of linguistic politics which surfaced after the Union. Along with this public matter, there was a private concern which Boswell felt as strongly as anyone, conveyed in the words "the Scotchman who had not yet acquired the cadence of the English." In this essay I shall first consider briefly the broader political issue as it was manifested in Boswell's adult lifetime. This is chiefly by way of background to the second part of the essay, which will examine Boswell's own interest in the "Scotticism" in oral or written expression.[2]

I

It was generally agreed by Scots of all persuasions at the time of the Enlightenment that the Scottish language had become, to all intents and purposes, a variant of the main linguistic stock, i.e. English. This had happened, it was felt, not because of any inherent weakness in the older tongue, but simply as a consequence of the dependence – political, economic, moral – which had been imposed by the Union. This view is most succinctly expressed by William Robertson, in Book VIII of his *History of Scotland* (1759). If the Union had not taken place, Robertson argues, two distinct nations could have continued to support two distinct languages, or at least dialects of comparable standing. "But, by the accession," he proceeds, "the English naturally became the sole judges and lawgivers in Language, and rejected, as solecisms, every form of speech to which their ear was not accustomed."[3]

The two best-known responses to this situation are the list of banned Scots idioms compiled by David Hume, and the efforts of the Select Society in the early 1760s to improve native usage in the English language. One could suggest that at a deeper level the efforts of creative writers to reclaim a living Scots idiom, as displayed most prominently in the work of Robert Fergusson and Robert Burns, reflect a parallel effort to undo the damage of the Union; but this was a less conscious process, impelled partly by the imaginative drives of highly gifted poets.

The simpler case to analyze of the two just mentioned is the strong programmatic campaign of the Select Society.[4] The purpose in view was "the correction of Scottish pronunciation," following a remark by the English politician Charles Townshend: "Why can't you learn to speak the

English language as you have already learnt to write it?" Despite public lectures and various publicity devices, not to mention the advocacy of men like Robertson and Hugh Blair, the campaign excited derision in Edinburgh. This was at a juncture when anti-Scottish mania, already visible at the time of John Home's *Douglas* in 1757, was about to attain new fervour in England with the rising unpopularity of Bute's ministry.[5] The activities of the Select Society bespeak an awareness that anti-Scottish sentiment could be whipped up simply on the basis of their peculiar, or at least readily identifiable, manner of speech.

That a course of public lectures should have been undertaken is in itself significant. The outstanding figure in this growing profession was undoubtedly Thomas Sheridan the younger, son of Swift's friend and father of Richard Brinsley. In this very year of 1761, Sheridan lectured in Edinburgh to an impressive audience of "three hundred nobles, judges, divines, advocates, and men of fashion."[6] Sheridan notoriously spoke in a strong Irish brogue of his own, and it can be seen as either fitting or ironic that he advocated a standardization of the four British languages. There is an obvious link here with Boswell, who attended Sheridan's Edinburgh lectures and soon made Sheridan (as F. A. Pottle has put it) his "guide, philosopher, and friend."[7] The details of this relationship cannot be considered fully in this essay: it is enough here to note that the young Boswell became a member of the Select Society at the end of 1761; his own awareness of the issues surrounding what might be called Scottish English, it follows, grew up in the context of this wider national concern.

As for Hume, there is much that could be said. His list of solecisms has been often ridiculed, as though he ought to have realized that this was an insult to the resources of native Scots idiom. In fact the list was originally compiled for private use, though it was printed in some copies of the *Political Discourses* (1752) and later reprinted in the *Scots Magazine* (1760). There is in any case no need to apologize for Hume's defensiveness on this score; ample evidence exists that many others were ready to criticize Scottish authors, Hume included, when they were felt to have departed from the norms of polite English usage. In this sense Townshend's confidence that Scottish people had learnt to write English in a fully acceptable fashion is not borne out by the facts.[8]

Hume was by no means unique in feeling anxious on this score. James Beattie admitted to nervousness about Scotticisms in his writing, and thanked Elizabeth Montagu for providing a model of pure English – certainly there is a degree of flattery towards his patron, but we need not doubt that the worry was any the less genuinely felt.[9] (Montagu had savored the manner of Adam Ferguson's *History of Civil Society*, contending that it was impossible for anyone but a Scotsman to have written so.) Hume himself had advised his friendly antagonist, the clergyman and pamphleteer Robert Wallace, around 1751, to expunge Scots words such as "expiscate" from his work.[10] As late as 1802 the historian Malcolm Laing, best known today for his inquiry into the authenticity of Ossian, sent Dr. Samuel Parr his work for the specific purpose of identifying and removing Scotticisms.[11] Very few authors were immune from this feeling of uneasiness. One exception is Adam Smith, who set down his early conviction that someone born north of the Tweed could yet attain "a correct and even elegant style."[12] But Smith had a wider cultural, educational, and social background than most of his countrymen by the time he came to write *The Wealth of Nations*. Stay-at-home Scots, who moved in restricted circles, naturally risked a greater appearance of provinciality or even rusticity, though in practice it was a certain pedantic formalism of language which often bespoke the Caledonian to English eyes and ears.

A well-known passage in Boswell's *Life* records Johnson's reactions to Hume's list:

> I told him that David Hume had made a short collection of Scotticisms. "I wonder, (said Johnson), that *he* should find them." (II, 72)

Malone's gloss on this passage in the third edition of the *Life* reads, "The first edition of Hume's *History of England* was full of Scotticisms, many of which he corrected in subsequent editions." It is certainly true that some niggling occurred when Hume's *History* first appeared, and since Malone could still unabashedly use the verb "corrected" in this context, forty years later, it is no wonder that a Scot of Hume's generation would think it prudent to guard against such criticisms.[13] Two further glosses are possible. The first concerns Boswell's own plans for a Scottish dictionary, of which Johnson was well aware and which will be mentioned in connection with Boswell's career, in the later part of this essay. The second relates to the grounds of Johnson's prejudice. Insofar as his dismissive remark cannot be explained by a rooted aversion to the philosopher on account of his religious views, it may perhaps owe something to Hume's reputation in England for a mixture of Scottish and French idiom in his writing. Very soon after Boswell's first meeting with Johnson, he recorded the following under July 20, 1763:

> The conversation now turned to Mr. David Hume's style. JOHNSON. "Why, sir, his style is not English; the structure of his sentences is French. Now the French structure and the English structure may, in the nature of things, be equally good. But if you allow that the English language is established, he is wrong. (I, 439)

Most people, Scottish as well as English, had got used to the idea that the English language was the "established" vehicle for polite communication – the great Dictionary may have played some part in this. It is characteristic of

Johnson's more analytic approach to language that he should mention "structure" – presumably syntax, word-order, cadence – rather than simply diction, which was the usual criterion of a "Scottish" style. Hume's friend John Peach is said to have discovered more than two hundred Scotticisms in the first edition of the *History*: this relates much more to individual words than to any broader consideration of phrasing.[14]

There is of course, too, the related issue of pronunciation, which in Boswell's day was sometimes kept separate but more often merged into the broad topic of Scotticism. Hume was not immune from criticism on this score: the most forthright statement is that of Lord Charlemont, who asserted that "his speech in English was rendered ridiculous by the broadest and most vulgar Scottish Accent, and his French was, if possible, still more laughable." This Irish testimony may appear tainted; equally suspect, on grounds of social prejudice, is the waspish comment by Horace Walpole: "Mr. Hume is fashion itself [in Paris], although his French is almost as unintelligible as his English."[15] Boswell does not say much about Hume's manner of speech, though we know that as a young man he had mimicked the philosopher ("I had not only his external address, but his sentiments and mode of expression").[16]

Other notable figures of the age did not escape so lightly, especially in England. Henry Dundas, as we shall see in reviewing Boswell's relationship to the issue, was known as a broad Scots speaker who had made a virtue of this apparent defect. William Robertson, according to Alexander Carlyle, spoke with a particularly broad "accent and tone," though he nevertheless manifested great taste in the way he used language.[17] An interesting case is provided by Francis Jeffrey, a generation later, who set out as a young man to eliminate his native burr: in Cockburn's words, he was "bent on purifying himself of the national inconvenience." The results were mixed: as John Gross has put it, "he came back from Oxford with a queer accent which astonished his friends and delighted his enemies."[18] Among the latter may be counted the famously demotic speaker, Lord Braxfield, who said of Jeffrey, "The laddie has clear tint his Scotch, and found nae English."[19] It is worth adding that Boswell's own father commanded a rich Scots idiom when he chose, and the young James cannot have failed to become aware of the potentialities which a sudden leap into the vernacular could open up, in the court-room or elsewhere. On one occasion he imitated "the rude Scots sarcastical vivacity" when he met Jean-Jacques Rousseau at Moutiers in 1764.

The issue of pronunciation had a number of ramifications in politics, too. The wholly unlikely story that George III when he came to the throne spoke with a Scottish accent seems to be part of a scare-story directed against the influence of Bute on him (according to Lord Holland, the King on opening his first Parliament stressed the word *allies* on the first syllable, which is a somewhat sophisticated case to take).[20] Sometimes the Scottish language is parodied in cartoons which identify wild Highlanders with Jacobitism, though in truth the Scottish establishment was overwhelmingly Lowland in origin, and from quite early in the century consistently, if unenthusiastically, Hanoverian in allegiance. After the Union it was sometimes claimed that the new Scottish members of the Westminster Parliament were barely understood and consequently laughed at: only with a second generation, it has been argued, did the Scottish block achieve a ready hearing when their more anglified background gave them ease in speaking "pure" English.[21]

A more direct concern for most people was facility in spoken English sufficient to conduct business and (the crucial thing for Boswell) to advance a professional career. When Roderick Random came to London, he was told by Strap that a London schoolmaster would be ready to teach him "the pronunciation of the English-tongue, without which (he says) you will be unfit for business in this country."[22] Political and social prejudice reinforced this need for any aspirant Scotsman seeking to make his way in England, or in a field dominated by English taste, as was the profession of letters. Even if Boswell had not been split by personal conflicts, family quarrels, feudal dreams, and literary ambitions, he would necessarily have run into a whole set of disruptive ideological pressures which centered on the use of English, in print and in speech. As we have seen, most writers, from Hume downwards, were subject to intense pressure in respect of the "correctness" of their English usage. Much less self-confident by nature than a Hume or a Smith, it is not surprising that Boswell reflects in his own person an acute form of this anxiety state.

II

As Scotland sought for a national identity in the era of the Enlightenment, so Boswell coveted a sense of the self which would include a proper mixture of the Scottish – proper, that is, in terms of fulfillment of his notions of the world and of his own needs. His background might fairly be said to be multicultural. There was his upbringing amid the closes and wynds of the old city of Edinburgh; his occasional visits to the ancestral seat at Auchinleck, his studies at the ancient universities of Edinburgh and Glasgow, followed by his elopement to London, his spell at Utrecht and his Grand Tour, his involvement with the Scottish Bar and his hankerings after success in London. This complex heritage mirrors the divided loyalties of Scotland after the Union, with its proud indigenous culture, its close continental similarities and its inevitable economic involvement with its larger neighbor. Some of this split makes itself apparent in linguistic areas; the mixed feelings we have seen in a number of figures concerning the dubious "correctness" of Scottish usages serve to express this inheritance.

The young man began on his projected dictionary of Scottish words at least as early as January 1764, when he was at Utrecht.[23] It was one of several planned works never to see the light, though enough of a manuscript survived to be sold from his son's library in 1825. It will be best known to most readers from a passage in the *Life of Johnson*, under October 19, 1769:

> He advised me to complete a Dictionary of words peculiar to Scotland, of which I shewed him a specimen. "Sir, (said he,) Ray has made a collection of north-country words. By collecting those of your country, you will do a useful thing towards the history of the language." He bade me also go on with collections I was making upon the antiquities of Scotland. "Make a large book; a folio." BOSWELL. "But of what use will it be, Sir? JOHNSON. "Never mind the use; do it." (II, 91–2)

Probably Boswell's motives were less pure than the antiquarian values suggested by Johnson would indicate. In his youth he had realized that distinctive Scottish vocabulary was a racial marker, and since he both clung to his nationality tenaciously and yet resisted its cramping effects on his career and personality, a lot hung for him personally on the state of his language.

Abundant evidence exists to show that he kept this awareness throughout his adult life. Selective quotation will demonstrate the point.[24] For example, in February 1767, back in Edinburgh after his years of travel, he received a letter from Sir John Pringle, giving high hopes for Boswell's advancement. He would shine at the Bar and "give the tone for a new eloquence." The reason for this superiority to other candidates for fame was that "you have the advantage of possessing the English language and the accent in a greater degree than any of your rivals, and a turn for expressing yourself in a clear and energetic manner, without those hyperbolic modes of speech that were introduced long ago, and were still kept up during my youth, and which slipped from the bar to the tea tables at Edinburgh."[25] Pringle was more far-sighted than he knew, though Boswell's ultimate preeminence turns out to have lain in his biography and journals rather than in the court-room. What Pringle said was of course exactly what Boswell wanted to hear. He would not have been quite so pleased if he could have known what Fanny Burney would write in her *Memoirs of Dr. Burney*, long after his death: "He spoke the Scotch accent strongly, though by no means so as to affect, even slightly, his intelligibility to an English ear."[26] Boswell was proud of his own "ear," and according to G. M. Young this enabled him to pass sufficiently for an authentic English writer, unlike Hume: Boswell could "detect provincialisms in the speech of Garrick and Johnson himself, and very rarely will a phrase be found to show that the writer was not born on Attic soil. Hume to the end had to keep by him a list of things that are not said. . ."[27] This is a peculiar way of putting the matter, not least because one may well feel that Attic soil lay closer to the Athens of the north than to the purlieus of Fleet Street.

The most striking single glimpse of Boswell's attitudes occurs in a brief phrase, found in his journal for March 24, 1775. He is describing a meeting at the Club; naturally the section was excised when he wrote up the passage for the *Life of Johnson*:

> I was disgusted by [Dr. George] Fordyce, who was coarse and noisy: and, as he had the Scotch accent strong, he shocked me as a kind of representative of myself. He was to me as the slaves of the Spartans, when shown drunk to make that vice odious. His being a member lessened the value of The Club. (*Ominous Years*, p. 94)

Admittedly Boswell was so displeased with the election of Adam Smith a year later ("Smith too is now of our Club. It has lost its select merit") that he actually had thoughts of seceding to form a new club.[28] But the hostility against Fordyce is also a gesture of self-hatred, and the fear of exposure as a coarse drunkard is closely allied to fear of exposure as a raw Scot. A couple of weeks later, Boswell reverted to his obsession in conversation with Burke:

> I maintained a strange proposition to Burke: that it was better for a Scotsman and an Irishman to preserve so much of their native accent and not to be quite perfect in English, because it was unnatural. I would have all the birds of the air to retain somewhat of their own notes: a blackbird to sing like a blackbird, and thrush like a thrush, and not a blackbird and other birds to sing all like some other bird. Burke agreed with me...I said it was unnatural to hear a Scotsman speaking perfect English. He appeared a machine. I instanced Wedderburn...Lord Lisburne and I had afterwards a discussion on this subject. My metaphor of the birds he opposed by saying, "A Scotsman may do very well with his own tone in Coll; but if he comes into the House of Commons, it will be better if he speaks English. A bagpipe may do very well in the Highlands, but I would not introduce it into [Johann Christian] Bach's concert." "This," said I, "shows what it is to argue in metaphors. One is just as good as another." But I maintained to my Lord that it put me in a passion to hear a Scotsman speaking in a perfect English tone. It was a false voice. He speaks as if he had some pipe or speaking instrument in his mouth. And I thought always, "Can't he take this confounded pipe out, and let us hear him speak with his own organs?" I do still think I am right.

The exchange with Burke proceeds after this prolonged metaphoric contest:

> I said to Burke, "You would not have a man use Scotch words, as to say a *trance* for a *passage* in a house." "No," said he, "that is a different language." "But," said I, "is it not better, too, to try to pronounce not in the broad Scotch way and to say *passage* and not *pawssage*." "Yes," said Burke, "when once you're *taught* how they pronounce it in England; but don't *try* at English pronunciation." Said Richard Burke, "Better say *pawssage* than *pissage*." And indeed some Scotsmen, such as Rae, the advocate, make blunders as bad as this. (*Ominous Years*, pp. 124–5)

One may wonder whether Boswell's dislike of a truly perfect English accent may derive from a recognition that he himself had not quite achieved this, or indeed quite *wanted* it consistently. It is also noteworthy that the subject crops up in the company of the Irish immigrants Edmund and Richard Burke; Lisburne, though he held an Irish peerage, was actually Welsh. Boswell had been shocked earlier in the same day, at a Commons committee reviewing the Clackmannan election, by Rae's "barbarous Bath-metal English." He alternates between the idea that it is unnatural for a Scot to acquire an English indistinguishable from that of a southerner, and acute embarrassment when he hears broad Scottish speakers in an English forum.

Just a few months later, the topic recurs:

> I began today a curious bargain which I made with the Hon. Henry Erskine in order to acquire correctness in writing. We were to give to each other a copy of every one of our printed [legal] papers, and each was to be censor on the other. For every ungrammatical expression and every Scotticism except technical phrases, a shilling was to be incurred. (*Ominous Years*, pp. 228–9)

This was when Boswell was no beginner: he was thirty-five at the time, ten years older than the future Lord Advocate Erskine. His prolonged tutelage in English expression went on almost to the end of his life. And the whole issue is seldom out of his head for long. In 1769 he quotes Thomas Sheridan on Thomas Reid's *Essay on the Human Mind* (1764): "Sheridan said that Reid's book was the most correct of any that North Britain had produced, for he had not found one Scotticism in it." Two weeks later, he cites Dr. John Armstrong, "whom I found as worthy, as lively in his way, and as splenetic as ever. He is a violent Scotsman. He said the only advantage the English had over us was the *recitativo*, the tone of speaking."[29] Nine years later, Boswell noted that one "Logic" Bayne (according to Lord Kames) prospered despite failure at the Bar and knowing "very little law," such were the effects of "a slow, formal manner, a neatness of expression and the English accent."[30] Thus Bayne became professor of Scots law at Edinburgh. We might remind ourselves here that the Master of Edinburgh Academy was required as late as 1823 to have "a pure English accent" – merely to have been born in England was not enough to guarantee this desirable asset.[31]

The fullest single examination of the issues under review occurs in a passage which does find a place in the published *Life*. The topic surfaces on March 28, 1772, in the company of Sir Alexander Macdonald (later the object of a bitter quarrel) as well as Johnson. Macdonald remarks, "I have been correcting several Scotch accents in my friend Boswell," adding for Johnson's consideration the generalized reflection "I doubt, Sir, if any Scotchman ever attains to a perfect English pronunciation." This provokes Johnson into his most sustained treatment of these matters: the gist of his comments is that Scotsmen may attain perfect English pronunciation, but usually relax after getting near to perfection. Johnson knows that people are able to discover from his speech his own local origins. "So may Scotchmen be found out. But, Sir, little aberrations are of no disadvantage. I never catched Mallet in a Scotch accent; and yet Mallet, I suppose, was past five-and-twenty before he came to London." The editors of the *Life* quote Johnson's later biography of Mallet, from the prefaces to the English poets, where he describes Mallet's efforts to distance himself from his Scots origins (in terms of name as well as accent) and the unpopularity he thus incurred with other Scots – "he was the only Scot whom Scotchmen did not commend" (II, 158–9). Boswell, reading this, can scarcely have been unaware of the possible applicability to his own case. He too worried about having alienated his fellow-countrymen, especially after his ill-advised move to the English Bar. In 1788 he wondered in the pages of his journal, "Perhaps it is not wise in me to keep myself so much abstracted as I do from Scotchmen of all ranks"[32] (though at the same time he was still put off by any "vulgar Scotch" speech he encountered). It should be added that independent testimony confirms Johnson's assessment of Mallet: "Mallet wrote good English," wrote Giuseppe Baretti, "and I remember that Richardson, author of the famous *Pamela*, used to say that Mallet was the only Scotchman who never confused 'shall' and 'will' in the future tense."[33]

The conversation in 1772 prompted a further section in Boswell's narrative, revealing to us Johnson's wider views. Quotation at length is necessary for the full point to emerge:

> Upon another occasion I talked to him on this subject, having myself taken some pains to improve my pronunciation, by the aid of the late Mr Love, of the Drury-lane theatre, when he was a player at Edinburgh, and also of old Mrs Sheridan. Johnson said to me, "Sir, your pronunciation is not offensive." With this concession I was pretty well satisfied; and let me give my countrymen of North-Britain an advice not to aim at absolute perfection in this respect; not to speak *High English*, as we are apt to call what is far removed from the *Scotch*, but which is by no means *good English*, and makes "the fools who use it," truly ridiculous. Good English is plain, easy, smooth in the mouth of an unaffected English Gentleman. A studied and factitious pronunciation, which requires perpetual attention, and imposes personal constraint, is exceedingly disgusting. A small intermixture of provincial peculiarities may, perhaps, have an agreeable effect, as the notes of different birds concur in the harmony of the grove, and please more than if they were exactly alike.

This is plainly a more considered version of the views set forth in the exchange with Burke, cited above (p. 63). And possibly Boswell has Burke, amongst others, in mind when he proceeds:

> I could name some gentleman of Ireland, to whom a slight proportion of the accent and recitative of that country is an advantage. The same observation will

apply to the gentlemen of Scotland. I do not mean that we should speak as
broad as a certain prosperous member of Parliament from that country [Henry
Dundas]; though it has been well observed, that "it has been of no small use to
him; as it rouses the attention of the House by its uncommonness; and is equal
to tropes and figures in a good English speaker."

After this dig at his *bête noire*, Dundas, Boswell goes on to commend his
erstwhile friend, the late Sir Gilbert Minto, whom Lord Lisburne would also
mention during the conversation from April 1775. The discussion then
merges into consideration of the need for a dictionary to fix English
pronunciation; this in turn leads to the merits of Sheridan's dictionary, and
to what Johnson calls the "disadvantage of being an Irishman" in this context
– "what entitles Sheridan to fix the pronunciation of English?" (II, 159–61).

This last remark has two barbs from the point of view of Boswell: it
challenges his own competence as a Scot to pontificate on matters of English
usage; and it casts doubt on the wisdom of his period of tutelage under
Sheridan. Nevertheless, the exchange ends amicably, and for the most part
the two men maintained a fairly comfortable relationship in regard to
national differences. By the end of Johnson's life, Boswell was approaching
the stage he had reached when John Courtenay's poem (quoted in the *Life*)
described him as "scarce by North Britons now esteem'd a Scot" (I, 223).
Years before, Johnson had paid Boswell a cheerfully back-handed compliment: the passage in the *Life* is dated May 1, 1773:

> He observed that "The Irish mix better with the English than the Scotch do;
> their language is nearer to English; as a proof of which, they succeed very well
> as players, which Scotchmen do not. Then, Sir, they have not that extreme
> nationality which we find in the Scotch. I will do you, Boswell, the justice to
> say, that you are the most *unscottified* of your countrymen. You are almost the
> only instance of a Scotchman that I have known, who did not at every other
> sentence bring in some other Scotchman." (II, 242)

The verdict that Boswell was "unscottified" is true in one way, but it
neglects the passionate, if romantic, attachment to Scottish history which
marks Boswell's general view on life. He could indeed be said to manifest
"extreme nationality" in certain of his affinities. As Janet Adam Smith has
finely said, Boswell's Scotland "is the past as well as the present, a virtue to
be practised, a source of feeling, with which sober rationality has little to
do."[34] It was to this degree a concept of the nation that had little to do with
wealth and virtue in the Enlightenment sense, that is with the concept which
belonged to political economists and philosophers, social thinkers and
lawyers, who were shaping the real world of eighteenth-century Scotland. It
is not very much of a simplification to say that the unscottified Boswell lived
in the prose world of London, whilst the scottified Boswell clung on to the
poetic world of Auchinleck.

The state of affairs just outlined can be sensed behind any number of short moments of byplay in the *Life*: to take a single example, the entry for May 12, 1778, when Johnson is asked by Boswell whether he values his friend for being a Scotchman. "Nay, Sir," replies Johnson, "I do value you more for being a Scotchman. You are a Scotchman without the faults of a Scotchman. You would not have been so valuable as you are, had you not been a Scotchman" (III, 347). Here Johnson does recognize Boswell's otherness, the quality of an unscottified individual who was able to provide insights and experience not available to Johnson himself. It follows that the situation underlines a much greater enterprise, the tour of the Hebrides. Boswell for his part owed his anxiety to get Johnson to Scotland in some measure to a desire to redeem and validate his own Scottish identity. And from Johnson's point of view Boswell was valuable as a mediator and interpreter. Though Boswell did not have the Gaelic, this must surely have extended on many occasions to a role as literal interpreter, when Johnson found difficulty with local speech – perhaps more often in Edinburgh and the Lowlands than in the remote stages of the journey.

Boswell's joking insistence on *scottifying* Johnson's palate, mentioned early in the tour on August 18, 1773, is another comic extension of the metaphor (v, 55). The more serious side of the issue turns up in Boswell's admission in footnotes of certain Scotticisms, when he published his account. Even as late as the great *Life* itself, Boswell reverted to criticisms he had received on this score, and inserted a small riposte in the text of his biography (v, 425). It is a final indication that, first and last, Boswell was open to the impress of the age, and could not escape a strong awareness of his nationality, expressed most commonly in the identifiable use of English, both written and spoken, which almost all Scottish men and women displayed wherever they went.

III

Not all contemporaries would have agreed with Thomas Blacklock, when he wrote of the difficulties which Scotchmen had to endure before they could write "with that facility & Chastness which occur naturally to an Englishman."[35] As far as the written language was concerned, Alexander Carlyle believed that English was to some degree "a foreign tongue," which had to be learnt as a special exercise, and which tended to abound in circumlocutions or "additional epithets" when used by writers such as Hume and Robertson.[36] Other commentators took different views; but no one doubted the visibility, or rather audibility, of the Scotticism. Response to this awareness could take the form of guilt, or defensiveness, or aggressive counterclaims, or fierce national pride: Boswell exemplifies many of these attitudes at one time or another. As John Clive has written, "The sense of inferiority that expressed itself in imitation of English ways, and a sense of guilt regarding local mannerisms, was...only one aspect of the complex meaning of provincialism."[37] The link with the continent of Europe expressed itself in education, law, and medicine, but this distinctly anti-provincial force could not operate effectively in the area of language. Hence many stern patriots could be shamefaced about their "incorrect" English usage. David Hume, the favorite of Paris, the luminary of half of the civilized world, could seek the advice of undistinguished English scribblers. So James Beattie, taken up by fashionable London, could write in 1775, ("I become every day more and more doubtful of the propriety of publishing Scotticisms. Our language (I mean English) is degenerating very fast; and many phrases, which I know to be Scottish idioms, have got into it of late years."[38] Beattie was one who believed that the Scots learnt English as a dead language. Such views did not promote a living engagement with current English.

In these circumstances it was almost inevitable that Boswell, with his feeble sense of a determinant self, should catch the general anxiety about the subject. He was certainly pleased to be told by Burke that he spoke "very good English," but embarrassed by an implicit contrast with Gibbon.[39] He was probably just as proud to be informed by his friend Andrew Erskine, "when you was in England you spoke Scotch to Englishmen and English to Scotchmen," suggesting a kind of linguistic ambidexterity many Scots aimed at.[40] Without doubt it would have been the utmost mortification to him could he have read Nancy Temple's remark to her mother (wife of Boswell's great friend), "You cannot conceive a more unpolished girl than Miss B. is [Veronica Boswell]. She is really vulgar, speaks broad Scotch..."[41] By such standards did many English people judge matters of social acceptability. He possibly remained always as puzzled as he had been in Utrecht that "although an Englishman often does not understand a Scot, it is rare that a Scot has trouble in understanding what an Englishman says."[42] There were so many grounds for nervousness.

John MacQueen has recently observed that Boswell "cannot be properly understood save in the context of the Scottish life and thought of the eighteenth century."[43] This is nowhere more true than in that muddled area of sociolinguistics which is the home of the Scotticism.[44]

NOTES

All references to *Life* are included in the text.

1 Tobias Smollett, *The Expedition of Humphry Clinker*, ed. L. M. Knapp (London: Oxford University Press, 1972), pp. 199–201.

2 In addition to general studies of the Scottish Enlightenment, a valuable background to the issues considered in this essay is provided in particular by two items in *Scotland in the Age of Improvement*, ed. N. T. Phillipson and Rosalind

Mitchison (Edinburgh: Edinburgh University Press, 1970). These are Janet Adam Smith, "Some Eighteenth-Century Ideas of Scotland," pp. 107–24; and John Clive, "The Social Background of the Scottish Renaissance," pp. 225–44.

3 Quoted by Janet Adam Smith, p. 112: see also p. 110 for Hume's letter to Gilbert Elliot in 1757, on the "very corrupt Dialect" heard in both "Accent & Pronunciation" of the Scottish ruling class – paradoxically when the Scottish people were "the most distinguish'd for Literature in Europe."

4 Information on the Select Society is available in many standard sources, but the best general account is Davis D. McElroy, *Scotland's Age of Improvement* (n.p.: Washington State University Press, 1969), pp. 48–67. Material particularly relevant to the present discussion can be found in E. C. Mossner, *The Life of David Hume* (Oxford: Clarendon Press, 2nd ed. 1980), pp. 372–3 (noting the subscriptions mounted to pay for English tutors); and Alastair Smart, *The Life and Art of Allan Ramsay* (London: Routledge, 1952), p. 77. A good overview of the Society is given by John Robertson, *The Scottish Enlightenment and the Militia Issue* (Edinburgh: John Donald, 1985), pp. 85–6.

5 For some Scottish reactions to this hostility, see Dorothy Yarwood, *Robert Adam* (London: Dent, 1970), pp. 97–8. Yarwood mentions Boswell's difficulty in making friends at this time.

6 Clive, "Scottish Renaissance," p. 239. For fuller details on the course of lectures, see Pottle, *Earlier Years*, pp. 64–5, 473.

8 A representative (though here positive) reaction of one English reader is a comment by Gray on Adam Ferguson's *History of Civil Society*: see his letters to James Beattie of August 12, 1767, in *The Correspondence of Thomas Gray*, ed. P. Toynbee and L. Whibley, rev. H. W. Starr (Oxford: Clarendon Press, 1971), III, 975. It might be added that Gray took notes of Scottish words when he made a visit to Glamis in 1765: see W. P. Jones, *Thomas Gray; Scholar* (Cambridge, Mass.: Harvard University Press, 1937), p. 177.

9 Quoted by C. B. Tinker, *The Salon and English Letters* (New York: Macmillan, 1915), p. 193. For Montagu's praise of Ferguson, see Mossner, *Life of David Hume*, p. 543.

10 *Life of David Hume*, p. 263.

11 Warren Derry, *Samuel Parr* (Oxford: Clarendon Press, 1966), p. 124. A curious instance, which might well have come to Boswell's attention through Johnson, is the employment of Theophilus Cibber as nominal author of the *Lives of the Poets* (1753), to guard against both Scotticisms and possible Jacobite sentiments.

12 Quoted by R. H. Campbell, A. S. Skinner, *Adam Smith* (New York: St. Martin's Press, 1982), p. 37.

13 Hume wrote to John Wilkes of the "desperate and Irreclaimable" tongue he inherited: cited by Mossner, *Life of David Hume*, p. 370.

14 *Life of David Hume*, p. 89. For a fuller discussion of Hume's alleged inability to avoid Scottish forms of words, see Boswell, *Life*, II, 72 n. 2.

15 Mossner, *Life of David Hume*, p. 214; *The Yale Edition of Horace Walpole's Correspondence*, ed. W. S. Lewis *et al.* (New Haven: Yale University Press, 1937–83), XXXI, 49 (letter to the Countess of Suffolk, September 20, 1765); see also XL, 385.

16 See *Earlier Years*, p. 93, which cites the "Harvest Jaunt" of 1762.

17 Alexander Carlyle, *Anecdotes and Characters*, ed. J. Kinsley (London: Oxford University Press, 1973), p. 253. Carlyle similarly said that Robertson's language was "good honest natural Scotch."

18 John Gross, *The Rise and Fall of the Man of Letters* (London: Weidenfeld and Nicolson, 1969), p. 8: see also Boswell, *Life*, II, 159, n. 6; Karl Miller, *Cockburn's Millennium* (Cambridge, Mass.: Harvard University Press, 1976), p. 264.

19 *Grand Tour I*, p. 260.

20 *The Life and Letters of Lady Sarah Lennox 1745–1826*, ed. the Countess of Ilchester and Lord Stavordale (London: John Murray, 1901), I, 14.

21 See Yarwood, *Robert Adam*, p. 33.

22 Tobias Smollett, *The Adventures of Roderick Random*, ed. P.-G. Boucé (Oxford: Oxford University Press, 1981), p. 96 (from chapter 18).

23 See *Boswell in Holland*, pp. 158–64 and *passim*.

24 Some further examples are provided by Janet Adam Smith, "Some Eighteenth-Century Ideas of Scotland," p. 113.

25 *In Search of a Wife*, p. 31.

26 Fanny Burney, *Memoirs of Dr. Burney* (London: Moxon, 1832), II, 191. For Johnson's opinion of Boswell's accent, see *Life*, III, 105.

27 G. M. Young, "Boswell – and Unashamed," in *Daylight and Champaign* (London: Cape, 1937), p. 277.

28 To W. J. Temple, April 28, 1776; *Letters*, I, 250. See also rough notes for May 10, 1776, cited by D. M. Low, *Edward Gibbon 1737–1794* (London: Chatto and Windus, 1937), p. 229.

29 *In Search of a Wife*, pp. 312, 323. Hume sent Reid a detailed commentary on the *Inquiry*, with a lapse from "good English" noted – in fact a Scotticism. See *The Letters of David Hume*, ed. J. Y. T. Greig (Oxford: Clarendon Press, 1932), I, 375–6.

30 *Boswell in Extremes*, p. 213.

31 Miller, *Cockburn's Millennium*, p. 47.

32 *English Experiment*, p. 204.

33 Quoted by L. Collison-Morley, *Giuseppe Baretti* (London: John Murray, 1909), p. 164, from *La Frusta letteraria*, no. 9. See also p. 163 on Hume, "whose history is pleasant reading, in spite of his frequent Scotticisms."

34 Janet Adam Smith, "Some Eighteenth-Century Ideas of Scotland," p. 115. This is part of a judicious survey of Boswell's feelings about Scotland.

35 *The Correspondence of Robert Dodsley*, ed. J. E. Tierney (Cambridge: Cambridge University Press, 1988), p. 283.

36 Quoted by Janet Adam Smith, p. 110.

37 Clive, "Scottish Renaissance," p. 239.

38 William Forbes, *An Account of the Life and Writings of James Beattie, Ll.D.* (New York: Brisban and Brannan, 1807), p. 399.

39 *Boswell in Extremes*, p. 238 (another passage in the journal suppressed in the published *Life*).

40 *Boswell in Holland*, p. 172.

41 *Diaries of William John Temple*, ed. L. Bettany (Oxford: Oxford University Press, 1929), p. 70.

42 *Boswell in Holland*, p. 159.

43 John MacQueen, *Progress and Poetry* (Edinburgh: Scottish Academic Press, 1982), p. 109.

44 For a primary definition in answer to the question "What is Scots?," and useful background on the state of the language at the end of the eighteenth century, see the excellent study by Graham Tulloch, *The Language of Sir Walter Scott* (London: André Deutsch, 1980), esp. pp. 167–81. The work is relevant insofar as it was the dominance of Walter Scott in the literature of his time which spearheaded the efforts, much more evident in modern times, to recapture a form of Scots as the medium of a living literature. Boswell, like Burns, died just too soon to witness this movement.

5

BOSWELL AS CRITIC

Joan H. Pittock

Few eighteenth-century literary figures are more congenial to the twentieth than Boswell. Had he lived today it can hardly be doubted that he would have excelled in the art of the interview. His alertness to the strategy of the situation, his sensitivity to the potentialities of his own role, are unrivalled. He is as happy interviewing a porter at the door of a cockfight ("I have great pleasure in conversing with the lower part of mankind, who have very curious ideas") as interrogating General Paoli, Rousseau, or Voltaire, and he is fully aware of the value his public will assign to each. His wish is for fame and money: in his time the pursuits of literature and criticism might seem to offer unrivalled opportunities for both.

Boswell's criticism, however, is not that of the professional, but the amateur. Unlike Johnson, who was responsible to booksellers, to his public, to the tradition of authors and critics whose values he interpreted for his own times in the "common pursuit of true judgement," Boswell chose as his models the fashionable and the successful. The instincts of the journalist seem to dissipate his recorded literary interests into the occasional sensitive response or commonsense observation. Even in the series of papers he wrote for the *London Magazine* he discusses only four specifically literary topics: Periodicals, Authorship and Revision, Criticism, and Diaries. It is hardly surprising that, although on occasion he may seem to challenge Johnson to advantage in specific critical judgements – notably on Fielding, for example – there has been little attention paid to criticism as one of Boswell's strengths (*Life*, II, 175). In 1966 Irma Lustig published an article on Boswell's criticism in the *Life of Johnson*, where most of it seems to cluster round Johnson's opinions in the text and in editorial comments.[1] Concerning Boswell on genres, and Boswell on contemporary writers in response to Johnson's views on literature (as expressed in the *Life*), there can be little more to say. More recently, however, the business of criticism has expanded into areas of theory which call into question the relevance of truth and value, foregrounding instead a web of discourse and ideology. Perception of structures and styles, hermeneutics and reader response, the pleasures and differences of the text, existentialism and alienation, separates us from the Christian–humanist tradition of which Johnson, not Boswell, was a part. Johnson's concern to establish a canon of authors expressing for his own and future generations firm perspectives of human values to extend the understanding of the common reader is a profoundly serious view of literature: "What should books teach but the art of living?" He might question the status of existing texts as classics, but he assumed the importance of continuance of esteem rather than novelty, of human relevance rather than formal distinction. Up to the middle of this century respect for national traditions in literature and criticism was the keystone in the arch of English as a university discipline. The arbitrement of taste was considered an essential part of education. This consensus has been eroded and the status of the classic text put into question. Boswell, unlike Johnson, is a master of the strategies of questioning which characterize our age: his best work has all the appearance of openness to character and text which imbues much of our interest in fictional worlds. Differences in style, in narrative structure, in levels of discourse, are his métier. Catering for the not particularly discerning is recognized by Boswell as a social necessity, and a potential source of fame and fortune. The disclosure it involves of one's own ego is an additional source of pleasure. It appeals to the awareness of the existential in us, while the highly developed consciousness of self in its private and social ramifications has the moment by moment potentiality for endless re-invention of character of modern fiction. Boswell has also, however, his envelope of consciousness: this sets him apart and alone. Within that envelope he is aware of an inevitable alienation from himself. It is interesting to pinpoint elements in Boswell's critical perspective which have a decidedly modern quality.

That the business of literature was with the generality of mankind and its everyday appetites was Boswell's personal conviction and his social experience. Johnson's dismissal of mediocrity in art is well known. When he refused to distinguish between the merits of a louse and a flea Boswell might have recalled an earlier dispute with Sheridan:

> We disputed about poems. Sheridan said that man should not be a poet except he was very excellent; for that to be a *mediocris poeta* was but a poor thing. I said I differed from him. For the greatest part of those who read poetry have a mediocre taste: consequently one may please a great many. Besides, to write poems is very agreeable, and one has always people enough to call them good; so that a man of a tolerable genius rather gains than loses. (*London Journal*, p. 151)

The entertainment of the public is its own justification. When Johnson objected that *The World* and *The Connoisseur* "wanted matter" Boswell admitted that the latter periodical lacked the "deep thinking" of Johnson's own work, but observed that it had "just views on the surface of life, and a very sprightly manner" (*Life*, I, 420).

Social circumstance encouraged his keen awareness of the pleasures of literature and the theatre, the pursuit of diversion which the metropolis held for him and into which he plunged as a relief from the small worlds of Scottish village and Edinburgh society alike. With Erskine he enthuses over a place where a man "may enjoy whatever is to be had in this transitory state of things" where "Every agreeable whim may be enjoyed without censure," dwelling happily on the promising prospects such an environment offered for personal fame and wealth:

> I told him I wondered how Mr. Lloyd got so much poetry for his magazine. "I wonder," said he "that he does not get more of such poetry. It is as if one were making a collection of whinstones in Scotland, where you may get them in every field. We talked with relish on publishing and on the profits made by books and pamphlets ... It is very agreeable to look forward and to imagine that we shall probably write much, get much fame and much gold. (*London Journal*, p. 179)

At about the same time Johnson wrote in *The Rambler*, no. 93:

> To commence author, is to claim praise, and no man can justly aspire to honour, but at the hazard of disgrace...The duty of *criticism* is neither to depreciate, nor dignify by partial representations, but to hold out the light of REASON, whatever it may discover; and to promulgate the determinations of TRUTH *whatever she shall dictate.*[2]

No such reflections hindered Boswell from publishing his correspondence with Erskine, his *Ode to Tragedy*, his pamphlet on Foote's production of *The Minor*, his *Critical Strictures on Elvira*, *The Cub at Newmarket* or his several poems in the second volume of the *Collection of Original Poems by Scotch Gentlemen* in the period 1760–3. Nor was he to be inhibited by professional decorum from rushing into print in defence of the Douglas cause, or trying the mode of romance in *Dorando*. The happy possession of a "facility of manners" which Adam Smith had praised in the student at his lectures on rhetoric and belles lettres likewise prompted a happy facility in burlesque in the *Letters*, Shandean parody in the comments on *The Minor*, and extremes of sensation, whimsicality, and introspective sentiment in the poems.[3] As for the *Ode to Tragedy*, no stops were left unpulled:

> 'Tis thine the soul to humanize
> By fancied wo – Goddess! 'tis thine
> To bid compassion meet the eyes,
> And all the feelings soft refine.
> 'Tis thine. With great Apollo's skill,
> The inmost springs of life to thrill;
> 'Tis thine to move a breast of stone,

And make a brazen heart to own,
That solemn tragic numbers are of force,
To stop a villain in his bloody course.

Characteristically, however, it is the promulgation of self with heroic–comic zest that is most striking. The pamphlet on Foote is by "A Genius," the Ode to Tragedy is dedicated to Mr. Boswell, in the *Collected Poems* there is "B – A Song" ("Boswell of Soapers the King"), "An Epistle from a London Buck to his Friend" (by "a Gentleman of Scotland"), and "The Race. An Heroic Ballad" by "A Genius." The Erskine–Boswell letters contain several references to their geniuses: "we great geniuses" (November 17, 1761), "enormous geniuses" (December 3, 1761), "my genius" (November 20, 1762). The recurrence of "genius" can be placed in context. It is not only part of the rapidly growing interest in modes of perception as self-realization – one of that group of words: imagination, taste, fancy, sublime, pathetic, picturesque, sentimental, sensational, gothic – in which a whole shift in sensibility was recorded. A spiritual base had been claimed for the word in Young's *Conjectures on Original Composition* (1759). Boswell admired the author of *Night Thoughts* in terms of the pathetic fallacy:

> He who does not feel his nerves shaken, and his heart pierced by many passages in this extraordinary work, particularly by that most affecting one, which describes the gradual torment suffered by the contemplation of an object of affectionate attachment, visibly and certainly decaying into dissolution, must be of a hard and obstinate frame. (*Life*, IV, 61)

He opens a letter of January 11, 1762 with "original conjectures of my own" and begins his *London Journal* with Young's adjuration to "Know thyself." Young continues "Reverence thyself," but a group of writers with a higher social profile were giving a more congenial interpretation of the genius which Young saw as the inner potential of every man. The "London Geniuses" whom Boswell met as a group on May 24, 1763 had already been connected with a series of periodical publications, such as *The Student*, to which Johnson had contributed, and, more successfully, with *The World* and *The Connoisseur*. The fashionable London literary world was dominated by them and the periodicals gave back to the world a flattering reflection of its concerns.

The spirit of "Every man shall soap his own beard" of Boswell's Soapers Club is that of the Nonsense Club or the Geniuses of London. One of the group, George Colman the Elder, contributed fifteen papers under that name to *The St. James's Chronicle*. In the first of these, of June 11, 1760, the Genius is described as needing "neither diligence nor assiduity. Supported by confidence, he disdains to halt along on the crutches of application... Almost every man is an adept of every art; acquires learning without study; improves good sense without meditation; writes without reading..."[4]

Colman and the rest may have been mocking Young's prescription as they were to parody Gray and pillory Hogarth. Of the group, Churchill (whose *Rosciad* Boswell much admires in his correspondence with Erskine – "He is certainly a very able writer: he has great powers of numbers") was the most formidable satirist, Wilkes the source of excitement and partisanship as the furore concerning his election and imprisonment unfolded through this decade. In both a kind of reckless cynicism expressed itself in demonstrating the threadbare and corrupt assumptions of contemporary society and enshrining their dissatisfaction in new abstractions, which they might exploit for their own ends. The restlessness, transitoriness, and role-playing of life in the town was too much for some of their early members. Smart and, later, Cowper retired hurt: the first after entertaining the town with the farcical jocularities of *Mrs. Midwife* and the second after his suicide attempt. The group also focused their critical appraisal on the theatre, in terms of Churchill's successful *Rosciad* and Robert Lloyd's *The Actor*. Boswell was likely to find the ideas of the group, their success, their place in London literary society, and their self-publicity both glamorous and congenial: in the same decade Chatterton was to assume the world-weary cynicism that was one of their hallmarks. They had no illusions about the nature of their own success; they perceived the shallowness of their concerns and those of the town and took advantage of both. So, to return to the keyword "genius," Robert Lloyd wrote in "Genius, Envy and Time " of genius as "a bustling lad of parts"

> Who all things did by fits and starts,
> Nothing above him or below him,
> Who'd make a riot or a poem,
> From excentricity of thought,
> Not always do the thing he ought.

There is the young Boswell to the life.

He had already seen Wilkes and Churchill at the Beefsteak Club on his first visit to London but he was to become involved more closely with them when Bonnell Thornton wrote a favorable review of his correspondence with Erskine, and May 24 Boswell was introduced by Thornton to Churchill, Wilkes, and Lloyd. On the following day he writes the memorandum: "Go on with Geniuses moderately. Call Wilkes and leave card, with full directions. Cultivate acquaintance with wits to be *bel esprit*."[5] That he succeeded in this is proved by his long and happy acquaintance with Wilkes.

Much of Boswell's criticism is of the theatre and theatrical performances. It was a favorite amusement, partly because it linked him with and separated him from his Edinburgh youth:

> I then called on Mr. Lee, who is a good agreeable, honest man, with whom I
> associate fine gay ideas of the Edinburgh Theatre in my boyish days, when I

used to walk down the Canongate and think of players with a mixture of narrow-minded horror and lively-minded pleasure; and used to wonder at painted equipages, and powdered ladies, and sing "The bonny bush aboon Traquair," and admire Mrs. Bland in her chair with tassels, and flambeaux before her. (*London Journal*, p. 85)

He might become the man of the world in a theatre audience, observe the fashion like any town-bred buck, and indulge his role-playing with the legitimate preoccupation of the dramatic critic. He enters into the thick of the civilizing process itself. It affords a topic of conversation of which he does not tire. Boswell records his disagreement with Johnson over Foote and Garrick in the *Life* and assesses performances of roles frequently and freely in the *London Journal*:

I dined with Mr. Sheridan. He was quite enthusiastic about oratory. He said Garrick had no real feeling; that his talents for mimicry enabled him to put on the appearance of feeling, and that the nicety of his art might please the fancy and make us cry, "That's fine." But as it was art, it could never touch the heart. Mr. Sheridan's distinction was just, but does not apply to Garrick, because he often has touched the heart and drawn tears from multitudes. (p. 57)

and again:

Sheridan in his usual way railed against Mr. Garrick, and I as strenuously defended him against Tommy's attacks. He gave us, however, a most ingenious dissertation on the character of Hamlet that atoned for all his wrong-headed abuse of the great modern Roscius. (pp. 234–5)

Another London acquaintance probably affected him more deeply, entering into the very marrow of his perceptions. He had met Sterne, then famous and successful, on his first visit to London: the *Letters* contain allusions to Yorick, and Tristram, and the Douce MS in the Bodleian, published in *Boswell's Book of Bad Verse*, contains an account of a meeting with Sterne:

> My verses, be they good or ill,
> Have been, dear foes – do laugh your fill –
> By Sterne approv'd; when in the Mall
> I've even kept him back from Hall.
> For Fame I would not tell a lie,
> So don't endeavour to deny;
> For this bid mem'ry backwards post,
> The day she'll show if not quite lost.
> Have you not caper'd at my *Cub*,
> Like puritanic priest in tub?
> And did you not my shoulder pat,
> And call me child of Dorset's Mat?[6]

Boswell's subject is the transformation of the country parson, Sterne as Yorick, to the fashionable author: "That there is he – do, Thomas look! – / Who's wrote such a damn'd clever book."

> Beg pardon, Sir, for this intrusion;
> Before *you* I'm in some confusion.
> "Before me? Bless my soul, my dear,
> Am I an object of your fear?
> Go on, I prithee – do not stare –
> I have enough of time to spare."
> Permit me, doctor, then to show
> A certain Genius whom you know,
> A mortal enemy to strife,
> In diff'rent periods of his life.
> To country curacy confin'd
> (Ah! how unlike his soaring mind)...
> He had of books a chosen few,
> He read as humour bid him do;
> If Metaphysics seemed too dark,
> Shifted to Gay from Dr. Clarke...
> Sometimes our priest, with limbs so taper,
> Before his glass would cut a caper,
> Indulging each suggestion airy,
> Each whim and innocent vagary.
> The Heliconian stream he'd quaff,
> And by himself transported laugh.

The "metamorphosis" takes place with Dodsley's help, "To reap a crop of fame and pelf," as a consequence of the new fashionable furore reported from the Duke of York's table in 1760. Even Sterne's sermons have become popular: the first volume of the *Sermons of Mr. Yorick* was published in 1760.

> A strange enthusiastic rage
> For sacred texts now seiz'd the age,
> Around St. James's ev'ry table
> Was partly gay and partly sable.
> The manners by Old Noll defended
> Were with our modern chit-chat blended:
> "Give me some macaroni, pray."
> "Be wise while it is call'd today."
> "Heav'ns! How Mingotti sung last Monday!"
> "Alas! How we profane the Sunday!"
> "My Lady Betty! Hob or nob?"
> "Great was the patience of old Job,"
> Sir Smart breaks out, and one and all
> Adore St. Peter and St. Paul.

Boswell would not worship, but praised Sterne, whether in or out of favor, for "Sweet Sentiment, the certain test / Of goodness, commendation best," as well as for his "Judgment, imagination bright, / True erudition, polish'd taste, / Pure language – (tho' you write in haste)." Boswell imagines Sterne asks on what authority he has the right to judge, and the modest youth replies:

> Bards may commend their friends, 'tis true,
> But pray, sir, what pretence have you?
> Are you a Poet? Yes I am...
> A heart and head for musing fit,
> With levity, sure sign of wit;
> A little spark of Fancy's fire
> Whose wings excursive seldom tire;
> A decent faculty to chime
> And put my foolish thoughts in rhyme.

The young Boswell considers himself a poet; he also feels affinities with Sterne. But he is a gentleman, and from a distinguished line. On neither count would he feel obliged to take account of system in criticism or scholarship. He enters into the spirit of Shandy in the notes at the end of the epistle to Sterne: "*Design*. – A few Compliments – Stay stay – not so fast – what little have you – Are you a Poet? – Yes – An infant son of Apollo – You have told me so – I have the marks – a happy levity of head etc..."[7] He is already using the shifts of mood, consciousness, and feeling in his prose, and these are augmented by his facility in role-playing. Pondering the possibility of a career in the law – "I might have the wit and humour of Sir David Dalrymple, the jollity of Duncan Forbes, the whim of Baron Dalrymple, the show of Baron Maule, and the elegant taste of Baron Grant. I thought I might write books like Lord Kames and be a buck like Mr. James Erskine" (*London Journal*, p. 200).

On July 16, 1763 Johnson advises him "to keep a journal of my life, fair and undisguised":

> He said it would be a very good exercise, and would yield me infinite satisfaction when the ideas were failed from my remembrance. I told him that I had done so ever since I left Scotland. He said he was very happy that I pursued so good a plan. And now, O my journal! art thou not highly dignified? Shalt thou not flourish tenfold? No former solicitation or censures could tempt me to lay thee aside; and now is there any argument which can outweigh the sanction of Mr Samuel Johnson? (p. 305)

The self-communing, self-reflective modes are part of the sensitivity to mood and circumstance which Johnson was frequently to reprove. "Variety of fine cheering ideas glanced athwart by blest imagination, ideas which gave me exquisite sensations at the time but which are so very nice that they elude endeavours to paint them" – this suggests that capacity for sentiment already noted in Sterne and valued so highly as a mark of the poet in himself (p. 201). The egotistical element with which he enhanced the importance of such perceptions and feelings has broad affinities with those of *A Sentimental Journey* or *Rêveries d'un promeneur solitaire*. Boswell, however, lives too rapidly and with too strong a sense of circumstance to sink into egotism undiluted by a sense of proportion. In the *Tour* he recalls the discomfort of too attentive hospitality:

> I was uneasy to think myself too fastidious, whilst I fancied Dr. Johnson quite satisfied. But he owned to me that he was fatigued and teased by Sir Alexander's doing too much to entertain him. I said, it was all kindness. JOHNSON. "True, sir: but sensation is sensation" BOSWELL. "It is so: we feel pain equally from the surgeon's probe, as from the sword of the foe." (*Life* v, 95)

Just as Johnson insisted that "It is our business to exempt our selves as much as we can from the power of external things," so Boswell fastens on the detail, the circumstantial reality, the reality of the moment (III, 363). He can enter deliberately into what he supposes to be the character of the true Englishman, who eats beefsteaks and goes to a cockfight:

> An old cunning dog whose face I had seen at Newmarket sat by me a while. I told him I knew nothing of the matter. "Sir," said he, "you have as good a chance as anybody." He thought I would be a good subject for him. I was young-like. But he found himself balked. I was shocked to see the distraction and anxiety of the betters. I was sorry for the poor cocks. I looked round to see if any of the spectators pitied them when mangled and torn in a most cruel manner, but I could not observe the smallest relenting sign in any countenance. I was therefore not ill pleased to see them endure mental torment. Thus did I complete my true English day, and came home pretty much fatigued and pretty much confounded at the strange turn of this people. (*London Journal*, p. 87)

There is none of the luxuriating in sentimental sensation of Sterne or Rousseau here: the experience itself fills his powers of observation. The journalist is satisfied with the adventure.

The sensationalism of experience for which Boswell is notorious can be steadied by observation of fact, as on his meeting with Captain Cook (*Life*, III, 7).[8] The difference in the attention to detail between Johnson's *Journey to the Western Isles* and Boswell's *Tour to the Hebrides* emphasizes the specificity of Boswell's observation and the power of his memory. His wit and power of recall is happily caught in the farewell to Inch Keith when Johnson asks him to "pay a classical compliment to the island on quitting it":

> I happened, luckily, in allusion to the beautiful Queen Mary, whose name is upon the fort, to think of what Virgil makes Aeneas say, on having left the country of his charming Dido:

Invitus, regina, tuo de littore cessi!
[Unhappy queen, / Unwilling I forsook your friendly state (Dryden)]
"Very well hit off," said he. (IV, 56)

Boswell may have lamented his early education as merely consisting in reading books, but he displays an elegant acquaintance with a wide variety of classical authors in his periodical essays. His easy correspondence and conversation with many of the great legal and philosophical minds of his time – it was after all to Boswell that Adam Smith confided the desperation of his early wish to become a soldier – confirms the ease and facility of his conversation; its wit and fluency are shown in the *Correspondence*, and particularly in the happy audacity of his reply to Hume's letter in the *London Journal* (pp. 236ff). At Glasgow he attended Adam Smith's lectures on rhetoric and belles lettres and on moral philosophy. Not only did Smith insist in his lectures on the value of specific detail in observation (his instance of learning that Milton wore latchets on his shoes instead of buckles is well known) but he foregrounded the importance of an easy style and facility of communication. He recommended the style of Swift as a model (and Sterne is not unindebted to this). Smith's own syntax and diction are admirably lucid and a model of coherence and cogency. He is a man of his time, himself an example of its advancing thought, writing with flexibility and from a position which places in perspective the achievements and priorities of the past. Set the opening lines of Johnson's pamphlet on the Falkland Isles, for example, beside those of Smith's *Wealth of Nations* and the difference is clear. Smith is analytic and instructive, not general and ethical. His sentences are varied to keep the attention of his audience. He is clear in his requirements of style: "the perfection of style consists in expressing in the most concise, proper and precise manner the thought of the author, and that in the manner which best conveys the sentiment, passion or affection with which it affects or he pretends it does affect him and which he designs to communicate to his reader." For Smith the use of language is related to its prime function, communication in its several aspects.[9] This contrasts with the belle-lettriste approach of Blair in his Edinburgh lectures.

From the outset in writing his journal, Boswell is concerned with keeping the attention of his reader and consequently with varying his presentation. A sense of the facts of entertainment and amusement in the context of the town in art and life, and the ways in which this may be conveyed, leads him to insert episodes in dialogue. He can present this so as to convey his own awareness of the gap between ideal and actual response to artists:

SATURDAY, 1 JANUARY
DIALOGUE AT CHILD'S

1 CITIZEN. Pray, Sir, have you read Mr. Warton's *Essay on the Life and Writings of Pope*? He says he had good sense and good versification, but wants the warm imagination and brilliancy of expression that constitute the true

poetical genius. He tries him by a rule prescribed by Longinus, which is to take the words out of their metrical order and then see if they have the sparks of poetry. Don't you remember this?
2 CITIZEN. I don't agree with him.
1 CITIZEN. Nor I, neither. He is fond of Thomson. He says he has great force.
2 CITIZEN. He has great faults.
1 CITIZEN. Ay, but great force, too.
2 CITIZEN. I have eat beef steaks with him.
3 CITIZEN. So have I. (*London Journal*, p. 113)

He realizes that to be readable the creation of scenes and episodes, short snatches of anecdote, and changes of subject will best amuse his reader. In the *Letters* Erskine writes, "You think you have a knack of story-telling."[10] Boswell's sensitivity to narrative fastens on the problem of realism Gissing described in *New Grub Street*, and Joyce exploited in Bloom:

To relate gravely that I rose, made water, took drugs, sat quiet, read a book, saw a friend or two day after day, must be exceedingly poor and tedious. My journal must, therefore, like the newspapers, yield to the times. Yet I may take some incidents to insert. At any rate, I shall soon again be roaming abroad in search of amusing adventures. (*London Journal*, p. 196)

He is alert to levels of language, not only delighting in parody and burlesque but observing his own skill with pleasure:

How easily and how cleverly do I write just now! I am really pleased with myself; words come skipping to me like lambs upon Moffat Hill; and I turn my periods smoothly and imperceptibly like a skilful wheelwright turning tops in a turning loom. There's fancy! There's simile! In short, I am at present a genius: in that does my opulence consist, and not in base metal. (p. 211)

The hero of a romance or novel "must not go uniformly along in bliss, but the story must be chequered with bad fortune" to hold the attention of the reader (p. 226). The structuring of his narrative and the development of a relaxed and entertaining style are his priorities. So he admires Burke's mastery of the trope on first hearing him speak in the Commons:

It was a great feast to me... It was astonishing how all kinds of figures of speech crowded upon him. He was like a man in an Orchard where boughs loaded with fruit hung around him, and he pulled apples as fast as he pleased and pelted the Ministry... It seemed to me however that his Oratory rather tended to distinguish himself than to assist his cause. There was amusement instead of persuasion. It was like the exhibition of a favourite Actor. But I would have been exceedingly happy to be him. (*Corr: Garrick, Burke, Malone*, pp. 84–5)

Boswell does not need to search for the trope or the analogy when he is interpreting a play of emotion. There is, to take one example, his account of the dinner he gave for Johnson on October 16, 1769 when Reynolds, Garrick, Goldsmith, and others were present. "Garrick played round him [Dr. Johnson] with a fond vivacity, taking hold of the breasts of his coat, and, looking up in his face with a lively archness, complimented him on the good health which he seemed then to enjoy; while the sage, shaking his head, beheld him with a gentle complacency" (*Life*, II, 82–3). Boswell interprets the detail of behavior, what we should now call the signs, the body language, with exactness. He does not diminish the atmosphere by generalizing language or unnecessary reticence. This is again true of other descriptions in which he keeps to the truth of emotions, writing to our feelings unblocked by the decorum of his own day.

The encouragement and care given by Edmund Malone to Boswell in the writing and revision of the *Life* is a remarkable tribute from one of the most professional and distinguished scholars of the day to another professional. Though it was done for love of Johnson it is clearly also done for love and respect for Boswell. As the editor shows in his introduction to the *Correspondence*, Malone often achieves a blurring of Boswell's account:

> I have emphasized that Malone generally treated Boswell's text with great respect, but now must undercut my argument by admitting that on a very few occasions he introduced changes not only without Boswell's approval but against his directives. This he did to soften Boswell's expressions of his own emotions or opinions, which might (Malone feared) expose him to public ridicule. Boswell wrote in the first edition, "I loved to behold Dr. Samuel Johnson rolling about in this old magazine of antiquities [the Advocates' Library]." Malone thought "I loved" should be changed to "It gave me pleasure," but Boswell rejected the change, writing, "I think 'I loved' a good warm expression." Malone nevertheless submitted "I was pleased" without Boswell's knowledge. Again, Boswell wrote in the first edition that he "several times burst into tears" on hearing the story of the battle of Culloden. When Malone suggested a change to "I could not refrain from tears," Boswell replied, "Since I have once acknowledged the *fact* let *burst into tears* remain." Malone made the change anyway. (*Corr: Garrick, Burke, Malone*, p. 177)

Boswell's perceptiveness takes him beyond the fashionable. His sense of the authentic emotional fact, his alertness to the enduring importance of the reader, place him at the centre of literary experience.

It is clear from Boswell's journalistic conquests, the expedition to Corsica, the interviews with Rousseau and Voltaire and the tour to the Hebrides, that he inhabits a different dimension from that of his London acquaintance. He comes from a different tradition, a different country and a different past. Even in London he had naturally gravitated toward the company of other Scots; when abroad he insists on the importance of his family connections, and the country from which he says he comes is Scotland. He refers to the "shocking familiarity" with which Rousseau's simplicity of manner might be met in Scotland:

BOSWELL. "But they would say, 'Poh! Jean Jacques, why do you allow yourself all these fantasies? You're a pretty man to put forward such claims. Come, come, settle down in society like other people.' And they would say it to you with a sourness which I am quite unable to imitate for you."
ROUSSEAU. "Ah, that's bad."
  There he felt the thistle, when it was applied to himself on the tender part. It was just as if I had said, "Hoot, Johnnie Rousseau man, what for hae ye sae mony figmagairies? Ye're a bonny man indeed to mauk siccan a wark: set ye up. Canna ye just live like ither fowk?" It was the best idea could be given in the polite French language of the rude Scots sarcastical vivacity. (*Grand Tour I*, pp. 253–4)

A more specifically literary discussion with Voltaire not only introduces Shakespeare but also Macpherson's Ossian, the "Homer of Scotland" as Voltaire sees him.

  Boswell had probably agreed with Erskine that although Ossian might well be the Homer of Scotland his fame would be shorter-lived than the Greek's. He called Macpherson, with whom he was on familiar terms in his London visit of 1762–3, the "Sublime Savage" and disagreed with Macpherson's attack on social reserve and dignity of behavior. Boswell appreciates the civilizing behavior of modern society, while Blair and Macpherson rail against it (*London Journal*, p. 291). Gentlemanliness gives way to patriotism, however, when Johnson discounts the beauties of natural scenery and Boswell recalls the delight with which he remembers Arthur's Seat as a wellspring of imaginative inspiration. For the Scottish community in London the patriotism is complex. There are the stories of old Scotland, pre-Union and Stuart with all the romance of legend and lineage and peculiar beauties of landscape which relate so closely to its history. There is also in living memory the feeling for a land where battles have been fought and blood spilt, where incredible faith, honor, and loyalty have been witnessed within their own lifetime and all the excitements of romance are caught in the ballads and songs on the miraculous escape of Bonny Prince Charlie, for whom Boswell was continuing to scheme until the late 1780s.[11] Something of the climate of nostalgic pride is reflected in the episode in Boswell's *London Journal* where he is laid up with venereal disease and is visited by Dalrymple, calling himself mysteriously "The Man in Black," a well-known figure in the stories of the '45. In his tour to the Hebrides Johnson was tracing the footsteps of the Wanderer Prince himself. Nonetheless his vendetta against Macpherson was pursued with the utmost rigor: as ever on this issue Boswell is silent. The legendary figure of Flora Macdonald is brought to reality on their journey; he feels less affinity with the remote myths of the Fianna.

  Whatever the shifting perspectives of criticism may be, Boswell is clear on the question of his own values: he reacts with horror to Holbach's *Système de la nature* with its mechanistic interpretation of human existence (*Life*, IV, 47).

Of his own "wretched changefulness" he observes "It was most comfortable to me to experience in Dr Johnson's company, a relief from this uneasiness. His steady vigorous mind held from before me those objects which my own feeble and tremulous imagination frequently presented, and in such a wavering state, that my reason could not judge well of them." In *The Rambler* above all may be found "bark and steel for the mind...[to] brace and invigorate every noble and manly sentiment" (III, 193; I, 215).

As in his own "wretched changefulness" Boswell opens for us the vicissitudes of his life, real and imagined, so in his assumptions and literary preoccupations he rehearses with a happy frankness the diverse but continuing interests of criticism. No matter from what perspective, or in terms of what *durée*, we now view the criticism of the eighteenth century, Boswell's percipience and dynamism inform his thinking about literature, which therefore remains of enduring interest.

NOTES

1 Irma S. Lustig, "Boswell's Literary Criticism," *Studies in English Literature*, 3 (1966), 529–41.
2 Samuel Johnson, *The Rambler*, ed. W. J. Bate and Albrecht B. Strauss, 3 vols. (New Haven: Yale University Press, 1969), II, 134.
3 *Letters Erskine*, p. 109.
4 See Lance Bertelson, *The Nonsense Club: Literature and Popular Culture 1749–1764* (Oxford: Clarendon Press, 1986), p. 129. Bertelson quotes Colman and Lloyd.
5 See Ian Finlayson, *The Moth and the Candle: A Life of James Boswell* (London: John Constable, 1984), p. 39f.
6 *Boswell's Book of Bad Verse*, ed. Jack Warner (London: White Lion Publishers Ltd., 1974), p. 140.
7 *Boswell's Book of Bad Verse*, p. 201
8 Boswell reports, "I gave him [Johnson] an account of a conversation which had passed between me and Captain Cook, the day before, at dinner at Sir John Pringle's: and he was much pleased with the conscientious accuracy of that celebrated circumnavigator, who set me right as to many of the exaggerated accounts given by Dr Hawkesworth of his Voyages."
9 Adam Smith, *Lectures on Rhetoric and Belles Lettres*, ed. J. C. Bryce (Oxford: Clarendon Press, 1953), p. 55.
10 *Letters Erskine*, p. 109.
11 See Donald Cross Bryant, *Edmund Burke and his Literary Friends*, Washington University Studies in Language and Literature, No. 9 (St. Louis, 1939), p. 123.

Part II

CONTEXTS FOR THE *LIFE OF JOHNSON*

6

BOSWELL'S LIBERTY-LOVING
ACCOUNT OF CORSICA AND THE
ART OF TRAVEL LITERATURE

Thomas M. Curley

Boswell's *Account of Corsica* appeared at a remarkable moment of eighteenth-century English travel. Its publication in 1768 occurred when Captain Samuel Wallis returned from his discovery of Tahiti, Lieutenant James Cook took command of his momentous Pacific voyages, Samuel Johnson renewed his promise of a Highland tour that resulted in a magnificent travel book, and a dying Laurence Sterne finished his exuberant paean to cosmopolitan touring in *A Sentimental Journey through France and Italy by Mr. Yorick.* Few modern commentators of Boswell recognize that *An Account of Corsica* is a distinguished example of eighteenth-century travel literature worthy of comparison with Sterne's fiction and yet anticipates the more famous biographical studies of Johnson. This first of Boswell's major publications made creative use of travel book conventions for a radical romantic celebration of liberty behind the maturation of both primitive Corsica and young Boswell himself on the Grand Tour. There was a conscious artistic shaping of his experiences abroad around the theme of liberty in the life of the narrator, the nation, and its leader, Paoli, for the propagandistic purpose of uniting England to Corsica's struggle for freedom. Although the entire geographical description is an integrated, pseudo-Rousseauistic exploration of the impact of freedom on the observer and the observed, it was the final autobiographical portion of the book with the *Memoirs of Pascal Paoli* that provided Boswell with a narrative model for his *Journal of a Tour to the Hebrides* (1786) and *Life of Samuel Johnson* (1791).

Travel was a national enthusiasm and a prime manifestation of the irrepressible Georgian curiosity to seek and see new truths about life on the world's intellectual fronts. Pope's imperial prophecy in *Windsor Forest* (1713), "The Time shall come, when free as Seas or Wind / Unbounded Thames shall flow for all Mankind," was a fitting prelude to the unprecedented expansion of territorial dominion under the Georges. Englishmen conquered Canada and almost half of India, lost American colonies but gained Pacific possessions in Australasia and Polynesia, sent embassies to China and adventurers into Africa, and bequeathed to

89

Victorians an empire more extensive than ancient Rome's. To match their growing global supremacy, Britons emerged as the most active tourists and most accomplished explorers in Europe. A vast store of travel books chronicled their discoveries and profoundly influenced the arts and sciences.[1] Most authors, like Smollett and Johnson, wrote in a firmly defined tradition of travel literature and sometimes, as with Sterne and Boswell, wrought changes in the genre. The most famous Grand Tourist of all was Boswell himself, whose modern reputation depends upon his *Life of Johnson* but whose eighteenth-century notoriety rested initially on his description of Corsica.[2]

Travel literature had well-established conventions which, despite inevitable variations, can be found in *An Account of Corsica*. Reflecting a scientific revolution and Royal Society guidelines, a codified format promoted the Baconian call for an accumulation of accurate data world-wide, even though it also caused a tedious uniformity in geographical reporting. The usual procedure was to offer a first-person narration of foreign sights on a journey according to a comprehensive checklist of topics of inquiry under the three general headings of geography, natural history, and anthropology. A comparable coverage of the flora, fauna, and inhabitants is present in Boswell's travel book, which ends with a first-person narrative of his adventures with Paoli. His description also incorporates features found in travelogues about Grand Touring. The stress is similarly on the moral and cultural education of the young narrator from his encounters with continental people and places. If accounts of distant voyages and travels usually recorded encyclopedic findings, tourists' descriptions tended to focus on the distinctly human phenomena of foreign culture and government to the neglect of natural history and scenic observation.[3] Boswell, in the true *terra incognita* of Corsica, made sure to combine encyclopedic reporting with a Grand Tourist's journal of his political education at the hands of Paoli and his followers. Boswell also imitated tourists like Joseph Addison in his *Remarks on Italy* (1705) in interjecting ennobling quotations from the classics to provide instructive comparisons between the past and present state of a nation. However, a good writer of travel literature was as much hampered as helped by the formal restrictions of the genre that sacrificed racy individuality for a scientific thoroughness. Boswell, like Sterne and Johnson, faced the problem of standardization and happily found a solution that parallels innovations in the contemporaneous *A Sentimental Journey* for an age of sensibility.

The second half of the century witnessed a greater autobiographical emphasis in English travel accounts, and Yorick's self-oriented Grand Tour fully epitomizes the new trend. Authors consciously exploited the subjective elements of the genre so as to engage the reader's imagination in the vicarious experience of travel. Giuseppe Baretti wanted readers of his *Journey from London to Genoa* (1770) to "see what I saw, hear what I heard, feel what I felt, and even think and fancy whatever I thought and fancied myself."[4] Travel books were a literature of process with an obvious potential for creating an imaginative bond between the reader's mind and recorded scenes through the medium of the author's subjective flow of impressions. Boswell's work has a psychological aim of making readers empathize with the changing sights and sensations through the traveller's enthusiastic personality and peripatetic mode of inquiry. He, like the protagonist of Sterne's *A Sentimental Journey*, assumes the role of an impressionable Grand Tourist being liberated and educated into a cosmopolitan appreciation of human simplicity and freedom by means of a heartfelt imaginative rapport with continental strangers. Boswell's bracing attempt to capture an emotional communion in travel helps to explain why Johnson preferred the closing autobiographical report of Paoli to the impersonal description of Corsica filling the bulk of the book: "Your history was copied from books; your journal rose out of your own experience and observation. You express images which operated strongly on yourself, and you have impressed them with great force upon your readers. I know not whether I could name any narrative by which curiosity is better excited, or better gratified."[5]

Johnson's comment pinpoints the appeal of the concluding *Journal and Memoirs of Paoli* but overlooks this section's inseparable ties to the preceding *Account of Corsica*. The entire book, like *A Sentimental Journey*, has a consciously crafted narrative unity that is unusual for contemporary travel literature. Like Sterne, Boswell fixed upon the concept of liberty for the work's coherence.[6] Although Johnson initially urged Boswell to think of publishing a narrative of his continental rambles, Rousseau seems to have been responsible for both the jaunt to Corsica and the preoccupation with liberty in the travel book. The well-known visits to the *philosophe* in December of 1764 appear to have intoxicated Boswell, then a fan of the *Nouvelle Héloise*, with the dream of testing the radical ideas of the *Contrat social* (1762) concerning ideal government and a primitive state of nature in an actual breeding-ground of freedom in primitive Corsica. He would go there as Rousseau's unofficial "Ambassador Extraordinary" armed with letters of introduction from a political philosopher who praised Corsica in the *Social Contract* and had just received a request to draft a constitution for the emergent nation.[7] Under these circumstances, Boswell's patriotic vision of the country in his travel book may usefully be seen as his very free translation of the *Social Contract* – heavily colored by classical traditions of golden ages and heroes in Plutarch, Virgil, Homer, Livy, and others, and modified by the realities of the Corsican political situation.

Corsican politics constituted a long historical struggle to establish a national identity and independence from oppressors as ancient as Carthaginians and Romans to their current counterparts, the Genoese and the French. With the end of the War of Austrian Succession under the peace of

Aix-la-Chapelle in 1748, England's half-hearted efforts at intervention ceased, and France pursued a patient policy of acquiring the island from Genoa, the uneasy conqueror of Corsica since the fourteenth century. Supported by Corsican family connections, Pasquale Paoli (1725–1807) returned in 1755 to become supreme general, introducing a remarkable peace and order among the normally feuding insurgents. This truly selfless man saw Boswell's visit (from October 11 to November 20 of 1765) as an opportunity for persuading the Scot to return home on an unofficial diplomatic mission to gain British support for Corsican independence and abrogate the British proclamation of 1763 forbidding subjects to assist Corsicans. As fantastic as Paoli's expectations may seem in entrusting such an assignment to an obscure young Briton, *An Account of Corsica* was to spearhead the mission. While Paoli played his improbable British card through the little-known Boswell, he secretly negotiated with the French minister, Choiseul, for a declaration of independence, but balked at making any territorial concessions to France. Exactly three months after the publication of *An Account of Corsica*, the French sealed the island's doom by signing a treaty of purchase with the Genoese on May 15, 1768. Suspecting Paoli of diplomatic double-dealing, the divided English government could do nothing.[8] Corsica became a French province, and Paoli an English exile.

No hint of this sorry political outcome infiltrates the pages of the high-spirited travel book. Public interest in the account of awakening Corsican liberty was no doubt heightened by the glamor of the brash narrator self-consciously playing the part of a freedom-fighter defying Britain's ban against giving aid and appealing for a foreign policy in support of a burgeoning third-world nation. Boswell, the sole British reporter of the guerilla resistance, aimed to arouse the sympathy of his liberty-loving countrymen but from a radical Rousseauistic viewpoint echoing the *Social Contract* ("Man is born free; and everywhere he is in chains... To renounce liberty is to renounce being a man"). Rousseau's tract called European attention to Corsica as a unique place prepared to receive legislation creating a social contract of pure political liberty. Boswell quotes and translates the pertinent paragraph from the *Social Contract*, summarizing the purpose and perspective of his entire travel book: "M. Rousseau in his Political Treatise, entitled DU CONTRAT SOCIAL, has the following observation... 'There is yet one country in Europe, capable of legislation; and that is the island of Corsica. The valour and the constancy with which that brave people hath recovered and defended its liberty, would well deserve that some wise man should teach them how to preserve it. I have some presentiment that one day that little island will astonish Europe.'"[9] *An Account of Corsica* transforms Rousseau's rousing presentiment into Paoli's astonishing achievement of an emergent body politic resting on a social contract of freedom.

What points of resemblance exist between the theoretical formulations in the *Social Contract* and the actual portrayal of Corsica by Boswell? First, there is a common stress on liberty as the greatest good and end of legislation. Second, there is the traditional equation of a ruler with a father – except that Paoli established a patriarchal bond of love which Rousseau expressly denied could exist between a governor and the governed. Third, there is an analogous insistence on a virtually superhuman legislator, who is a Lycurgus of wisdom, disinterestedness, and providential authority in creating a state of moral equality and communal freedom.[10] Rousseau himself is associated with such a legislator in Boswell's closing discussion of a Corsican constitution. But it is Paoli who is the dramatic personification of this idealized figure by virtue of his constituting a free government out of anarchy – even if he wields powers not permitted the law-giver of the *Social Contract*, such as the execution and maintenance of law in his capacity as a benevolent dictator–magistrate of the island. There is nothing in *An Account of Corsica* exactly parallel to Rousseau's major and most radical political doctrine that the state is essentially the collective sovereignty of the people (the "general will"), unless its counterpart be the democratic Corsican nation responsible for Paoli's power. Most important, all the criteria listed in Book 2, chapter 10 of the *Social Contract* for singling out Corsica as ripe for utopian legislation cohere in Boswell's conception of the country. According to Rousseau, the people best suited for a state of liberty have (1) common interests and economic equality without the yoke of a highly developed government or of ingrained prejudices to stifle receptivity to new ideals; (2) self-sufficiency, moderation, and the courage both to resist invasion and to dissociate themselves from quarreling neighbors; and (3) the solidity of an ancient race combined with the docility of a new citizenry ready to preserve primitive simplicity and yet to accept those innovations necessary for ideal government. The Corsicans, as presented by Boswell, are the fulfillment of Rousseau's prerequisites for political formation.

Boswell's publication is artful propaganda transforming personal experience and historical research into a coherent case for British support of Corsican independence. It is a fact-based artifact having a romantic libertarian perspective shaped in part by Rousseau and the classics but nevertheless containing a reliable British description of the country. The topic of liberty becomes the focal point of the narrative, around which revolve three interrelated concerns: the development of primitive Corsica; the education of naive Boswell; and the inspiration of father-figure Paoli behind the nurturing of the nation and the narrator. The full title of the travel book reflects these triple preoccupations: *An Account of Corsica, The Journal of a Tour to that Island; and Memoirs of Pascal Paoli*. The very epigraph, taken from a Latin chronicle of ancient Scotland, initiates the theme of liberty.[11] The ensuing *Dedication to Pascal Paoli* concedes the propagandistic end of publishing the General's panegyric and implicitly testifies to his influence upon Boswell's education: "But I wish to express to the world, the admiration and gratitude with which you have inspired me" (p. VII). The Preface to the first edition of "my little monument to liberty" (p. XIV) sets forth Boswell's credentials as an historical researcher, a geographical explorer of unknown regions, and an accurate biographer of Paoli the conversationalist in a manner prophetic of the authorial claims in the *Life of Johnson*. There is even the same, slightly disingenuous, profession of "scrupulous" fidelity in recording his subject's sayings.

So much of Boswell's autobiography here and elsewhere in his writings is a recounting of his lifelong pursuit of a reconciliation of opposites within his personality by emulating authority-figures of acknowledged greatness. The principal interest in the Preface is his avowed ambition to be a successful writer. His desire for literary fame is integral to his autobiographical concern with acquiring an education – through the inspiration of General Paoli – that will reconcile the dualities of his personality by unleashing his creative impulse for liberty under the necessary constraint of performing civilizing public service. Authorship would fulfill this educational ideal of balancing release and restraint, imperfection and respectability, self-absorption and the public's gratification, nature and art, and freedom and civilization:

> A man who has been able to furnish a book which has been approved by the world, has established himself as a respectable character in distant society, without any danger of having that character lessened by the observation of his weaknesses. To preserve an uniform dignity among those who see us every day, is hardly possible; and to aim at it, must put us under the fetters of perpetual restraint. The authour of an approved book may allow his natural disposition an easy play, and yet indulge the pride of superiour genius when he considers that by those who know him only as an authour, he never ceases to be respected. Such an authour when in his hours of gloom and discontent, may have the consolation to think that his writings are at that very time giving pleasure to numbers; and such an author may cherish the hope of being remembered after death, which has been a great object to the noblest minds in all ages. (pp. XX–XXI)

By 1769, in the third printing, there is a prefatory affirmation of having attained this tranquil state of literary celebrity, owing to the popularity of the travel book. His search for authorial fame in the Preface hides a deeper quest for maturation through a synthesis of liberation and civilization that coincides exactly with the underlying principle of progress in Corsica's emergence as a nation under Paoli.

No better proof of this conflation of personal and public modes of maturation exists within the travel book than in the first paragraph of the ensuing Introduction. This passage enunciates the thesis uniting every physical, historical, and personal detail reported by Boswell:

Liberty is so natural, and so dear to mankind, whether as individuals, or as members of society, that it is indispensibly necessary to our happiness. Every thing worthy ariseth from it. Liberty gives health to the mind, and enables us to enjoy the full exercise of our faculties. He who is in chains cannot move either easily or gracefully; nothing elegant or noble can be expected from those, whose spirits are subdued by tyranny, and whose powers are cramped by restraint. (p. 1)

This paean to liberty bridges private and political realms of being via a common principle of creativity that smacks more of William Blake or Sigmund Freud than of Jean-Jacques Rousseau at his most radical in *Émile*. To Boswell the "divine fire of liberty" (p. 6) is not only the end of human happiness but also its very means; it is deemed the creative force behind the progress of civilization in individuals and nations and, by extension, within himself, Corsica, and General Paoli: "Liberty is indeed the parent of felicity, of every noble virtue, and even of every art and science. Whatever vain attempts have been made to raise the generous plants under an oppressive climate, have only shewn more evidently the value of freedom" (p. 4).

Servitude implies inhuman stagnation; freedom is a civilizing vitality that Boswell, like Locke, Rousseau, and Jefferson, declared to be the ultimate sanction of good government and the rule of law forged by the social contract:

There is no doubt, but by entering into society, mankind voluntarily give up a part of their natural rights, and bind themselves to the obedience of laws, calculated for the general good. But, we must distinguish between authority, and oppression; between laws, and capricious dictates; and keeping the original intention of government ever in view, we should take care that no more restraint be laid upon natural liberty than what the necessities of society require. (p. 3)

This passage, so prophetic of the key premise of the *Declaration of Independence*, sums up the libertarian justification for Boswell's sympathetic treatment of Corsica's guerilla warfare against Genoa in the rest of the travel book. His political indoctrination of the reader continues in the Introduction with the assurance that all right-minded persons will catch the contagion of Boswell's enthusiasm for watching the birth of a noble nation weaned on freedom through Paoli:

It is therefore no wonder that the world has at all times been roused at the mention of liberty; and that we read with admiration and a virtuous enthusiasm, the gallant achievements of those who have distinguished themselves in the glorious cause; and the history of states who were animated with the principle of freedom, and made it the basis of their constitution. (pp. 4–5)

This indirect appeal for the audience's participation in Boswell's own later imaginative empathy with Paoli and his country's rebellion supposes the durability and universality of the force of liberty. The moral uniformity of human nature ensures that the "divine fire of liberty" inflaming the hearts of humankind throughout history has ignited the "advancement of civilization," whether in ancient Rome, among the Swiss and Dutch, or, most spectacularly, among the brave Corsicans, now "emancipating themselves for ever from a foreign yoke, and becoming a free and independent people" (pp. 5–7). The Introduction ends by advertising the geographical novelty of the travel book and by encouraging readers to identify emotionally with the Corsicans through Boswell the narrator, who has himself "felt as it were a communication of their spirit" (p. 9).

The first two-thirds of the work, dealing with the natural and political history of Corsica, involves impersonal and comprehensive reporting which, having been shaped by Boswell's eyewitness response to the island, remains a perfect complement to the autobiographical *Journal and Memoirs of Paoli* at the close. In accordance with the conventions of travel literature, Boswell surveys the country's geography and natural history, but then he departs from tradition, as Thoreau would do in *Walden*, in making landscape a physical symbol of a higher moral reality to be found in the people and their chieftain, Paoli: "Indeed the interiour parts of the island...have a peculiar grand appearance, and inspire one with the genius of the place; with that undaunted and inflexible spirit, which will not bow to oppression" (p. 27). The place is by nature a fertile seed-bed of liberty, an Eden of plentiful flora and fauna, and a bucolic Ithaca of primitive ruggedness and Spartan simplicity under the leadership of a modern Lycurgus. "Corsicans breathe a pure atmosphere" (p. 16), sweet rivers quench their thirst, rich iron-mines betoken their heroic character, and a wholesome wilderness – "so privileged by nature, that there is no poisonous animal in it" (p. 44) – nurtures a hardy, golden-age race of patriots aspiring to civilization through liberty. Propaganda demands the aggrandizement of the island's topography, such as its excellent harbors, to promote a diplomatic alliance that would satisfy Britain's self-interest and selfless defence of liberty simultaneously: "vessels stationed in the ports of Corsica might be formidable to France, as the western side of the island is directly opposite to the extensive coast of Provence, on which a descent might be made with cruisers in a very short time" (p. 21).

Such is the opening description of the physical environment which, implanted with the "spirit of liberty" (p. 63), engendered the rebellious political history recounted in *Chapter II. A Concise View of the REVOLUTIONS which CORSICA has undergone from the earliest times*. The meaning of Corsica's troubled past confirms the libertarian assumption of the Introduction, namely, that oppression by any invaders, be they Romans, Goths, Saracens, Franks, the Pope, or the Genoese, only activates a subject state's "right to liberty" (p. 70) by revolution. It was an assumption soon to be tested with different results by two groups of freedom-fighters, Corsicans, and American colonists, whom Boswell always applauded over Johnson's occasionally bitter opposition: "For however a people may, from indolence, from timidity, or from other motives, submit for a season to a certain degree of tyranny; if it is long continued, and pushed to an exorbitant length, nature will revolt, and the original rights of men will call for redress" (p. 72). The history of Corsica's revolutions climaxes in the person of Pasquale Paoli, whose endearing demeanor typifies his liberating and civilizing influence upon both Corsicans and Boswell: "His carriage and deportement prejudiced them in his favour, and his superiour judgment, and patriotick spirit, displayed with all the force of eloquence, charmed their understandings. All this, heightened with condescension, affability and modesty, entirely won their hearts" (p. 127). Paoli's edifying bearing was in keeping with his noble behavior in freeing his compatriots according to the "soundest principles of democratical rule" and criminal justice (p. 132) and then in cultivating their "exquisite degree of sensibility" (p. 133) to serve useful civic ends so that a love of liberty would not degenerate into chaotic rebelliousness. Boswell, who liked to think of himself as sharing the Corsican character traits of a lively sensibility and taste for freedom, came to see in Paoli's public policies against political anarchy some pertinent remedies for his personal restlessness and waywardness. The final paragraph of chapter 2 epitomizes the repeated presentation of the General as a patriarchal liberator and civilizer of Corsica:

> But Paoli improved the season of tranquillity to the best purpose, in preparing for future schemes of victory, and in giving perfection and stability to the civil constitution of his country; effectuating what ages had not been able to produce, and exhibiting an illustrious instance of what was said of Epaminondas; "Unum hominem pluris fuisse quam civitatem. That one man has been of more consequence than a whole nation." (pp. 142–3)

An Account of Corsica turns finally to the compelling topic of the inhabitants whom the natural and political history of the place had molded and whom Boswell's subsequent *Journal and Memoirs of Paoli* will document in more intimate detail. Therefore, occupying the strategic middle portion of the work between impersonal and personal reporting is his preoccupation with the people as summarized in *Chapter III. The Present State of CORSICA, with respect to Government, Religion, Arms, Commerce, Learning, the Genius and Character of its INHABITANTS*. Of chief interest is the government of a free nation, "a compleat and well ordered democracy" roughly conforming to the Rousseauistic ideal of a "progression of power flowing from the people" (p. 153) and having a legislative, executive, and judicial structure like the tripartite system of the later United States of America. The Corsican constitution suits the temperament of a citizenry whose Spartan ruggedness under the refining influence of a modern Lycurgus is offset by a humane liberty-loving sensibility ensuring the future greatness of the islanders. Rousseau praised this spirit of liberty, and an unproven Boswell played at being a radical, imagining a complete fellow-feeling with inhabitants of comparable exuberance and promise. The citizens already exhibited what Boswell was in the process of acquiring himself, specifically, a civilizing devotion to a patriarchal Paoli "ever ready to enlighten his countrymen" (pp. 149–50) and to keep their powerful sensibility under constructive control: "It is ... a species of despotism, founded, contrary to Montesquieu, on the affection of love" (p. 162).

Religion, of the tolerant kind favored by Rousseau, buttresses the islanders' constitution and displays "the same spirit of boldness and freedom, for which they are distinguished in civil affairs" (p. 164). Also bolstering a democratic government and burgeoning commerce is their strict moral code instilling temperate habits against luxury and punishing adultery with severity: "When morals are intimately connected with ideas of honour, and crimes of an alluring nature are not committed with impunity, we may expect that mankind will retain a proper awe, and be kept within the bounds of their duty" (pp. 217–18). Coming from a notorious womanizer guilty of the "licentious gallantry" criticized in the account, this sentiment might seem hypocritical or unintentionally ironic. Practice and belief did not, unfortunately, coincide for long in Boswell's personal life, although he fitfully struggled for a reconciliation of his inner contradictions under the influence of virtuous role-models. He was surely writing his description of Corsican morality in the glow of remembered examples of self-discipline in people like Paoli who offered the sexy Scot some salutary advice against immorality as part of his ethical education on the Grand Tour. In the end readers are invited to share Boswell's edifying communion with a nation dedicated to the task of liberating and civilizing itself. Whether or not his message is propaganda, the task undertaken by Corsicans had a personal as well as a political significance for an author intent on his own maturation to productive adulthood: "When we thus view the Corsicans gloriously striving for the best rights of humanity, and under the guidance of an illustrious commander and able statesman, establishing freedom, and forming a virtuous and happy nation, can we be indifferent as to their success? Can we Britons forbear to admire their bravery, and their wisdom?" (p. 225).

Boswell for one could not resist this patriotic challenge and very frankly revealed his admiration in the celebrated finale of the travel book, *The Journal of a Tour to Corsica; and Memoirs of Pascal Paoli*. After a formal and encyclopedic survey of the island, Boswell concludes with an impressionistic and unique response to the same subject matter in an autobiographical narration that continues the cohesive thematic vision of Corsican liberty so as to validate the preceding description by eyewitness testimony. The *Journal*, like the rest of the travel book, is by his own admission an artistic transformation of the experience abroad: "In writing this Journal, I shall not tire my readers, with relating the occurrences of each particular day. It will be much more agreeable to them, to have a free and continued account of what I saw or heard, most worthy of observation" (p. 276). The very first paragraph enunciates the principal autobiographical concern of the *Journal*, that of Boswell's education on an unusual Grand Tour to a place "where I should find what was to be seen no where else, a people actually fighting for liberty and forming themselves from a poor inconsiderable oppressed nation, into a flourishing and independent state" (p. 261). The spectacle of a primitive but progressive Corsica would be rich instruction for a wild tourist growing up in pursuit of his own liberty, refinement, and prosperity abroad. Rousseau the "wild philosopher" (p. 263) – a sobriquet suggestive of Boswell's later disllusionment – had himself endorsed both the political experiment in Corsica and the visit there by the author who was a like-minded "man of sensibility" (p. 320) sympathetic to democratic causes: "my enthusiasm for the brave islanders was as warm as his own" (p. 262). A considerable portion of the remainder of the *Journal* is a relatively uninhibited accounting of his cumulative enthusiasm for the country.

In keeping with current Romantic tastes in travel literature, there is an intimate, first-person unfolding of the tourist's gradual imaginative identification with the landscape, the inhabitants, and, ultimately, the leader of Corsica. The reader's sense of immediacy is enhanced by the startling naiveté of Boswell's autobiographical stock-taking of his growing oneness with the heroic nation. His continental rambles trained him to become a receptive citizen of the world, possessed with a fine freedom-loving sensibility "fully able to enter into the ideas of the brave rude men whom I found in all quarters" (p. 288). Whether rowing beside the simple peasants "which gave me great spirits" (p. 269) or eating like "one of the 'prisca gens mortalium'" (p. 286) or climbing their mountains "in great health and spirits" (p. 288), he found himself greatly attracted to the primitive way of life: "I enjoyed a sort of luxury of noble sentiment" (p. 295). Successive encounters with Corsicans stimulated increasing empathy to the point of his conceiving himself a guerilla chieftain "mounted on Paoli's own horse...to indulge a momentary pride in this parade" (p. 294) and even addressing his new countrymen on the topic of liberation and civilization at the heart of his own maturation and Corsica's independence:

> I expatiated on the bravery of the Corsicans, by which they had purchased liberty, the most valuable of all possessions, and rendered themselves glorious over all Europe. Their poverty, I told them, might be remedied by a proper cultivation of their island, and by engaging a little in commerce. But I bid them

remember, that they were much happier in their present state than in a state of
refinement and vice, and that therefore they should beware of luxury. (pp.
288–9)

The subsequent meeting with Paoli, as vividly recorded in the climactic
Memoirs of Paoli, is certainly the capstone of Boswell's emotional communion
with the Corsican cause of liberation and civilization. The eventual easing of
the General's reserve forges a friendship productive of conversations that
present Paoli as a Platonic (as well as Plutarchan) and Rousseauistic
philosopher-prince of gravity, clemency, and piety and as a paternal teacher
of liberty and civility for both Boswell and the Corsicans:

> He said his great object was to form the Corsicans in such a manner that they
> might have a firm constitution, and might be able to subsist without him. Our
> state, said he, is young, and still requires the leading strings. I am desirous that
> the Corsicans be taught to walk of themselves...We are now to our country
> like the prophet Elishah stretched over the dead child of the Shunamite, eye to
> eye, nose to nose, mouth to mouth. It begins to recover warmth, and to
> revive...The arts and sciences are like dress and ornament. You cannot
> expect them from us for some time. But come back twenty or thirty years
> hence, and we'll show you arts and sciences, and concerts and assemblies, and
> ladies, and we'll make you fall in love among us, Sir. (pp. 299–300)

Just as Paoli resurrects and refines the dormant country in freedom and
prosperity, so too he inspires and instructs an immature Boswell to entrust
his future success to the creative force of his own liberty-loving sensibility
disciplined by noble, public-spirited goals:

> "If a man would preserve the generous glow of patriotism, he must not reason
> too much...Virtuous sentiments and habits, said he, are beyond philosophical
> reasonings, which are not so strong, and continually varying"... Paoli told me
> that from his earliest years, he had in view the important station which he now
> holds; so that his sentiments must ever have been great. (pp. 326, 329)

Paoli thus becomes a moral as well as a political catalyst of maturation.
Boswell's desire in the Preface to harmonize personal freedom and public
respectability by literary fame ultimately springs from the magnanimous
role-model of Paoli, who had himself integrated passionate release and
virtuous restraint in his life:

> His notions of morality are high and refined, such as become the Father of a
> nation...He told me that his father had brought him up with great strictness,
> and that he had very seldom deviated from the paths of virtue. That this was
> not from a defect of feeling or passion, but that his mind being filled with
> important objects, his passions were employed in more noble pursuits than
> those of licentious pleasure. I saw from Paoli's example the great art of
> preserving young men of spirit from the contagion of vice, in which there is
> often a species of sentiment, ingenuity and enterprise nearly allied to virtuous
> qualities.

> Shew a young man that there is more real spirit in virtue than in vice, and
> you have a surer hold of him during his years of impetuosity and passion than
> by convincing his judgement of all the rectitude of ethics. (pp. 302–3)

This "great art" of moral synthesis is the overriding lesson that Boswell witnessed in the formation of a free Corsica and hoped to practice in his own pursuit of greatness through the art of travel literature. Ethical precepts were best learned from life, rather than from books of philosophy, and hence he went directly to Paoli, as he would seek out Samuel Johnson, for his schooling in manhood. The leader of a young nation was a suitable father-figure of heroic sensibility for a callow tourist with an undisciplined sensibility: "The contemplation of such a character really existing, was of more service to me than all I had been able to draw from books, from conversation, or from the exertions of my own mind...I saw my highest idea realized in Paoli" (p. 328). Appropriately in the *Memoirs of Paoli*, Boswell's increasing imaginative communion with the nation peaks in his parting recognition of having achieved intimate fellowship with Corsica's philosopher-prince: "I said I hoped that when he honoured me with a letter, he would write not only as a commander, but as a philosopher and a man of letters. He took me by the hand, and said, 'As a friend'" (p. 351).

An Account of Corsica is an excellent and extraordinarily unified specimen of eighteenth-century travel literature exhibiting the new Romantic turn for an exuberant imaginative empathy with foreign scenes. Its overwhelming popularity with readers of the Age of Johnson is a touchstone of its enduring literary and historical value. There is the additional interest of the book's close ties with Boswell's other major publications in his lifetime. The travelogue proved to be a successful literary experiment in Grand Touring with an admixture of autobiography, conversational immediacy, and ennobling portraiture of an edifying celebrity that paved the way for the two memorable biographies of his later years. Differences obviously exist in the three works. Following travel book conventions, *An Account of Corsica* is oriented more to geography and autobiography than to chronicling another man's life. Propagandistic aims and Rousseauistic sentiments made it less psychologically subtle and more politically radical than either of the more famous studies of Johnson touring the Hebrides or dominating the intellectual world of London.[12] Maturity, different role-models, and professional preoccupations subdued, without ever eradicating, Boswell's self-centered and sometimes superficial enthusiasm for liberty and heightened his respect for law and order so visibly symbolized by "the literary Colossus" from Lichfield at a time of disturbing, epoch-making revolutions. He had played at being a radical citizen of the world, as he would later dabble at being a Scottish advocate upholding the rules of the British establishment.

Indeed, when in 1779 his thoughts strayed again to Corsica in one of his *Hypochondriack* essays, the emphasis was now on political authority, not personal freedom: "we know that in that nation where liberty was adored, the supreme power was in fact exercised by their general; and while they threw off a foreign yoke, they submitted with willing confidence to decisive government at home."[13] Nevertheless, his two later biographies capitalized on literary techniques developed in his travelogue, that of blending art and fact to create a coherent study of a great man and patriotic father-figure who embodied and inculcated a nation's ideals for the education of the narrator and his readers:

> From having known intimately so exalted a character, my sentiments of human nature were raised, while, by a sort of contagion, I felt an honest ardour to distinguish myself, and be useful, as far as my situation and abilities would allow; and I was, for the rest of my life, set free from a slavish timidity in the presence of great men, for where shall I find a man greater than Paoli? (pp. 351–2)

There would be another, more crucial influence upon Boswell's fame and formation. That greater man was Samuel Johnson.

NOTES

1 See especially Percy G. Adams, *Travelers and Travel Liars: 1660–1800* (Berkeley: University of California Press, 1962) and *Travel Literature and the Evolution of the Novel* (Lexington, Kentucky: University Press of Kentucky, 1983) as well as Charles L. Batten, Jr., *Pleasurable Instruction: Form and Convention in Eighteenth-Century Travel Literature* (Berkeley: University of California Press, 1978).

2 The absence of any modern edition of the complete *Account of Corsica* is a glaring omission in Boswell scholarship and calls for redress, despite lukewarm and, I believe, deficient assessments of the book's worth by even eminent devotees of the author like the late Frederick A. Pottle in *Earlier Years*, p. 362. Professor William Paul McCarthy of Iowa State University kindly transmitted a contemporary poetic tribute to Boswell's fame as a tourist, entitled "Corsica. Written in the Year 1769" by Anna Letitia Barbauld, some excerpts of which appear below:

> Hail, generous Corsica! unconquered isle!
> The fort of freedom; that amidst the waves
> Stands like a rock of adamant, and dares
> The wildest fury of the beating storm...
> Such were the working thoughts which swelled the breast
> Of generous Boswell; when with nobler aim
> And views beyond the narrow beaten track
> By trivial fancy trod, he turned his course
> From polished Gallia's soft delicious vales,
> From the grey reliques of imperial Rome,

From her long galleries of laureled stone,
Her chiseled heroes and her marble gods,
Whose dumb majestic pomp yet awes the world,
To animated forms of patriot zeal;
Warm in the living majesty of virtue;
Elate with fearless spirit; firm; resolved;
By fortune nor subdued, nor awed by power.

(*The Works of Anna Letitia Barbauld*, 2 vols. [London, 1825], I, 1–2)

3 See Thomas M. Curley, *Samuel Johnson and the Age of Travel* (Athens, Georgia: University of Georgia Press, 1976), chapters 1 and 2.

4 Giuseppe Baretti, Preface to *A Journey from London to Genoa* (London, 1770).

5 Samuel Johnson, *The Letters of Samuel Johnson with Mrs. Thrale's Genuine Letters to Him*, ed. R. W. Chapman, 3 vols. (Oxford: Clarendon Press, 1952), no. 222, I, 230.

6 For the influence of Plutarch's *Parallel Lives* upon Boswell's quest for liberty, see Stanley Brodwin, "'Old Plutarch at Auchinleck': Boswell's Muse of Corsica," *Philological Quarterly*, 62 (1983), 69–93. William R. Siebenschuh affirms the unity of the travel book in *Form and Purpose in Boswell's Biographical Works* (Berkeley: University of California Press, 1972), pp. 10–30.

7 *Grand Tour I*, p. 254.

8 Pottle, *Earlier Years*, pp. 244–50.

9 *Account of Corsica*, pp. 361–2. All future references to this first edition of the work will be cited in the text.

10 Jean-Jacques Rousseau, *Le Contrat social*, I, 2 and II, 3, 7, and 10 for references to patriarchal government, Lycurgus, the legislator, and Corsica.

11 "Non enim propter gloriam, divitias aut honores pugnamus, sed propter libertatem solummodo, quam nemo bonus nisi simul cum vita amittit. Lit. Comit. et. Baron. ad Pap. A.D. 1320" ("For we fight not for glory, riches or honors, but solely for liberty, which no good man loses except with his life").

12 See, for example, Marshall Waingrow, "Boswell's Johnson," pp. 45–50, and Sir Harold Nicolson, "The Boswell Formula, 1791," pp. 74–8, in *Twentieth-Century Interpretations of Boswell's Life of Johnson* (Englewood Cliffs, New Jersey: Prentice-Hall, 1970) for Boswell's conservative view of Johnson and the connection between the travel book and the biography.

13 Essay no. 19 on Subordination in Government, *Hypochondriack*, p. 245. The conservatism in his biographical studies of Johnson, who as a Boswellian role-model differed significantly from Paoli, did not by any means erase all of Boswell's former libertarianism from these later works. For example, the famous summary "character" ending the *Life* (IV, 426) criticizes Johnson for narrowness in religion and politics: "His being impressed with the danger of extreme latitude in either, though he was of a very independent spirit, occasioned his appearing somewhat unfavourable to the prevalence of that noble freedom of sentiment which is the best possession of man."

7

BOSWELL AND SYMPATHY: THE TRIAL AND EXECUTION OF JOHN REID

Gordon Turnbull

Boswell's account in his journals and legal records of his passionate but unsuccessful defense, in Edinburgh's High Court of Justiciary in August 1774, of an accused sheep-stealer named John Reid documents the most intense of his several engagements with capitally condemned criminals. His report of the trial and its aftermath – in which Boswell worked frantically to gain Reid a reprieve and even devised a plan, perfectly serious and abandoned only at the last minute after many of the preparations had been made, to make off with Reid's body after the hanging and attempt to revive it – provides his diary with the longest, most detailed, and most self-revealing of his criminal narratives. After this defeat, though he would labor at the law for many years more, Boswell made a critical emotional swerve away from the Whig, Lowland, Presbyterian Scotland embodied most notably, in this context, by his father, Lord Auchinleck, one of the judges in the cause who sent John Reid to the scaffold: a swerve away, that is, from the ethos of the Edinburgh judicial establishment, in which language had the capacity to incarcerate and destroy, into fulfillment of his ambitions instead to be a biographer, to enter a world in which language might sustain human significance by conferring a textual immortality. Part of Boswell died with Reid: it was defeat in this cause which, in Frank Brady's words, "crystallized his distaste for the Scottish bar" and "destroyed his momentum as a lawyer."[1]

Boswell's interest in his often guilty and sometimes capitally condemned clients did much to block his prospects of a Scots judicial career, occasionally impelling him to strenuous and impolitic legal and extralegal efforts to rescue them from the punitive processes of the courts.[2] His powerful sentiments of identification, fellow-feeling, and guilty complicity with his doomed clients provide, as it were, a lived or street-level version of aspects of the theory of sympathy in Adam Smith's *Theory of Moral Sentiments* (Boswell as a student at the University of Glasgow heard Smith deliver the lectures on which the book was based, in 1759–60). Boswell's journal, a protracted attempt to fix or "know" himself in written form, is

aligned with the Scottish Enlightenment's great historiographical endeavor
to reinscribe the British identity from the perspective of the post-Union
Scot, and his lifelong experimentations with the theatrical qualities of
character parallel Enlightenment interrogations of the structure and
continuity of identity.[3] But Boswell's relation to Smith's theory, which
reinscribes in a theater/spectator paradigm Humean arguments about the
instability of the ordinary boundaries of human identity, exposes complexities in his response that signal some of the impulses behind what can be
seen as a later realignment of Boswell's sense of sympathy away from
Smith's "theatrical" theory towards Burke's account of tragic spectatorship
in his "Essay on the Sublime and Beautiful." In this change of affinity we
find more subtly nuanced intellectual and emotional depths in Boswell's
rejection of Edinburgh (for which, as his native city, he would retain
nonetheless a nostalgic fondness) for London. When studied in the context
of some of Boswell's most considered opinions on death and executions,
stated mainly in his essays for the *London Magazine* as The Hypochondriack,
the Reid trial discloses much about the less frequently examined roots of his
decision against a career as a practicing Scots lawyer, in favor of the liberal
and liberating discourse of biography, and about his deeper beliefs in
biography's central assignment – the recuperation of character in discourse.
But to arrive at conclusions like these means taking on the undeservedly
neglected task of treating Boswell's legal career seriously, and exploring one
of the most notorious and least palatable features of his life – a compulsive
excited attendance at scenes of execution.

Reid's trial came in the summer immediately following the tour to the
Hebrides in 1773 with Samuel Johnson, during which Boswell kept the
journal record that would later form the basis of the first stage of his
Johnsonian biographical endeavor. Boswell's capacity for entering imaginatively into, or adopting the characterological style of, his high-life
biographical subjects like Paoli and Johnson – in his famous remark in the
Life of Johnson, his mind in time became "strongly impregnated with the
Johnsonian aether" (July 1, 1763) – shows up too, in a different register, in
the criminal lives of the remarkable biographical underworld of the private
journals. Here is found a biographical narrator, less convinced of the
monumental stability of character he would in the *Life* ascribe to Johnson,
driven by guilty identification and complicit fellow-feeling with malefactors
who, resembling himself, failed as rebels against Scots religio-legist
authority. Throughout most of his adult life, Boswell attended executions
regularly. He closely questioned prisoners on their way to death, and stood
as near as he could to the fatal trees of Edinburgh's Grassmarket and
London's Tyburn and Newgate, studying conduct and deportment, catching
and sometimes publishing last words, as the objects of legal vengeance
stepped into eternity, and always wondering how he himself would have

behaved in the same predicament. Until his later years, when frequent attendance had steeled him, he suffered afterwards, as he did after the execution of the Macheath-like Paul Lewis who figures notably in the *London Journal 1762–63*, from "gloomy terrors."[4] The word terror is recurrent in his writing, and important: the second stage of the Aristotelian catharsis in tragic spectatorship, it will reappear in this account. The execution in April 1779 of the Rev. James Hackman (who in a fit of amatory jealousy shot Martha Ray, mistress of the Earl of Sandwich) led Boswell to some self-revealingly apprehensive and monitory newspaper meditations on the murderous nature of masculine erotic passion.[5] He resolved to attend no more executions after Hackman's (he relapsed in June 1784) but mere thoughts of them obsessed him and he suffered through them imaginatively: "I shunned the execution of Daniel Mackay for stealing from the post-house, though I felt an inclination to see it...I was dreary at night, thinking of the execution" (*Laird*, p. 391).

In three essays for the *London Magazine* in 1770, "On the Profession of a Player," Boswell puzzles over the theatrical quality of the barrister's adoption of his client's part in court. He ponders the "mysterious power" by which a player "really is the character which he represents," and explains it by "a kind of double feeling," through which "the feelings and passions of the character which he represents must take full possession as it were of the antechamber of his mind, while his own character remains in the innermost recess." This double feeling "is experienced in some measure" also "by the barrister who enters warmly into the cause of his client, while at the same time, when he examines himself coolly, he knows that he is much in the wrong, and does not even wish to prevail."[6] In Smith's *Theory of Moral Sentiments*, the court-room appears as a metaphoric site of moral spectatorship of the self, and the criminal trial a figurative *locus* of ethical self-appraisal:

> When I endeavour to examine my own conduct, when I endeavour to pass sentence upon it, and either to approve or condemn it, it is evident that, in all such cases, I divide myself, as it were, into two persons; and that I, the examiner and judge, represent a different character from that other I, the person whose character is examined into and judged of.[7]

There are traces here of a secular Calvinism that marks much earlier and later Scots writing, of a good self and an evil self, Hogg's good brother and evil brother, Stevenson's Jekyll and Hyde, and anticipations of the divided self of a much later Scots cultural theorist, R. D. Laing. In Smith's theory, as David Marshall has put it in his discussion of the *Theory of Moral Sentiments*, moral philosophy "entered the theater," with an acount of sympathy turning on a complex set of theatrical identifications and substitutions between observer and sufferer.[8] But for Edmund Burke, fictional spectacle proves inadequate in an age whose punitive and judicial practices provided public spectacles of actual pain and death:

> Chuse a day on which to represent the most sublime and affecting tragedy we have; appoint the most favourite actors; spare no cost upon the scenes and decorations; unite the greatest efforts of poetry, painting and music; and when you have collected your audience, just at the moment when their minds are erect with expectation, let it be reported that a state criminal of high rank is on the point of being executed in the adjoining square; in a moment the emptiness of the theatre would demonstrate the comparative weakness of the imitative arts, and proclaim the triumph of the real sympathy.[9]

Much in this famous and resonant passage deserves commentary – the class or "rank" interest, the air of quasi-sexual arousal in the scene of death, and not least Burke's disturbingly interesting implication that tragic fiction itself has had a real role in sharpening the appetites of the theater-going public for the enjoyment of the spectacle of death. Boswell, an avid and responsive theater-goer all his life, is nonetheless compelled like Burke's hypothetical spectator, by temperament as well as by profession, to the real-life drama of the capitally condemned. In his legal reports, court-room and theater are conflated, and Boswell notably occupies Smith's metaphoric site literally.

In his criminal clients, failed rebels against religious and legal authority, Boswell saw aspects of himself, "that other I," paying, as Patricia Spacks puts it, "the high penalties of social deviation."[10] His fascinated sympathy for clients like Hay, Raybould, and Reid goes far beyond even the imagined identifications with the other wretches at whose executions he was merely a spectator. "I had," as he puts it at the height of his exertions in the Reid cause, "*by sympathy* [emphasis added] sucked the dismal ideas of John Reid's situation, and as spirits or strong substance of any kind, when transferred to another body of a more delicate nature, will have much more influence than on the body from which it is transferred, so I suffered much more than John did" (*Defence*, p. 288). The night before Reid's hanging, Boswell reports himself "so affrighted that I started every now and then and durst hardly rise from my chair at the fireside" (September 21, 1774, *Defence*, p. 336). At first, Boswell thought of Reid that he "need not insert any account of him in my journal" (July 30, 1774, *Defence*, p. 236), intending to preserve a distinction between personal life and professional career and restrict Reid to his Register of Criminal Trials. But Reid invaded Boswell's life despite his firm intentions. By the time he came to write a petition to the King for clemency, he "could think of nothing else" (August 20, 1774, *Defence*, p. 275). Near the end, Reid thanks Boswell for his strenuous legal and extralegal efforts, and says that "few would have done so much for a brother, though a twin" (September 14, 1774, *Defence*, p. 317). Resuming his journal after an eleven-day lapse (September 25, 1774 written October 6, *Ominous Years*, p. 6),

Boswell is moved to notice how Reid "required so much writing in it."
Boswell's persistent interrogations of Reid about the alleged sheep-stealing
yield only shifting and equivocal versions of the truth, and while Boswell
remains adamant that the evidence presented in court was insufficient to
convict his client, he is in agony that he cannot actually *know* whether Reid's
denials are the truth: the struggle to know Reid is assimilated to Boswell's
overriding journalistic struggle, announced at the head of his *London Journal*,
to obey the ancient philosopher's wise counsel to know himself.

Reid has special claims on Boswell not just because they shared a common
imprisonment by Scots judicial institutions, with Boswell standing in the
court-room, almost as reluctantly as Reid, in obedience to Lord Auchinleck's wishes. Reid's predicament touches the deepest impulses in Boswell's
aspirations to biography. What Boswell dreaded most in Edinburgh was of
course social insignificance, and what he found most distressing about the
conduct of legal life there was its refusal to concede significance to individual
human identity:

> Death makes as little impression upon the minds of those who are occupied in
> the profession of the law as it does in an army. The survivors are busy, and
> share in the employment of the deceased. Archibald McHarg, writer, died this
> session, and though he had a great deal of business, he was never missed. His
> death was only occasionally mentioned as an apology for delay in giving a
> paper. The succession in business is so quick that there is not time to perceive
> a blank. (*Defence*, p. 266)

What distresses him is the absence from the impersonal processes of
institutional justice of Boswellian sympathy.

Moreover, Reid in Boswell's estimation was the victim of the capacity of
the authoritative social uses of language to construct character, not to
immortalize but to imprison and destroy. In a court-room, character is
turned into discourse for the purpose of knowing and morally appraising it,
and trial becomes the institutionalized contestation of rival versions in words
of the same character. Much of Boswell's court-room defense of Reid
turned on the issue of *official* constructions of character. Character is, of
course, etymologically, an inscribed or written thing. Reid had been
Boswell's first criminal client – a matter of great importance to Boswell, who
was much given to the ceremonial marking of firsts in his life. In an earlier
trial for sheep-stealing some eight years before, Boswell had, despite strong
prosecution evidence, won a verdict of "not proven" for Reid.[11] Boswell now
argued in 1774 that the court was prejudiced against Reid because of the
earlier trial, in which Boswell's ingenious defense strategies had won the
improbable verdict of "not proven" – a verdict which the judges at the trial
had denounced as preposterous and against the evidence. Now, Reid was
charged with theft, reset of theft (receiving sheep knowing them to be

stolen), and with being in "habit and repute" a thief. A succession of
prosecution witnesses produced little other than circumstantial evidence of
Reid's part in the theft, but had much to say on the subject of Reid's
character and reputation. (This would prove in the end decisive; as Boswell's
colleague Michael Nasmith put it afterwards, "habit and repute bore all
before it.") That community sentiment, Boswell argued, had been created by
the judges themselves, who in the 1766 trial had conveyed "to the minds of a
numerous audience that notwithstanding [the] verdict [Reid] was still a guilty
man" (*Defence*, p. 250). It is "well known that when a man has had the
misfortune to be tried for any crime, a prejudice is thereby created against
his character which is seldom entirely removed from vulgar minds" (*Defence*,
p. 241).[12] The official legal text which inscribes Reid's character is, in
Boswell's estimation, lethally wrong. The very Scots law terms themselves,
we might note, imply the role of textuality in criminal legal process: the
charge is contained in an "indictment"; the part of the indictment stating the
grounds of the charge is the "libel" (from the Latin word for book); Reid is
charged with being a "guilty actor" in theft and reset of theft; "panel"
(defendant) derives analogously from the original slip or parchment on which
was written the indictment or names of the indicted; and Reid is sent to
death, of course, by a "sentence" (from the Latin for opinion or maxim). In
his journal, the quarrying-ground for his later biographies, Boswell inscribes
a rival version of Reid, an innocent or at least not demonstrably guilty man,
doomed by a false construction of character, and constructs him in a
discourse – Boswellian biography – opposed to the punitive and destroying
discourses of the law, religion, and conservative, malevolent, or scapegoat-
seeking community sentiment. Just as Boswell's journal notices and remarks
on the unremarked death of Archibald McHarg, writer, who had left a
"blank" not even noticed amid the flurries of paper in the Court of Session,
and gives McHarg a kind of permanence, Boswell's narrative strives to keep
life in Reid even when his schemes for resurrection of Reid's body falter.

Crucially, Boswell's desire to believe in Reid's innocence deepens quite
precisely when Reid's story becomes his own in the telling of it, when, as it
were strongly impregnated with his client's aether, he has internalized his
specular other; or, to use his own striking figure for internalization quoted
above, "sucked" the dismal ideas of Reid's situation. He interrogates Reid in
prison, and does not believe the protestations of innocence until he finds
himself reporting the scene to Michael Nasmith: "In telling him John's
explanation of his behaviour when taken up, I became impressed that it
might be true, and enlarged on the uncertainty of circumstantial evidence"
(September 7, 1774, *Defence*, p. 306). Next, Boswell simply appropriates
Reid's identity, and decides to produce a broadside in his name: "a curious
thought struck me that I would write the case of John Reid as if dictated by
himself on this the day fixed for his execution. I accordingly did it, and hit off

very well the thoughts and style of what such a case would have been." (The printer adds "taken from his own mouth" to this "case," and Reid himself is angry about the fraud.) And Boswell turns Reid, like himself, into a confessional autobiographer: "I desired John to write his life very fully, which he promised to do" (August 10, 1774, *Defence*, p. 264). Boswell remains Reid's voice in the community after his execution, providing accounts of it, that day, for the Edinburgh newspapers, and forever, in his journal.

The pattern of Boswell's own behavior after the trial follows closely the rhythms of Reid's fortunes. Wisely, Boswell had resolved on sobriety, declaring that he would "taste no wine till the trial was over" (July 30, 1774, *Defence*, p. 236). When word leaks out that the jury has settled on a guilty verdict, Boswell drinks freely in Walker's Tavern and reverts to his own guilty habit and repute. "I was much in liquor, and strolled in the streets a good while – a very bad habit which I have when intoxicated" (August 1, 1774, *Defence*, p. 253). (At many moments recorded in his journals, Boswell's bouts of drunkenness and strolling around after whores accompany fits of gloom, guilt, depression, and worries about death.) Three weeks later he marks a period of intoxication as a period of oblivion, a blank in his pages like the blank left by death: "*Perdidi diem*" [I have lost a day] (August 23, 1774, *Defence*, p. 279). When the letter finally arrives (September 17, 1774) confirming that there would be no reprieve for Reid, Boswell and his associates Nasmith and Charles Hay feel impelled to match Reid's now certain death with a deeply drunken oblivion:

> We were fain to fly to wine to get rid of the uneasiness which we felt that, after all that had been done, poor John Reid should fall a victim...We drank two bottles of port each. I was not satisfied with this, but stopped at a shop in Leith and insisted that we should drink some gin...I grew monstrously drunk, and was in a state of mingled frenzy and stupefaction. I do not recollect what passed. (*Defence*, pp. 319–20)

What passed emerges the next day, when biographical narrative fills in the blank:

> It gave me much concern to be informed by my dear wife that I had been quite outrageous in my drunkenness the night before; that I had cursed her in a shocking manner and even thrown a candlestick with a lighted candle at her. It made me shudder to hear such an account of my behaviour to one whom I have so much reason to love and regard; and I considered that, since drinking has so violent an effect on me, there is no knowing what dreadful crime I may commit. (*Defence*, p. 321)

Reid, too, in his "Last Speech," blames his descent into crime on drunkenness: "And one evening in coming from the town of Linlithgow, along with a comrade, being pretty drunk, we went into a fold belonging to

John Bell and turned out his whole flock of sheep, of which flock I carried off four..." (*Defence*, p. 343). Boswell, in mingled frenzy and stupefaction, lashes out at his wife, who has been aligned all along with the official and community sentiment ranged against Reid. (After the execution, when "gloom" came upon Boswell, he went home but found his wife "no comforter, as she thought I had carried my zeal for John too far, might hurt my own interest and character by it, and as she thought him guilty" – September 21, 1774, *Defence*, p. 336). He knows not what "dreadful crime" he may commit; liquor, imbibed in a rush of sympathy for the doomed Reid, releases the violently criminal in himself. When Margaret Boswell is obliged to perform the office of Boswell's biographer, speak for him (as Boswell does for Reid) and fill in the blank left by his oblivion, she too is obliged to provide a criminal narrative.

In his youthful London journals, Boswell sought to deflect guilt and terror by modelling himself on Mr. Spectator. As Steele wrote in no. 266, "I am wholly unconcerned in any Scene I am in, but merely as a Spectator" (January 4, 1712). For the younger Boswell, watching himself play Macheath turns transgression into comic theater, but the execution of Paul Lewis destroyed the fiction of spectatorial distance and detachment and shocked him out of conscious literary self-construction. He freely confesses to his reader, John Johnston of Grange, his nights full of "gloomy terrors." Boswell in 1774 does indeed attempt to deflect John Reid's situation into artistic spectacle: he is struck at one point with the "curious thought" of turning Reid's story into a didactic Hogarthian visual narrative, "the Sheep-stealer's Progress in the manner of Hogarth's historical prints" (August 27, 1774, *Defence*, p. 283). But nothing comes of this idea: it is the didactic function of Reid's punishment that the judicial spectacle of execution supports, and which Boswell's secret biographical account of him seeks to subvert.

Conscious artistic construction of Reid founders also on Boswell's gloomy terror that he and Reid have both been doomed by a more potent mode of characterological inscription. The origins of the journal form, Ian Watt and others point out, were in Calvinist self-scrutiny. The journal is a record of guilt, a colloquy between self and Creator of that self, the Supreme Author, and brought into existence by sin: the Fall was a fall into self-record. Boswell, recording his own transgressions in his candid diary, "indicts" himself in his own "libel" (etymologically, a "little book"). Not surprisingly, Reid's plight releases Boswell's own seldom quiet Calvinist anxieties about fore-ordination, with the court's judgements standing as the secular analogue to the Supreme Being's irrevocable dispensations of election and damnation. The Divine Word, as much as the Sentence of the Law, and the self-indictments in Boswell's own candid record of sin, enact the metaphysical drama of the creating and destroying power of the word. Is Reid merely a "guilty actor" in a divine script, or a script written for him by the judicial institution bent on vengeance for the original sin, the first Reid trial in which Boswell aspired to be as judges and got Reid off in the teeth of judicial opinion, leaving the judges angry and bent on punitive retribution? Moreover, does Boswell inscribe himself and Reid into immortality in the journal – but to an immortality only of guilt? And if so, is this because Boswell has already been written into existence as a guilty man? Boswell seeks to resist belief in a predestinarian deity, or that he himself is a "mere machine" or a "reprobate from all eternity"; but there is not, Boswell remarks, "absolute demonstration to the contrary" (August 23, 1782, *Laird*, p. 474).

Boswell's escape from a legal career in Presbyterian Edinburgh into a biographical career in Episcopal London issues, then, from profounder desires for escape from confinement, and is, as the Reid trial discloses, an escape from a language that fixes character and destroys it into a language that resurrects character and immortalizes it. In the *Life of Johnson*, Boswell constructs a monumentally heroic Johnson, setting up a rival version of the text produced, as he words it, by the "dark uncharitable cast" of Sir John Hawkins and the "slighter aspersions" of Hester (Thrale) Piozzi. The biographer naturally shares some of the hero's moral space, and allows him scope outside social or metaphysical determinisms for the construction of character as a matter of the conscious moral will. Between biographer and subject there can be what Boswell calls in the *Tour to the Hebrides* a "generous attachment" – the cooperative interchange of identity that underpins, in a way that the barrister–client relationship more upsettingly replicates, Boswellian "sympathy."

Of all the capital convicts Boswell saw hanged, none impressed him more than James Gibson, an attorney executed for forgery in March 1768. Boswell wrote in his journal: "I always use to compare the conduct of malefactors with what I suppose my conduct might be. I never saw a man hanged but I thought I could behave better than he did, except Mr. Gibson, who, I confess, exceeded all that I could ever hope to show of easy and steady resolution" (March 23, 1768, *In Search of a Wife*, p. 141). The young Boswell, characteristically, transposes himself to the scaffold, and is concerned with himself as theater – with what he might hope to "show." Adam Smith thought the man on the scaffold suffered less than the man in the pillory, because the former is supported by spectator sympathy, but the latter is not; Smith himself would sympathize with the pilloried man because he suffers, as David Marshall puts it, "the worst of all miseries, theatrical exposure."[13] So impressive was James Gibson – that Other James on the scaffold – that Boswell wrote not only a careful journal account of his deportment and death, but worked it up into a letter to the *Public Advertiser* which he then reproduced fifteen years later, with revealing additions, as his *Hypochondriack* essay on executions.

Those additions in 1783 contain a most startling recommendation for punitive reform – shocking even allowing for the gloomy and melancholic persona of the *Hypochondriack*. The *Hypochondriack* essayist thinks that "the punishment of throwing criminals from the Tarpeian rock in ancient Rome was a very judicious one"; but the "best" mode of execution he has ever discovered

> is one practised in Modern Rome, which is called "*Macellare – to butcher.*" The criminal is placed upon a scaffold, and the executioner knocks him on the head with a great iron hammer, then cuts his throat with a large knife, and lastly, hews him in pieces with an ax; in short, treats him exactly like an ox in the shambles. The spectators are struck with prodigious terrour; yet the poor wretch who is stunned into insensibility by the blow, does not actually suffer much. (*Hypochondriack*, II, 284)

The opening part of Boswell's 1768 letter is an anxious meditation on cruelty, of which he deeply disapproves, and an attempt, with references to Burke, Lucretius, and the Abbé du Bos, to account for the "irresistible impulse" he nonetheless feels to be present at executions. He insists with Justinian, in his 1783 additions, that "as *mild punishments* as are consistent with terrour" should be inflicted on malefactors, and he declines even to discuss with his readers the various horrible sentences and tortures that criminals have suffered. What seems to Boswell "most eligible" is "a mode of death which strikes terrour into the spectators, without excruciating the unfortunate objects of legal vengeance." When he first attended executions, he says, he was "convulsed with pity and terror." What, plainly, he longs to eliminate with his ancient and modern Roman methods of execution concerns the first half of Aristotelian tragic catharsis – "pity," that is to say, the compassion, fellow-feeling, guilty identification, or, in a word, sympathy, of which Boswell in his relations with the condemned can never be free. If the guilty wretch is not actually suffering much, suffering has been transposed from the scaffold to the spectator, in whom the guilt is expiated by terror.

Boswell seeks in his "best" mode of public death fully to deflect the actual pain of fellow-feeling back where his own drift in affinities from Smith to Burke, from Edinburgh to London, from complicity in legal vengeance to biographical immortalizer, has shown it cannot be – in mere spectacle or ritual, an ancient classical ceremony, a public *disjecta membra*. John Reid, sent into the world perhaps to suffer for sinners like Boswell, would be a *pharmakos*, thrown out of sight from the Tarpeian rock, back into *mere* text – ancient writing, legend, history – and out of sensibility, the reverse, we might say, of the fate of Lewis's Monk, thrown down at the end of his story upon rocks to suffer, in a seven-day anti-creation, the worst tortures sensibility could know. In an impossible straining after a radical obliteration (in its root sense of eliminating the written letter), Boswell would have the wretch torn up – like the pages of a journal, his own self-indictment. The grim ceremony he advocates here, like the Reid trial, exposes the profoundest anxieties of Boswell the criminal advocate and Boswell the biographer. In the last and most disastrous of the quasi-filial associations of his life, Boswell attached himself to James Lowther, Lord Lonsdale. Boswell's familiar response was to write Lonsdale into his journal. "All [his] traits I mark as *disjecta membra* out of which I may afterwards complete the *real* character of one whom I *imagined* so highly" (December 10, 1786, *English Experiment*, p. 116). In law, the living body is torn up; in biography, character, the construction of identity in and by discourse, is recuperated in the verbal piecing together of the scattered limbs. Boswell's biographies of Paoli and Johnson confer immortality. But the healing, creating, or resurrecting power of the word – properties typical of the genre of comedy – vanish in the secret criminal histories of the journal. The criminal biographer is sent instead to a tragic spectacle, impelled there, if it is in some sense Boswell's guilt for which Reid must die, by a profound sympathy that is not separable from a prodigious terror.

NOTES

1 *Later Years*, p. 105. For Brady's discussion of the Reid trial, see pp. 96–104. I draw chiefly on Boswell's journal record of the trial and subsequent events, and various documents he preserved, as published in *Defence*.
2 See Pottle, *Earlier Years*, pp. 309, 355.
3 For Boswell's relationship to post-Union Scottish culture, see Gordon Turnbull, "James Boswell: Biography and the Union," in *The History of Scottish Literature, 1660–1800*, ed. Andrew Hook (Aberdeen: Aberdeen University Press, 1987), pp. 157–73. See also Kenneth Simpson, *The Protean Scot: The Crisis of Identity in Eighteenth-Century Scottish Culture* (Aberdeen: Aberdeen University Press, 1988), esp. chapter 5, "The Chameleon Scot: James Boswell," pp. 117–43, and Andrew Noble, "James Boswell: Scotland's Prodigal Son," in *Improvement and Enlightenment: Proceedings of the Scottish Historical Studies Seminar, University of Strathclyde 1987–88*, ed. T. M. Devine (Edinburgh: John Donald, 1989), pp. 22–42.
4 See *London Journal*, pp. 250ff.
5 See *Laird*, pp. 86–9.
6 *On the Profession of a Player, Three Essays by James Boswell, Reprinted from "The London Magazine" for August, September, October, 1770* (London: Elkin Mathews and Marrot, 1929), p. 18.
7 Adam Smith, *Theory of Moral Sentiments*, ed. D. D. Raphael and A. L. Macfie (Oxford: Clarendon Press, 1976), p. 113.
8 David Marshall, *The Figure of Theater: Shaftesbury, Defoe, Adam Smith, and George Eliot* (New York: Columbia University Press, 1986), p. 169. Colby H. Kullman has also discussed the "dramatic" quality of Boswell's handling of the Reid episode, in "Boswell's Account of the 'Flesher of Hillend': A Total Plan for a Criminal Drama," *Ball State University Forum*, 23 (1982), 25–34.

9 Edmund Burke, *A Philosophical Enquiry into the Origins of our Ideas of the Sublime and Beautiful*, ed. T. J. Boulton (Notre Dame and London: University of Notre Dame Press, 1958; 1968), pt. I, sect. xv, p. 47.

10 *Imagining a Self: Autobiography and Novel in Eighteenth-Century England* (Cambridge, Mass.: Harvard University Press, 1976), p. 295.

11 For summaries of the first Reid trial see *In Search of a Wife*, pp. 11–12, and *Earlier Years*, pp. 308–10.

12 Some years later in England, attending the Carlisle Assizes, Boswell sees a defendant named John Forrest tried for sheep-stealing, and summarizes the trial in his journal as an idealized version of the Reid cause. "I was much afraid for *Jack*," Boswell remarks, because his character was "notoriously bad," and "there was only such *suspicion* against my client *John Reid*" (*Laird*, p. 8; for the whole episode see pp. 8–10).

13 *The Figure of Theater*, p. 192.

8

BOSWELL AND HUME: THE DEATHBED
INTERVIEW

Richard B. Schwartz

He is "the greatest Writer in Britain," Boswell wrote in 1762. Years later he said, "I had really a good chat with him this afternoon. I thought also of writing his life." Samuel Johnson? No, Boswell is speaking of David Hume, a man with whose life his own was intertwined for many years. We know, for example, that early in his career Boswell tricked Hume into engaging in a correspondence with him; later he mimicked Hume's manner before friends, designed a mischievous print representing Hume and Rousseau, leased Hume's James's Court property for four years, and interviewed him while he lay on his deathbed.

Mossner considered it fortunate that Boswell did not write Hume's life, for, in his judgement and that of many others, Johnson is now less respected as a thinker because of Boswell's efforts. Had Boswell turned his full attention to Hume, we might now be spending our time reconstructing Hume's position as a philosopher rather than Johnson's as a professional writer, a point to which Donald Greene has added his agreement.[1]

One of the criticisms lodged against Boswell as a biographer of Johnson has been the disparity between their experience (in heritage, background, country, religion), a disparity narrowed with Boswell and Hume, who were not only fellow Scotsmen but neighbors. While some still think of Boswell and Johnson as Siamese twins connected at the head and heart,[2] few think of Boswell's linkages with Hume, despite the fact that, to Boswell at least, they were very important.

The point of contact between Boswell and Hume with which I will be principally concerned is Boswell's deathbed interview with Hume on July 7, 1776, Hume's death coming a few weeks later on August 25. Mossner calls it "an exceptionally brilliant piece of reporting"; "as journalism," he argues, "it is the most sensational 'scoop' of the eighteenth century," words often quoted with pleasure by Boswell's admirers.[3] But Mossner says more. He writes that the deathbed interview "is more than the graphic record of the dying thoughts of a great philosopher. It is also the graphic record of a moral crisis in the mind of a most unphilosophical reporter. The interview belongs, therefore, to the autobiography of James Boswell as well as to the biography of David Hume."[4]

This is the point which I would like to pursue. The thrust of my argument may be stated simply: if the deathbed interview is any indication of the sort of biography we might have expected from Boswell, we are fortunate indeed that he did not pursue the project further, for there is every indication that Boswell was not only not equal to the task of writing Hume's life, but, as in much of his biography of Johnson, unable to see past his own concerns and his own unique perspective. Troubled by Hume's remarks on identity, Boswell struggles constantly to retain a sense of the self, even if that requires him to reduce the experience of others to transmuted episodes in his own autobiography.

With regard to Boswell's qualifications for writing Hume's life, several years after Hume's death Boswell records a striking entry in his journal: "I borrowed today out of the Advocates' Library, David Hume's *Treatise of Human Nature*, but found it so abstruse, so contrary to sound sense and reason, and so dreary in its effects on the mind, if it had any, that I resolved to return it without reading it."[5] This, to say the least, is inauspicious. Even the stoutest defender of Boswell must consider it a reasonable expectation that a man who would write the life of a philosopher should at least be expected to read that philosopher's major philosophic statement with attention.

This is not to say that Boswell was ignorant of Hume's works, for he clearly read some of them and one cannot view Boswell as a philistine or fool. David Tarbet, for example, has often pointed out Boswell's learning, particularly his reading in the classics. In Boswell's case, however, one must always ask whether he is reading with the intention of seeking understanding or of seeking confirmation of his own beliefs. One is continually struck by the extent to which Boswell seeks confirmation and reassurance – in his reading, in his correspondence and conversation, and even in the odd personal behavior recounted in his *London Journal* where he runs about the city in disguise, heartened whenever that disguise is penetrated. On some occasions Boswell appears to be the pure Bloomian reader; there are no texts, only the self.[6]

This man who would write the lives of others has a great deal of difficulty seeing beyond his own experience and he is nearly always tempted to relate the concerns of others to his personal concerns, even if they are altered or diminished in the process. The extent of his self-absorption is not difficult to demonstrate. After seeing Hume in his final weeks and hearing him on the subject of death, religion, and immortality, Boswell is so personally shaken that he plunges into excess and indulgence.[7]

His editors (who are, of course, sympathetic to him) refer to his mental state at the time as one of neurosis (p. xix). This is interesting, for Hume once described Boswell as "very good-humoured, very agreeable, and very mad." It is the latter quality or condition which is most apparent in his behavior after Hume's death. For example, Boswell's editors note twenty-six instances of drunkenness on Boswell's part in the eight-month period between July 27, 1776 and March 25, 1777. In early October a tipsy Boswell attempts to demonstrate that he is still sober by walking across a rail-less bridge over the water of Doon. He survives but he has risked his life and the ruin of his family in what he himself describes as a "drunken delirium" (p. 39). On March 19 he is so drunk that, riding between Newmilns and Milrigs, he falls off his horse (p. 96).

The manner in which he handles his personal affairs is appalling. A month after his interview with Hume (p. 21) Boswell loses at brag and whist, at one point dropping six guineas at a single stroke. To put things in perspective, Boswell made 100 guineas that summer, losing 6 percent of it – perhaps $400 today – in an instant. Looking over his accounts for the past year the following January, he notes that in that twelve-month period he had an income of £600 (£300 from his father, £300 from fees) and expenses of £740. Yet, he writes, he "could not trace any great article of extravagance" (p. 72). He notes, however, the loss of 30 guineas on a single bet with Captain William Maxwell, perhaps $2,000 in modern currency. One must wonder what Boswell means by the word *extravagance*.

There are other curiosities, of course. On the day of Hume's burial, for example, Boswell goes with Grange to the grave site. Prior to the arrival of the mourners he looks into Hume's as yet unfilled grave. Then he hides behind a wall and watches the procession of carriages and the procession of the corpse. His journal entry for the next day begins with the statement (p. 27) "My mind was not right."

Lustig and Pottle have noted that Boswell faces death and mortality by, in their words, asserting "his animal vitality."[8] Years before, for example, his response to the news of his mother's death was a trip to a Parisian brothel. Once after seeing ten convicts hanged at Newgate he hurried to a prostitute named Betsy Smith, directing her to remove the "shocking sight" from his mind. This same pattern is repeated after his interview with Hume. Prior to Hume's death, for example, when Boswell is unable to get in to see him, he looks about for prostitutes in the old town of Edinburgh and confesses shock at the consciousness of his own situation. On December 1st, a few months after Hume's death, Boswell brings a prostitute named Peggy Grant to St. Andrew Square, the site of Hume's house, and has intercourse with her twice in a mason's shed (p. 63). By mid-February he is anxious to see Peggie Dundas, a woman he has twice enjoyed on the Castle Hill, though he was unable to see her face distinctly (p. 87), and eleven days later (p. 89) he picks up, in his words, "a big fat whore" and has intercourse with her upon a stone hewing in a mason's shed by David Hume's house, perhaps the same shed to which he had taken Peggy Grant on December 1st. At this time his "dear wife" is walking about on Castle Hill looking for him. The "vitality" of his sexuality has two sides. He is alive, expressing his physical presence and potency (when he has it); on the other hand he uses the little deaths simply to block out his consciousness of the larger ones.

When he is not drinking, gambling, or whoring he is buttonholing his friends, eliciting their opinions on questions of death and immortality. From the frequency with which the subject recurs it seems clear that Boswell is initiating the discussion. Among those he engages are: Johnson (pp. 154–5), Forbes (p. 206), Monboddo (p. 210), Kames (p. 213), Forbes again (p. 215), Crosbie (p. 219), Burke (p. 270), Johnson again (p. 285), and Dr. John Muir (p. 317). He is also, of course, writing *Hypochondriack* essays on these subjects.

In some cases the discussions border on the obsessive, as for example when Crosbie recounts his own efforts to conquer fear by forcing himself to be alone in dark rooms or lying at night upon a tombstone in a churchyard in an effort to conquer his fear of death, bizarre actions recalling for modern readers the activities of a G. Gordon Liddy. Boswell's search for consolation, confirmation, and counsel is, at the least, extreme.

That he should be deeply moved by Hume's death and by his deathbed interview with him should not occasion surprise; what is striking is the enormity of Boswell's behavior and the extent to which he loses that small degree of control over himself which he is sometimes able to sustain. One cannot help but seriously question his ability to look at the thoughts and circumstances surrounding Hume's death with that detachment, balance, and good judgement which one expects in a biographer.

What is it, after all, that has so troubled him? The actual account of the interview is brief, fives pages or so, and it is partly built upon his journal, partly augmented from memory. Hume's physical appearance strikes Boswell; he is "lean, ghastly, and quite of an earthy appearance" (p. 11); yet he seems placid and even cheerful, despite the fact that he is wasting away and knows that there will be no escape from his condition.

Boswell, characteristically, introduces the most sensitive and painful topic: mortality/immortality. (It is really appropriate to think of this interchange as an *interview*, for Boswell so often functions as a reporter rather than as a friend.) Hume tells him that he has entertained no belief in religion since he began to read Locke and Clarke. He says flatly that the morality of every religion is bad and that when he hears that a man is religious he concludes that he is a rascal.

Boswell presses him on the question of a future state; Hume holds his ground, saying "that it was a most unreasonable fancy that we should exist for ever" (p. 11). The thought of annihilation gives him no uneasiness (the most sensitive area of all for Boswell) and he confesses to finding no pleasure in the notion of a future state, for it is always connected in some way with hellfire and torment.

The reasons for Boswell's profound disturbance are twofold. He has great difficulty perceiving the fact that one may lack faith and yet be good. Thus, rather than attempting to appreciate all of the subtleties of Hume's position and his feelings, Boswell tends to stereotype him as an instance of that rare individual, the virtuous atheist, a type in whom Boswell finds it very difficult to believe.

The personal postures of the two are interesting, for it certainly seems that Hume is teasing Boswell, shocking the "pious" with overstatement. He knows that Boswell is bright, but he also knows that he lacks depth. Thus, he toys with him somewhat in an effort to open his eyes and expand his mind. Boswell, in attempting to dispute with Hume, however modestly, reveals his own naiveté but also draws Hume out and shows us a side of his personality. It is not a dimension that is unanticipated but it is a dimension that is nicely illustrated by the dialogue in the interview.

What most deeply troubles Boswell, of course, is the fact that when he personalizes the discussion he is uncomfortable with the result:

> In this style of good humour and levity did I conduct the conversation. Perhaps it was wrong on so awful a subject. But as nobody was present, I thought it could have no bad effect. I however felt a degree of horror, mixed with a sort of wild, strange, hurrying recollection of my excellent mother's pious instructions, of Dr. Johnson's noble lessons, and of my religious sentiments and affections during the course of my life. I was like a man in sudden danger eagerly seeking his defensive arms; and I could not but be assailed by momentary doubts while I had actually before me a man of such strong abilities and extensive inquiry dying in the persuasion of being annihilated. (pp. 12–13)

Boswell maintains his faith and continues the discussion, but it is fairly clear from what follows in the ensuing months that he is less comfortable facing life than Hume appeared to be facing death. He cannot, in short, get beyond the self. He cannot look upon Hume's actions and beliefs with detachment. He cannot seek some portion of Hume's calm; he can only thrash about in his own circumscribed world.

It is easy to fault Boswell for not saying or showing more in a five-page interview. There is, after all, some value in what he has left us. The troubling thing with Boswell, however, is not so much the fact that things are left out as it is that the things which are presented are so personalized. It is fair to ask, for example, whether or not questions of religion and mortality were as important to Hume at this time as the interview suggests. There is no question whatsoever that they were important to Boswell. In controlling the direction of the interview Boswell creates as well as records a scene that may (or may not) be a fair reflection of Hume's feelings and attitudes at the time. It is possible, as I will argue later, that Hume had other things on his mind and that while there may be no "lies" in the scene there may be far more Boswellian autobiography than Humean biography.

In some ways Boswell's reactions to Hume are surprising. After all, Hume's views on religion and faith and his reputation for personal equanimity and serenity were all matters of record. It is not as if Boswell had found Johnson doubting the existence of a future state and yet facing death calmly. Perhaps we should instead speak of Boswell's overreactions, for Hume's behavior and responses square exactly with what we know of him.

Boswell drinks, gambles, whores, and importunes. He offers his own responses candidly; what he does not give us are insights on Hume. He does not attempt to come to terms with real issues. For example, the question of Hume's beliefs is far from settled. Mossner, for example, claims that Hume was neither a theist nor an atheist but a skeptic.[9] Robert Ginsberg describes Hume as "simply a dispassionate atheist,"[10] while T. E. Jessop writes, "My own impression is that he was certainly not an atheist but somewhere between an agnostic and a deist, believing in a remote God of whom little can be said theoretically."[11] He who would write Hume's life must sort out these matters and it will be difficult if not impossible if the would-be biographer is unable to see past his own spiritual and intellectual turmoil and analyze Hume's thoughts and beliefs with dispassionate objectivity.

Boswell's "solution," however, is quite different. In January of 1784 he has what he describes as "a very agreeable dream" in which he finds a diary kept by Hume which shows that his skeptical treatises were published out of vanity, while Hume was, in reality, a pious man and good Christian.[12] In fact, the images so please Boswell that he "could not for some time perceive that it was only a fiction" (p. 177). I am not arguing that Boswell would have confused this dream with reality had he written Hume's life, but rather that the extent to which he turns experience into highly subjective autobiography is an ongoing shortcoming. He looks out at others but often sees only the self. We know exactly how Boswell felt – the thought of Hume's lack of faith was so intolerable that reality had to be rewritten in dreams. But how did Hume feel?

What else might have been done with this interview? I would like briefly to trace two possibilities, one general and the other more particular. I hope to show how the material at Boswell's disposal might have been employed. I do this not to argue that Boswell is patently inaccurate, but to demonstrate that other obvious possibilities would present themselves to a potential biographer.

Hume's final words to Boswell are, "If there were a future state, Mr. Boswell, I think I could give as good an account of my life as most people." Hume's personal and public lives were extremely important to him and the praise which he received for his posture, demeanor, and attitude is well known. One might even argue that his life was planned and designed in such a way as to embody the conclusions of his thought. Jerome Christensen has written a biography-length study of just this point.[13] Boswell, seeing Hume on his deathbed, might have discussed the manner in which Hume's behavior might have been calculated to make a point. There were, after all, a succession of Restoration and eighteenth-century deathbed scenes and interviews (Rochester, Addison, *et al.*) that every contemporary reader would carry with him as part of his literary and moral baggage. Boswell is operating within a well-established tradition and one might reasonably expect some commentary to that effect.

In his writings Hume is clearly at pains to address the question of how one lives and how behavior bears on philosophy. For example, in contrast to so many modern writers and thinkers whose aestheticist views enwrap them in an enclosed world of art and consciousness,[14] Hume believed that the mind was "insufficient, of itself, to its own entertainment." The mind "naturally seeks after foreign objects," just as the philosopher must leave his study and immerse himself in the real life of the real world.[15]

Boswell knows this. Mossner notes Boswell's comment in a letter of 1764 that Hume "wisely and calmly concludes that the business of ordinary life is the proper employment of man."[16] Popkin's excellent article published nearly thirty years ago, "David Hume: His Pyrrhonism and his Critique of Pyrrhonism,"[17] has never been more relevant, Popkin arguing that for Hume strict skepticism is an impossibility which the demands of real life will not permit. Hence Hume's critique of a skepticism which can never be practiced and hence Hume's philosophic strength that is built not only upon thought but upon life and experience. Nature, in short, is too strong for philosophy and one must consult it constantly. The fact that epistemological Pyrrhonism is the only possible conclusion of philosophical analysis does not, for Hume, cause us to adopt a practical Pyrrhonian attitude.[18] Indeed, we are caught between the force of thought and the demands of nature, but it is nature which must triumph. And, Popkin notes, although Hume remained a consistent anti-religionist, "he did contend that the belief in the existence of a deity was natural."[19]

This, it seems to me, would be serious grist for the mill of a would-be biographer of Hume. The conflict between thought and nature is at the heart of Hume's philosophy; what better setting in which to explore the issue than that of his deathbed? Ginsberg writes that "Hume's most astonishing triumph is his having lived his philosophy...he *proved* by his life the sense of his philosophy, just as his philosophy sprang from his character and experience." His theories, Ginsberg concludes, "do not...destroy an enlightened philosophy of man, but make it livable within the human frame."[20] This is the kind of subject to which a biographer should warm, including as it does the dual claims on our attention of personal experience and generalized reflection.

Consider, finally, Boswell's avoidance of what might be considered a crucial detail, a detail upon which one might build a larger argument, a detail whose dimensions should have been immediately apparent (and important) to Boswell. When he encountered Hume on that Sunday in July 1776 he was most struck by Hume's physical appearance, but unless one is prepared to permit Boswell to read Hume's mind based on his physical condition, the only external detail that Boswell reports that might reasonably suggest Hume's thoughts at that moment is the fact that he is reading Campbell's *Philosophy of Rhetoric*. "He seemed to be placid and even cheerful. He said he was just approaching to his end" (p. 11).

The fact that he "has before him" Campbell's *Rhetoric* may be of no consequence whatsoever. Boswell certainly makes nothing of it and Boswell was there. On the other hand, Boswell (not Hume) contrives to introduce the subject of immortality into their discussion and it is the course of that discussion which Boswell chooses to record.

Another reporter or would-be biographer would almost surely have discussed the presence there of Campbell's book. The reason – quite apart from the fact that it is there and Hume seems placid and even cheerful despite the fact that he is dying – is not far to seek. Campbell (1719–96) was one of the members of the Philosophical Society of Aberdeen, a group which in many ways gave rise to the so-called Common Sense School of philosophy. The Society's constant interest was the philosophy of David Hume and it spawned not only the important work of Reid but the more notorious work of Beattie.

Campbell had written a criticism of Hume entitled *A Dissertation on Miracles; Containing an Examination of the Principles advanced by David Hume, Esq; in an Essay on Miracles* (1762), but while arguing against Hume, Campbell made clear his positive indebtedness to Hume's thought, an action which drew a warm and appreciative response from Hume, who praised Campbell's civility and his ability to rise above the level of personal quarrel.[21]

Lloyd Bitzer has shown how Campbell's very important *Rhetoric* is built upon Humean thought, particularly in its analysis of the nature of belief. Hume's earlier antagonist has, in effect, now appropriated Hume's thought. Campbell, who was called at one time the "philosophical theologian of the Church of Scotland" demonstrated that a sense of reverence and a commitment to enlightened intellectual exchanges were not mutually exclusive, while Hume, on his deathbed, could lean back and trace the influences of his thought in the *magnum opus* of an old, genial antagonist. The theologian could debate with the skeptic and learn from him.

Established ideas could be challenged and progress be made with no
sacrifice of piety or blood. Enlightenment could be possible without excess.
It is a pretty image for Hume to ponder as his death approached.

Boswell says nothing of it, despite the fact that Common Sense
Philosophy (particularly Reid's) was his heart's darling and despite the fact
that he knew Campbell. He and Johnson met him, for example, in August
1773 in his capacity as Principal of Marischal College. Less than a year after
Hume's death, Boswell supped with Campbell and William Nairne. The
entry is interesting: "Supped Nairne with Principal Campbell; not pleased.
He thought not horribly of annihilation" (p. 129). Once again Boswell seeks
confirmation for his own beliefs and a quieting of his own fears but is
disappointed. And he does not go beyond the self. What does he record?
The fact that he was not pleased; a man did not agree with James Boswell.

It is interesting to speculate whether or not Boswell would have said more
about Campbell had he written Hume's life, but he certainly makes nothing
of Hume's reading Campbell's book on his deathbed. It may not be entirely
fair to characterize Boswell's behavior as Mossner does: that of a morbid,
impertinent busybody,[22] but the conclusion is inescapable that in this
instance as well as others Boswell finds it nearly impossible to escape his own
concerns and report clearly, objectively, and dispassionately. His own
reactions are made very clear but those reactions can be extreme, inordinate,
and solipsistic.

Finally, it is clear that while Boswell remains one of the principal literary
figures within that nexus of activity termed the Scottish Enlightenment, his
contacts with the figures who matter most were not matched with either the
philosophic depth or philosophic detachment that are reasonable requisites
for full participation in their discussions. As so often with Boswell, the
deathbed interview with Hume shows how a man's thoughts and actions
affected *him*; it shows the Boswellian self and the manner in which it was
affected by the experiences of others, experiences whose value in themselves
is subordinated to their role in his own continuing autobiography. Boswell
moved among the principals but he is neither the reliable recorder nor the
trenchant interpreter of what transpired there. Rather, he suggests the
stricken individual on an endless, sometimes pathetic, quest in search of
auditors who will listen to the endless tale of his own experience.

NOTES

1 Mossner, *The Forgotten Hume: Le Bon David* (New York: Columbia University
   Press, 1943), p. 169; Greene, "Reflections on a Literary Anniversary," *Queen's
   Quarterly*, 70 (1963), 207–8.
2 Note Harold Bloom's recent edited volume of criticism on "Dr. Samuel
   Johnson and James Boswell" (New York: Chelsea House, 1986). Why not
   Johnson and Burke? Johnson and Goldsmith? Johnson and Reynolds? Indeed,

why not Johnson and Hume? Both Mossner and, more recently, John Vance have shown striking points of contact between Johnson and Hume.

3 Mossner, *The Forgotten Hume*, p. 181.

4 *Ibid.*

5 *Laird*, p. 387.

6 See Imre Salusinszky, *Criticism in Society* (New York: Methuen, 1987), interview with Bloom, pp. 45–73, esp. pp. 67–73.

7 Parenthetical references in the text are to *Boswell in Extremes*.

8 *Applause* p. XVII.

9 "The Religion of David Hume," *Journal of the History of Ideas*, 39 (1978), 653.

10 "David Hume versus the Enlightenment," *Studies on Voltaire and the Eighteenth Century*, 88 (1972), 629.

11 "The Misunderstood Hume," in William B. Todd, ed., *Hume and the Enlightenment: Essays Presented to Ernest Campbell Mossner* (Edinburgh: Edinburgh University Press, 1974), p. 4.

12 *Applause*, p. 176. The next parenthetical reference within the text is to this volume of Boswell's journal.

13 *Practicing Enlightenment: Hume and the Formation of a Literary Career* (Madison: University of Wisconsin Press, 1987).

14 See, for example, the stunning study by Allan Megill, *Prophets of Extremity: Nietzsche, Heidegger, Foucault, Derrida* (Berkeley and Los Angeles: University of California Press, 1985).

15 See John A. Dussinger, "David Hume's Denial of Personal Identity: The Making of a Skeptic," *American Imago*, 37 (1980), 349.

16 Mossner, *The Forgotten Hume*, p. 173.

17 *The Philosophical Quarterly*, 1 (1951), reprinted in *Hume*, ed. V. C. Chappell (Garden City: Doubleday, 1966), pp. 53–98.

18 Popkin, "David Hume," p. 94.

19 Popkin, "David Hume," p. 81.

20 "David Hume versus the Enlightenment," pp. 645, 646.

21 See Mossner, *The Life of David Hume* (Oxford: Clarendon Press, 1970), p. 293. On the relationship with Campbell, see Lloyd F. Bitzer, "Hume's Philosophy in George Campbell's *Philosophy of Rhetoric*," *Philosophy & Rhetoric*, 2 (1969), 139–66.

22 Mossner, *The Life of David Hume*, p. 598.

9

"THIS PHILOSOPHICAL MELANCHOLY":
STYLE AND SELF IN BOSWELL AND HUME

Susan Manning

A man should not live more than he can record...a Diary...will not only be most immediately useful to the person who keeps it, but will afford the most authentick materials for writing his life.[1]

This was one of the blackest days I ever passed. I was most miserably melancholy...I was very dreary. I had lost all relish of London. I thought I saw the nothingness of all sublunary enjoyments. I was cold and spiritless.[2]

Boswell's journals record his melancholy moods as regularly as all his other sensations. This hypochondria or "Hyp" was at once another pose for the chameleon diarist (he wrote an entire series of periodical papers under the pseudonym "The Hypochondriack"), and the most intractable, unwriteable part of himself. Any eighteenth-century writer expressing melancholy was doubly conscious of its public and private dimensions: in Boswell's journals its presence focuses the problems of integrating life and writing with the degree of intimacy that his record tries to achieve.

Melancholy or hypochondria was a recognized medical condition also known as "spleen," which was supposed peculiarly characteristic of English persons of quality, idleness being the condition under which it flourished. It was accompanied by languor, disgust for worldly activities which charmed at other times, and the feeling of pointlessness identified by Boswell in his *London Journal*. Luxury it was to some extent, and even its victims recognized a fashionable dimension to their affliction. But it was also painfully real and intensely private: the silent resistance of the inner self to all the demands of social living.

The paradox of modishness and privacy was resolved in the acute self-consciousness of the melancholy state – at once entrapment within the self's perceptions and hypersensitivity to the image of oneself projected towards other people. Medical textbooks like Dr. George Cheyne's *The English Malady* (1733) or popular verse like Matthew Green's *The Spleen* (1737) anatomized the symptoms and recommended cures, but did not attempt to describe the experience of the affliction. The insufficiencies of the public language of analytic empiricism are nowhere more evident than in its attempts to contain melancholy by naming its manifestations. Resolutely unrecuperable, melancholy was the last refuge of the private self in the eighteenth century's very public world. Only a use of language which accepted and made room for the uncommunicable experience in the self-projection, the self within the style, could give a voice to melancholy's equivocations with the world.

When Pope's Eloisa writes of her dejection to Abelard, for example, the poetry at once respects her state of mind and reveals her self-dramatization. Her melancholy is both histrionic and real; the lines express a moving desolation *and* cast a sidelong glance at its self-deceptions.

> But o'er the twilight groves, and dusky caves,
> Long-sounding isles, and intermingled graves,
> Black Melancholy sits, and round her throws
> A death-like silence, and a dread repose:
> Her gloomy presence saddens all the scene,
> Shades ev'ry flow'r, and darkens ev'ry green,
> Deepens the murmur of the falling floods,
> And breathes a browner horror on the woods.[3]

In this double consciousness the poet deftly extricates himself from the melancholy state; the complex interaction of style and self-perception is a fully objectified characteristic of Eloisa herself. If the melancholy evoked in these lines were ever experienced by the poet, that state has been fully written out into the poetry. Pope's marriage of verbal and psychological precision combines echoes of Milton's "Il Penseroso" with textbook symptoms and adds a hint of mockery without disturbing the tone; he may not be in these lines, but melancholy most certainly is.

The melancholy state of Cowper's "The Castaway," on the other hand, is inescapably personal; rather than dissociating the description from himself the poet insists on the connection, indeed makes it the subject of the poem, as he implicates his desolation in the images of abandonment:

> Obscurest night involv'd the sky,
> Th' Atlantic billows roar'd,
> When such a destin'd wretch as I,
> Wash'd headlong from on board,
> Of friends, of hope, of all bereft,
> His floating home for ever left...
>
> Not long beneath the whelming brine,
> Expert to swim, he lay;
> Nor soon he felt his strength decline,
> Or courage die away;

But wag'd with death a lasting strife,
Supported by despair of life...

No voice divine the storm allay'd,
  No light propitious shone:
When, snatch'd from all effectual aid,
  We perish'd, each alone:
But I, beneath a rougher sea
And whelm'd in deeper gulphs than he.[4]

The rawness of the emotion and the verse form exist in tension here; the power of Cowper's language pulls at compassion and sympathy without engulfing the reader too in the formless inexpressibility of melancholy. What Cowper has lost of Pope's detachment, he has gained in immediacy. The balance is different, but the language of both poems is able to contain the mixture of self-consciousness and alienation, articulacy and silence which is the essence of melancholy. They represent two different ways of writing which successfully tread the tightrope between public and private, style and self, the complex interactions of the melancholy state.

Melancholy was for Boswell, as for Cowper, an ever-present reality of living. It is part of the self he is, but not of the self he wants to be; his journals record a constant tussle between the consistent social being he would like to project and his compulsive honesty towards the private experiences which will not accommodate themselves to his conscious shaping. Boswell cannot find a single frame to encompass his model of what a self ought to be and his account of how he acts in practice, because he puts too much faith in empirical accounts of sensations to add up, cumulatively, to the reality of a *self*. Melancholy acts as a negative focus for this failure of cohesion between description and experience, style and self. If the self is the sum of its sensations, it does not seem to be *a* self at all, but if he even begins to think about where else a self may be found, skeptical doubts envelop him in melancholy. His writing cannot sustain an integrity between the analytic intellect and the feeling self, as, in their different ways, both Pope's and Cowper's poems do.

Boswell's is the most naked version of the problem which faces all eighteenth-century writing which attempts to consider personal identity in the wake of David Hume's *A Treatise of Human Nature* (1739). His management of his melancholy in the journals enacts, I shall suggest, but fails to resolve the gulf which Hume had opened between thinking about self and perceiving one's own sensations. This gulf appears in his writing as an uncertain relationship between style and self, between public and private locations of identity, and arises because of the total equivalence he wants to create between the two.

Turning to Hume's own writing, we find him to have been a youthful victim of melancholy every bit as self-absorbed as Boswell. In a remarkable letter on "the present Condition of my Health" which he wrote in 1734 to Cheyne, the medical authority on melancholy and hypochondria, he described his symptoms and anxieties:

> all my Ardor seem'd in a moment to be extinguisht, & I cou'd no longer raise my mind to that pitch, which formerly gave me such excessive Pleasure...my Coldness proceeded from a Laziness of Temper, which must be overcome by redoubling my Application...I was continually fortifying myself with Reflections against Death, & Poverty, & Shame, & Pain, & all the other Calamities of Life...To keep myself from being Melancholy on so dismal a Prospect, my only Security was in peevish Reflections on the Vanity of the World & of all humane Glory.[5]

After this self-exposure, which was possibly suppressed and never sent, Hume, the lifelong analyst and exponent of passion and "feeling" as the only springs of human conduct, so fully absorbed his feeling self into his public style that no trace of the disruptive unsubduable sensations of melancholy remained. His short autobiographical account, "My Own Life," composed a few months before his death, condenses the whole anguishing episode described in his letter to Cheyne into a passing phrase with perfect equanimity. We do not know what process of maturing Hume underwent between 1734 and the publication of his *A Treatise of Human Nature* in 1739, what compromise was reached between the needs of the feeling self and the expository capabilities of the rational self. However he achieved his detached skeptical equanimity, though – and he never again exposed the raw Boswellian side of his consciousness to public view – the melancholy self is not silenced by, but completely integrated with, the philosophical positions of the *Treatise*.

In Book I of his *Treatise*, Hume demonstrates the "absurdity" of "the notion of external existence, when taken for something specifically different from our perceptions"; not only is knowledge of the external world limited to what we perceive of it, but the sense of identity, selfhood itself, appears at its most irreducible nothing more than impressions of sensation and reflection.[6] The self exists because through memory and imagination it constructs itself. Consciousness of identity is itself all the identity which may safely be posited, and our notion of selfhood comes from "the smooth passage of the imagination along the ideas of the resembling perceptions" (p. 205). Hume's account of identity is like the illusion of the moving cartoon picture: separate images are successively juxtaposed, the differences between any two adjacent pictures being so slight that in succession the overall impression is of continuity along a central axis of integrity.

In a similar way, Boswell's journals create his self retrospectively by fixing the momentary responses of experience as literary poses. His record of outward behavior is always accompanied by interrogation of the methods of recording: "proper" conduct can only be projected through "proper" style; the account must answer to both documentary and grammatical truths. The perfect tense becomes the mark of closure, completion, control: "I came home quiet, laid by my clothes, and went coolly to bed. There's conduct for you" (*London Journal*, p. 71). Clauses succeed one another in good order; the orderliness of the actions, contained within the past, earn the approbation of the present recording self. The account and the experience are mutually supportive and self-confirming.

Boswell's narrative runs most smoothly when his memory projects an ordered and sequential patch of life. There is particular satisfaction when life and narrative can be carried into a continuous present, when style and self promise and enact harmonious concordance:

> I got up excellently well. My present life is most curious, and very fortunately is become agreeable. My affairs are conducted with the greatest regularity and exactness. I move like very clock-work. At eight in the morning Molly lights the fire, sweeps and dresses my dining-room...I lie some time in bed indulging indolence, which in that way, when the mind is easy and cheerful, is most pleasing... (*London Journal*, p. 183)

But what happens when his imagination cannot make a "smooth passage," because the "perceptions" do not seem "resembling," but mutually contradictory, a series of superimposed but quite disjointed "frames"?

> What a curious, inconsistent thing is the mind of man! In the midst of divine service I was laying plans for having women, and yet I had the most sincere feelings of religion. I imagine that my want of belief is the occasion of this, so that I can have all the feelings. I would try to make out a little consistency this way. I have a warm heart and a vivacious fancy. I am therefore given to love, and also to piety or gratitude to GOD, and to the most brilliant and showy method of public worship. (*London Journal*, p. 54)

Boswell's journals attempt to establish his "character" by imposing continuity on his inconsistent behavior along Hume's lines. But however hard he tries to reconcile its contradictions narratively or conceptually, his sensations refuse to cohere with the fluid ease of a cartoon character. Hume had conceded that "the interrupted manner of [the perceptions'] appearance makes us consider them as so many resembling, but still distinct beings, which appear after certain intervals. The perplexity arising from this contradiction produces a propension to unite these broken appearances by the fiction of a continu'd existence" (*Treatise*, p. 205). This is very sanguine; weighted and rounded periods create confidence that consistency can be made where it cannot be found. Hume's style is willing – and able – to speak for his self, because that self is conceived in entirely public terms; he admits the *possibility* that the mind's natural inclination to ascribe identity to its successive perceptions may be obstructed, but the negative voice is easily neutralized and identified as aberrant within the urbane public tone of the philosophical exposition:

> This sceptical doubt, both with respect to reason and the senses, is a malady, which can never be radically cur'd, but must return upon us every moment, however we may chace it away, and sometimes may seem entirely free from it...Carelessness and in-attention alone can afford us any remedy. For this reason I rely entirely upon them; and take it for granted, whatever may be the reader's opinion at this present moment, that an hour hence he will be persuaded there is both an external and internal world. (p. 218)

The spectres of scepticism are amongst the greatest horrors of melancholy for Boswell. In the *Hypochondriack* essays he describes as an awful symptom of the condition that "[the melancholick] begins actually to believe the strange theory, that nothing exists without the mind, because he is sensible, as he imagines, of a total change in all the objects of his contemplation" (*Hypochondriack*, II, 42). Boswell would like to be convinced of the boundaries of the internal and external worlds; all his journals yearn for such certainty. But his very virtues as a diarist close off success at the point of possibility. His minute concern with successive impressions and sensations produces an unparalleled register of the movements of consciousness, but his sense of himself from within is so immediately transformed into self-projection that "being" is never separated from writing, self from the "styling" of self.

Boswell's vocabulary of self-analysis was learned from Hume and Adam Smith (whose lectures he attended as a student in Glasgow and whose *Theory of Moral Sentiments* developed the ethical dimension to Hume's empirical psychology), but he could not derive from them the counsel of how to live with it. Hume's philosophy of personal identity gave Boswell a way of describing himself in the double roles of spectator and actor, participant and observer, at once able to receive sensations and to reflect upon them. The "double consciousness" of observer and actor is embedded in the imagery of Hume's *Treatise*: "The mind is a kind of theatre, where several perceptions successively make their appearance; pass, re-pass, glide away, and mingle in an infinite variety of postures and situations" (*Treatise*, p. 253).

Here was a potent metaphor for Boswell – and an attractive opportunity to dramatize himself as all the characters he most admired: the self could become an actor on a stage, observed and recorded by the stylist in the audience. The "double feeling" by which the player at once enters his role fully and retains something of his own character as an observer is, Boswell writes in his exploration of the actor's craft, "experienced by many men in the common intercourse of life."[7] Indeed, such duplicity may be an essential safeguard against the emergence of our true, dangerous selves: "were nothing but the real character to appear, society would not be half so safe and agreeable as we find it." Luckily, though, all the world's a stage; a social voice always overlays the private self.

But the theater, as Hume has suggested, is internal to the mind as well; "how then," Boswell wonders, "can we represent, by a sensible image, the mind as a theatre to its own actings? Let us conceive a spacious saloon, in which our thoughts and passions exert themselves, and let its walls be encrusted with mirrour, for the purpose of reflection..." (*Hypochondriack*, I, 152).

This appears in the *Hypochondriack* essay on "Conscience," where Boswell draws extensively on Adam Smith's metaphor of the conscience as a kind of internal mirror to the acting self. Again, neither thought nor image is original to Boswell, but the literalness with which he applies it to understand himself in his journals has disconcerting consequences. The man of sensation as defined by Hume and Adam Smith only knows who he is by standing outside his own needs and looking back in on them as an impartial spectator. But this is, in both writers, an analysis of human identity, not an account of what it feels like to be a person. Boswell, however, adopts Smith's ethical psychology directly into the relationship between his own experience and the act of writing it down, between his style and himself. Smith's division of the self into observer and actor becomes Boswell's admonitory recollections in conversation with himself, set down in the journals. The writing out of memory on the page provides an opportunity for the observing, recording self and the acting self to meet in reminiscence and resolution:

> You talked of Smith's Sympathy, and said that when passion rose high you had a faculty in your own mind called Reason. You appeal to that. You find he disapproves; you dare not act. This is all within yourself. If you act, he condemns you. There is no occasion for a far-fetched appeal to others, which at best is but vague... At night you grew easy and renewed resolves of patience and firmness. (*Boswell in Holland*, p. 174)

The journal projects the acting self upon a visible stage – words – so that it can be looked at, reviewed, and ordered by the observing self. For the writer, the stage *is* words, "style"; the theater of the mind posited by Hume is projected on to the written page. In this "writing out" of action, the continuities of identity become syntactic and narrative, events are "scenes" projected back upon the memory as static tableaux, with Boswell the chief character center-stage. The style distances the observing self from its actions: Boswell "sees himself" or "feels himself" doing things. In this way he tries to absorb the inconsistency of his actual purposes within a "higher" literary consistency:

> I am vexed at such a distempered suggestion's being inserted in my journal, which I wished to contain a consistent picture of a young fellow eagerly pushing through life. But it serves to humble me, and it presents a strange and

curious view of the unaccountable nature of the human mind. I am now well and gay. Let me consider that the hero of a romance or novel must not go uniformly along in bliss, but the story must be chequered with bad fortune. Aeneas met with many disasters in his voyage to Italy, and must not Boswell have his rubs? Yes, I take them in good part. I am now again set a-going...(*London Journal*, pp. 205–6)

Consciously dividing himself into actor and spectator, he distanced the acuteness of sensation in its description, and discovered a potential solution to the ever-threatening silent negations of despair:

> I am rather passive than active in life...I may say, I act passively. That is, not with my whole heart, and thinking this or that of real consequence, but because so and so things are established and I must submit. (*London Journal*, p. 77)

In fact, though, what Patricia Meyer Spacks calls this "quality of self-withholding" from the world means that Boswell is unable, either in life or writing, fully to commit himself to its realities.[8] The actor is always part observer, watching and recording as well as being. This is why melancholy constantly threatens even his most active moments.

Boswell's journals are, in a very Humean sense, his identity: they are the written image of his experience, the operation of imagination upon memory. From his daily jottings he intends "at certain periods [to] make up masses or larger views of my existence" (*Defence*, pp. 225–6). He tries by imposing analysis upon sensation to *construct* integrity and selfhood:

> I have begun to acquire a composed genteel character very different from a rattling uncultivated one which for some time past I have been fond of. I have discovered that we may be in some degree whatever character we choose. Besides, practice forms a man to anything. (*London Journal*, p. 47)

Where Boswell tries to make the empirical chronicle of successive sensations a means to *self*-understanding at a personal rather than a philosophical level, Hume's observer in the *Treatise* stands clear of his subject but dramatically implicated in the style of the exposition. Subjective and objective occupy a verbal stage which has access at will to reason, order, logic, to contain the rampant anarchy of "response," unbridled sensation. But Hume's purposes – and his language – are also deliberately self-limiting, and reveal how much more than Boswell's his prose imposes structure on the presentation of sensations. What can be thought can be said, discursively, articulately; word and thought match, to the extent that there is even room in the writing for the feeling self to fight back at the logic of its own thought-processes. Melancholy and spleen emerge through metaphor as the mind's element of resistance to its own activities:

I am like a man, who having struck on many shoals, and having narrowly escap'd ship-wreck in passing a small frith, has yet the temerity to put out to sea in the same leaky weather-beaten vessel, and even carries his ambition so far as to think of compassing the globe under these disadvantageous circumstances. My memory of past errors and perplexities, makes me diffident for the future. The wretched condition, weakness, and disorder of the faculties, I must employ in my enquiries, encrease my apprehensions. And the impossibility of amending or correcting these faculties, reduces me almost to despair, and makes me resolve to perish on the barren rock, on which I am at present, rather than venture myself upon that boundless ocean, which runs out into immensity. This sudden view of my danger strikes me with melancholy; and as 'tis usual for that passion, above all others, to indulge itself; I cannot forbear feeding my despair, with all those desponding reflections, which the present subject furnishes me with in such abundance.

I am at first affrighted and confounded with that forelorn solitude, in which I am plac'd in my philosophy...I can give no reason why I shou'd assent to it; and feel nothing but a *strong* propensity to consider objects *strongly* in that view, under which they appear to me. Experience is a principle, which instructs me in the several conjunctions of objects for the past. Habit is another principle, which determines me to expect the same for the future; and both of them conspiring to operate upon the imagination, make me form certain ideas in a more intense and lively manner, than others, which are not attended with the same advantages. (*Treatise*, pp. 263–5)

The turn from melancholy, the self trapped within its own impressions, to a provisional but perfectly equable confidence in the propensities of mind to take their place in social discourse at the highest level, appears in Hume's smooth transitions through successive reflections, transitions which establish a unifying consistency of style over all the various sensations which the mind can muster. Personal alienation is projected fully forward into the public functions of the prose as the Calvinist metaphor of shipwreck serves a turn in advancing Hume's argument. This account of melancholy, after all, has a wholly public function not at odds with the analytic empiricism of the *Treatise* as a whole: it enlists the reader's sympathies through the recognizable literary language of hypochondria. Readily identifying the appropriate emotional key, the narrator projects the poses of melancholy to anticipate opposition, to intensify the enormous temerity of his philosophical proposition, and to stress how much confidence he has in it, being willing to plumb the furthest depths of spleen rather than abandon his quest. What this evocation of melancholy does not do is betray unwittingly anything of Hume's own private self. Cowper's castaway and Hume's are near relations in literature but not in life.

Boswell's writing cannot integrate the data of consciousness with anything like Hume's suppleness; the presence of melancholy has quite a different effect in his prose. It represents the ultimate failure of language to reflect sensations, of literature and life to match, and as such threatens the whole enterprise of constructing a self from the record of experience. This melancholy desolation paralyzes the faculties in the spaces beyond articulacy, because Boswell's language cannot, like Pope's or Cowper's, stretch to compass experience as well as its analysis. As his feelings go dead, so his words reduce to reiterated shorthand formulae: "was very bad...gloomy... dreary." Melancholy here is the refuge of the articulate self in the unsayable, where the word and the experience, style and self part company. Compulsively writing his life, Boswell tries to recuperate the melancholy self for the articulate one, by faithfully acknowledging its existence within the same framework as his social calendar – but he does it to deny that self within his projected model self. So his style neither incorporates nor excludes the unsayable part of selfhood, the *sense* of identity that will not be subdued to order, control, progress, and public maturity. The strain of trying to fit the private experience to the public identity shows in the tensely formal voice of his self-admonitions:

> I really believe that these grievous complaints should not be vented; they should be considered as absurd chimeras, whose reality should not be allowed in words. One thing I am sure of, that if a man can believe himself well, he will be really so. (*Boswell in Holland*, p. 212)

Hume, anticipating a possible corner of response in his reader, evokes the disorienting voice of melancholy indulgently in the conclusion to Book I of the *Treatise*, but once allowed, it is quickly contained within the public logic of the argument:

> Most fortunately it happens, that since reason is incapable of dispelling these clouds, nature herself suffices to that purpose, and cures me of this philosophical melancholy and delirium, either by relaxing this bent of mind, or by some avocation, and lively impression of my senses, which obliterate all these chimeras. I dine, I play a game of backgammon, I converse, and am merry with my friends; and when after three or four hour's amusement, I wou'd return to these speculations, they appear so cold, and strain,d, and ridiculous, that I cannot find in my heart to enter into them any farther. (*Treatise*, pp. 269–70)

Unlike Boswell's, Hume's "chimeras" really can be obliterated at will. Hume's style can dramatize sensation and reflection, participation and observation, at odds with one another, because it never risks naked self-exposure through the public voice. The fluctuations of mood which cumulatively compose a self are accommodated happily within a verbal play between the poles of passivity ("most fortunately it happens that...") and activity ("I dine...I am merry with my friends"). Embodying the abstract arguments over determinism and free will, Hume's prose refuses to be put out of countenance by the logical inconsistency of a human response which knows both within its own experience. His is a "philosophical melancholy" in two senses: it describes the melancholy sensations induced by philosophizing oneself into possible non-existence, and it evokes a literary state through metaphors which move flexibly between the realms of sensation and reflection, feeling and abstract thought.

Boswell's melancholy is not and cannot be transformed like this; this style has no means to resolve the relationship between sensation and reflection in his own life. During a high-spirited patch on his Grand Tour of Germany and Switzerland in 1764, he became convinced that he had solved the problem of melancholy once and for all:

> One great lesson to be learned is that man is a practical being. It is hard, but experience proves it to be true that speculation renders us miserable. Life will not bear to be calmly considered. It appears insipid and ridiculous as a country dance. Yet nothing is more certain than that the dreariest of all speculatists may be made to think as agreeably as others, provided he will rouse himself to action like them. (*Grand Tour I*, p. 32)

But this is little more than pious reiteration of the best specifics offered by conventional eighteenth-century wisdom on melancholy:

> To cure the mind's wrong biass, spleen,
> Some recommend the bowling-green;
> Some, hilly walks; all, exercise;
> Fling but a stone, the giant dies;
> Laugh and be well[9]

Boswell's combination of philosophical platitude, self-exhortation, and optimism ("nothing is more certain...") leaves no room in his writing for anything other than total self-reformation in response to the empirical analysis. When record and reality fail, as they must, to coincide, the self takes refuge once again in impenetrable negativity. Hume's game of backgammon or dinner with friends relieves his melancholy in the *Treatise* because it is "only" literary, and therefore responds to the writing down of the remedy; on the other hand, Johnson's recommendation (as recorded by Boswell himself in the *Life*) of a course of chemistry or rope-dancing as a cure for the condition recognizes by its self-mocking extremity the very private desperation for relief within the peremptory imperative voice. But the "mirth and gentle amusement" (*London Journal*, p. 154) which Boswell recommends to himself cannot in practice rouse him from his torpor; failing to follow his own recorded prescriptions for action, he seeks oblivion through excess, indulging sensation to the point of insensibility in whoring and drinking.

Resolutions or plans for life attempt to supply his want of an inner sense of self-coherence with an external model of character. The fullest of these was the "Inviolable Plan" he constructed in Utrecht to counteract the effects of perhaps his longest and most severely undermining bout of melancholy. The

"Plan" keeps speculation – and then madness – at bay. The journal is filled with memoranda "never [to] desist an hour from plan," exhortations to "indulge not whims but form into a man," and self-admonitions to "persevere. Consider that this happiness is wrought out by study, by rational conduct, and by piety. It is the natural effect of these causes; and you may ever be so. Be fixed in your general Plan, and never admit fancies to lead you from it" (*Boswell in Holland*, pp. 44, 54). The Plan's essential characteristic is its comprehensiveness: it has no silences, leaves no room anywhere for the unforeseen or the "unaccountable." As experience widens, so the "rational plan...may be enlarged" (p. 390). By constantly projecting resolutions on to the page where they become objects for contemplation – so that the self may, in effect, look on them as an impartial spectator and draw moral lessons from them – Boswell hopes to re-absorb them into his own life as *felt* desiderata of behavior.

Hume's *Treatise* and Boswell's journals are controlled and punctuated in much the same empirical way: a succession of model, experience, confirmation or denial, and re-adjustment. In the *Treatise*, this takes the form of hypothesis, evidence from observation, conclusion, consequent hypothesis; the driving force of Hume's prose style is a ruthless logic presented as self-evident observation. Within this scheme, the wayward and floundering movements of the mind's impressions are given space, but never allowed to disrupt the rigorous progression of hypothesis and modification. In Boswell's writing, on the other hand, the models are models for living, resolutions for conduct. In his journals there is always the hope – never fulfilled – that control over language will increase control over life, that rampant, often negative instinct may be harnessed by system. What Boswell is looking for is not a *relationship* between living and writing about living, but identity between the two, so that life and writing will reflect one another completely: the model or plan will become the reality. In the later journals when the distance between the projected model of the self and Boswell's actual experience becomes too great, the record is dislocated and abbreviated to obscure the discrepancy. Phrases are transliterated into Greek, sentences are truncated to words and words to letters: the style shrinks to deny or suppress the actions of self.

Unable to draw the thread of his various selves into a coherent whole, Boswell flies between dissipation and self-denial. Silence and effusion alternate uncontrollably, and verbal indulgence is but another form of relief from repressive control:

An Hypochondriack is sometimes so totally incapable of conversation, having a mind like an exhausted receiver, and organs of speech as if palsied, that when his ideas and his vivacity return, effusion is a pleasure to him, in which he can hardly resist an excess of indulgence. (*Hypochondriack*, I, 288)

Given this, it is easy to see why he must go to such pains to overwrite the silences of melancholy in his journals with positive resolutions in which the style leaves no room for the negative voice of the self. Stability is desired, planned for, projected, but never achieved:

> I am distracted with a thousand ideas...My mind is just as if it were in a mortification. O Temple! all my resolutions of attaining a consistent character are blown to the winds. All my hopes of being a man of respect are gone...what can I do? I cannot read. My mind is destroyed by dissipation. But is not dissipation better than melancholy? Oh, surely, anything is better than this...I would fain return to London and shelter myself in obscurity. Yet I would wish to stay some time abroad. I think I shall go to Brussels. It is a gay agreeable place, and may relieve me. (*Boswell in Holland*, pp. 8–9)

The difference between being able to analyze – to "say" – the condition and to affect it through writing brings home the impotence of words and emphasizes his suffering. The active recording self and the passive experiencing self separate. "Shape" – form – eludes both the prose and the man himself; the writing succumbs to the transitory moods. Boswell's journals and letters constantly expose the gap between his ability to observe and articulate, and his ability to shape or understand. His life, written, is a narrative without development, punctuated but not structured by repetitions and resolutions, an endlessly reiterated cycle of sensations, impressions, reflections, recriminations, and resolutions – the ingredients of biography or autobiography without the control or the distance of art. In both life and writing, the failure of Boswell's reflections upon his sensations to affect his future course leads to frustration and despair.

Melancholy repeatedly forces Boswell to acknowledge its unwelcome, disruptive presence: "Yet let me remember this truth: I am subject to melancholy, and of the operations of melancholy, reason can give no account" (*Boswell in Holland*, p. 225). Perhaps it can be, quite literally, *written* out of his life: "could I extract the hypochondria from my mind, and deposit it in my journal, writing down would be very valuable" (*Ominous Years*, p. 240). Or perhaps if it were not acknowledged, it might cease to exist altogether: "If I persist in study, and never mention my splenetic chimeras, am I not then a man? Can I not review my life with pride?" (*Boswell in Holland*, p. 223). This query is addressed to Temple rather than to himself, and the question is real not rhetorical: does (or might) the outward appearance of self and character equal (or become) the inward reality? A third alternative is to escape melancholy by escaping self, slipping into another role on the mental stage:

> Somehow or another, I was very low-spirited and melancholy, and could not relish that gay entertainment, and was very discontent. I left my company, and mounting on the back of a hackney-coach, rattled away to town in the attitude

of a footman. The whimsical oddity of this, the jolting of the machine, and the soft breeze of the evening made me very well again. (*London Journal*, p. 286)

But the self-consciousness of the escape ("in the attitude of a footman") transforms even violent action into another pose vulnerable to the contemplation of the melancholy self-observer.

More than anything else about his melancholy, Boswell fears its intractable silences, its unwriteability, that aspect of it that cannot be communicated or recognized by others as part of himself. In the *London Journal* he records a comment by a companion who "wondered how I could complain of being miserable who had always such a flow of spirits," and adds "Melancholy cannot be clearly proved to others, so it is better to be silent about it" (pp. 261–2). But where writing is being, and the reviewable record stabilizes memory, silence negates self; what cannot be recorded may not exist. Melancholy is a nothingness, it displays no positive or recuperable signs of identity, and refuses to subdue itself to style. It was quite vain for Boswell to exclaim melodramatically to Temple, "I have said to the Demon of Hypochondria, as the bold Highlander in *Fingal* says to his Deity of fanciful conjecture, 'show yourself to me and I will search thee with my spear'" (*Boswell in Holland*, p. 282); his "spear," his pen, has no resources to probe the Cave of Spleen and force its inhabitants into the daylight of discursive style. Neither do his self-consciously advertised metaphors and similes plumb the resources of poetic concentration with which Cowper wrestled his melancholy to form it into meaning:

> words come skipping to me like lambs upon Moffat Hill; and I turn my periods smoothly and imperceptibly like a skilful wheelwright turning tops in a turning-loom. There's fancy! There's simile! (*London Journal*, p. 187)

Measure this understanding of language against Cowper's "Castaway" and we see at once that Boswell's images are not a means to explore feelings, but a kind of gift-wrapping of known ideas. His metaphors represent a further element of conscious control through words rather than a link between private experience and public communication, a position Hume's and Cowper's shipwrecks both hold in different ways for the reader. Boswell's images are finally just another way of distancing reality, of severing the relationship between language and experience, and his style operates always between the tensions of conventionality and madness: the "ordinary" social, comprehensible, and orderly self is shadowed by its melancholy negation. Burdened with this unquestioning faith in the completeness of empirical description, he cannot express his melancholy other than as another conscious construction of style, another received mask of selfhood.

Melancholy remains in Boswell's journals a painfully observed condition faithfully recorded but insufficiently understood, a blank at the heart of the writing, alien and unassimilable to the self whose style can give no house-room to its meanings. Here is a mind, analytic and articulate, paralyzed by feelings it is able to describe but not to control, hoping to find relief from its symptoms by casting them out of the self on to the objectivity of the written page. The record may be looked at and identified as the feelings themselves cannot; it allows an observer – who may be the self or may be another – access to an experience whose meaning can be described but not touched.

Attempting to "fix" himself in a character, Boswell cannot accept that self may be composed of contradictory elements, and is not something uniform or single, that the social and the private may be continuous with one another without becoming the same thing. His journals aim to be a complete record of a man's – his own – selfhood in a way that Hume's analysis of the constituents of identity does not. But where Hume's public language can plunder the resources of metaphor to suggest the recesses of the private self recalcitrant to analysis without becoming lost in them, Boswell's is trapped in his minute adherence to a philosophy it cannot transcend. Hume's writing founds the *sense* of identity on "carelessness and inattention alone"; self-hood, Boswell's greatest and most constant desire in these journals, eludes him because it is to be looked for elsewhere than in the recorded sum of its passing sensations.

NOTES

1 *Hypochondriack*, II, 259, 263. This work will subsequently be cited in the text.
2 *London Journal*, pp. 213–14. This work will subsequently be cited in the text.
3 "Eloisa to Abelard," in The Twickenham Edition of the Poems of Alexander Pope, II: *The Rape of the Lock and Other Poems*, ed. Geoffrey Tillotson (London: Methuen, 1940), p. 312.
4 *The Poetical Works of William Cowper*, ed. H. S. Milford (Oxford: Oxford University Press, 1950), pp. 431–2.
5 *The Letters of David Hume*, ed. J. Y. T. Grieg, 2 vols. (Oxford: Oxford University Press, 1932), pp. 12–18.
6 *A Treatise of Human Nature*, ed. L. A. Selby-Bigge, 2nd ed. rev. Peter Nidditch (Oxford: Oxford University Press, 1978), p. 188. This work will subsequently be cited in the text as *Treatise*.
7 *On the Profession of a Player. Three Essays by James Boswell, Reprinted from "The London Magazine" for August, September, October, 1770* (London: Elkin Matthews and Marrot, 1929), p. 18.
8 *Imagining a Self: Autobiography and Novel in Eighteenth-Century England* (Cambridge, Mass.: Harvard University Press, 1976), p. 238.
9 Matthew Green, *The Spleen*, ed. W. H. Williams (London: Methuen, 1936), p. 8.

Part III

THE *LIFE OF JOHNSON* RECONSIDERED

10

THE ORIGINALITY OF BOSWELL'S VERSION
OF JOHNSON'S QUARREL WITH
LORD CHESTERFIELD

John J. Burke, Jr.

Johnson's letter to Lord Chesterfield is certainly one of the more memorable moments in Boswell's *Life*. It lingers on in the public memory and has become an indelible part of our inherited picture of Johnson. The sequence of events leading up to the publication of the *Life of Johnson* in 1791 suggests that this began to happen well before the biography was published. In his *Journal of a Tour to the Hebrides*, published at the beginning of October 1785, Boswell had included a note giving the public notice that Johnson had related to him "some particulars" "concerning his throwing off Lord Chesterfield's patronage," and that he was reserving these for the *Life* which was to be published later.[1] In 1790 Boswell had the letter to Lord Chesterfield printed separately, apparently as a foretaste of what he would provide for the public in the full *Life* which was to be published the following year.

A question necessarily arises here: why did Boswell believe the Chesterfield material was so important? The answer to that seems to come in many parts. Above all, Boswell seems to have believed that the quarrel with Lord Chesterfield brought himself and us into contact with something essential in Johnson's character. It was also, as far as he was concerned, a crucial event in the development of Johnson's public personality. The letter to Chesterfield was, at least in symbolic terms, Johnson's liberation, a key moment when he stood up for himself and so came of age, passing psychologically from dependence to independence. What may be even more interesting to us is what this incident reveals about Boswell himself. For there is no way to explain the attraction that the quarrel with Lord Chesterfield had for him without taking note of his own deep personal involvement in events in which, literally speaking, he had no part. So a fresh look at Boswell's account of the quarrel can yield valuable new insights into his practices as a biographer, but it can also provide us with a sobering perspective on the heated debate that currently rages over Boswell's trustworthiness as a biographer of Johnson.

Boswell's trustworthiness was once a given in literary studies, but like so many old truths it now appears to lie in ruins. In recent years he has become the object of ever more pointed attempts to discredit him.[2] His more extreme critics would dismiss him almost entirely from Johnson studies, to be replaced, at least for historical purposes, by Sir John Hawkins. Outrageous as such suggestions might seem, they have been slowly gaining some respectability, perhaps because as the eighteenth century recedes from view the memory of what we owe to Boswell grows dimmer. One way of reminding ourselves of how large that debt is would be to examine the work of the sixteen or so biographers of Johnson who preceded him, including Hawkins, to see which points Boswell contributed to our present understanding of the facts of Johnson's life. That would be a valuable but lengthy exercise. Fortunately, Boswell's account of the quarrel with Lord Chesterfield provides us with the concrete instance we need of what set him apart from his contemporaries.

The events that make up the quarrel can be divided into five stages. The first has to do with Johnson's taking on the task of compiling an English dictionary in the mid-1740s, and then at the instigation of Robert Dodsley, writing and publishing a *Plan* for the dictionary in early August 1747, and dedicating it to Lord Chesterfield. There is ample evidence to suggest that Chesterfield, in keeping with his reputation as the Maecenas of the age, took an active interest in the project. With the dedication of the *Plan* he assumed the public role of patron and as a token of that he gave Johnson a present of £10, a not inconsiderable sum. The second stage is marked by a cooling of this once warm relationship. At some point in this period, probably early on, Johnson was by his own later testimony kept waiting in the outward rooms of Lord Chesterfield's London residence and even repulsed from his door. We do not possess any detailed descriptions of these incidents, but whatever happened they were enough for Johnson to conclude that the "continued neglect" of his "patron" meant that there was no longer any point to their relationship and that he would have no more to do with Lord Chesterfield.

The third stage begins in the months preceding the publication of the *Dictionary* on April 15, 1755. It involves an expectation on the part of Lord Chesterfield, one that was shared by his circle of friends and supporters, that Johnson would dedicate the *Dictionary* to him. This stage can be dated from near the end of 1754, with the appearance of two highly flattering essays in the *World*. They appeared in the last week of November and the first week of December, some six months before the *Dictionary* would actually be published. The essays in the *World* were anonymous, but we are told that it was all about London that Chesterfield was the author; in fact it had to have been a very open secret since the essays were reprinted under Chesterfield's name in the December 1754 issue of the *Gentleman's Magazine*.

The fourth stage begins at the moment when Johnson becomes certain that there are widespread expectations that he will be dedicating his *Dic-*

tionary to Lord Chesterfield, thereby acknowledging him publicly as his patron; it ends when he writes the famous letter informing Lord Chesterfield that he does not think of him as his patron and that he will certainly not be dedicating his *Dictionary* to him. In the fifth stage there are some further attempts at reconciliation, but it becomes clear that there will never again be a meaningful relationship between them. There was a widespread (and erroneous) belief that Chesterfield later took his revenge on Johnson by describing him as the "respectable Hottentot" in his *Letters to His Natural Son*. There is a contrary story (with some evidence to support it) that Johnson's earlier anger eventually mellowed and that he even took steps to counter the damage that the quarrel had done to Chesterfield's posthumous reputation.[3]

The first question to be asked is: what was it that was known about this quarrel before Boswell appeared on the scene? Boswell after all did not become acquainted with Johnson until May 16, 1763, more than eight years after Johnson sent the famous letter. Our view of the quarrel really begins in the oral tradition, or as Patricia Mayer Spacks would have it, in gossip.[4] Johnson's letter to Lord Chesterfield, after all, was a personal communication between one person and another, and therefore a private matter. Yet William Adams, a close friend of Johnson's for many years, told Boswell that the letter was "the talk of the town" (I, 263). We do not know how it became the talk of the town, but we do know that Johnson confided in David Garrick at the time of the quarrel, and that he apparently told other friends about the letter. We also know that with prompting he would on occasion repeat the letter from memory within his circle of friends. William Cooke mentions an unnamed friend whom he once heard recite part of it from memory.[5] Presumably all this was done in confidence. Nevertheless, the story spread quickly by word of mouth, and soon took on a life of its own.

Chesterfield himself was also a means for spreading the story. We are told that, feigning indifference, he took pains to leave Johnson's letter upon the table in his receiving room for others to see when they visited him at home. We know that Chesterfield personally showed it to Robert Dodsley and pointed out the severest passages. The story, such as it has come down to us, remained a part of the oral tradition for many years before versions of it began to appear in print. In fact, there is no mention of their falling out, and none whatsoever of the famous letter in the first of the biographical accounts of Johnson reprinted by Brack and Kelley in *The Early Biographers of Samuel Johnson*.[6] These documents show the first biographical account appearing in one version in 1764, in another version in 1774, and then in yet another in 1782. It describes Lord Chesterfield as Johnson's patron, but only as the figure to whom he dedicated the *Plan* of the Dictionary in 1747.

The first account in print of the 1755 quarrel can be found in a piece by Isaac Reed that appeared in the *Westminster Magazine* in 1774, almost twenty years later. What is notable about Reed's account is that some of the elements in the Johnson–Chesterfield quarrel are already in place, including Chesterfield's two letters to the *World* and Johnson's repudiation of Lord Chesterfield's patronage. It also quotes a Johnsonian antithesis which had Philip Dormer Stanhope as a wit among lords, but only a lord among wits. The frequency with which this is quoted suggests that it was taken at the time as a deliciously wicked put-down.

> [Johnson's] intimacy with Lord Chesterfield was well known, which he gained by drawing up the original plan of his Dictionary, in a Letter to that Nobleman, who not only assisted him with hints for the Work, but also published two very elegant and friendly letters in a periodical Paper called the *World*, recommending the Doctor to the attention of the Public with great warmth. And here it will be necessary to mention an anecdote, which, if true, will serve as a proof how little the Doctor was inclined to return his Lordship's friendship. – A Gentleman of Dr. Johnson's acquaintance, on the first publication of his Dictionary, asked him, whether he was not in some respect indebted to Lord Chesterfield for assisting him in the Work? "Not at all, Sir (replied Johnson); the fact was only this: I had been sailing round the World of Learning for many years, and just as I got up to the Downs, my Lord Chesterfield sends out two little cock-boats to conduct me up the Thames. My Lord Chesterfield! No, no; he may be a Wit amongst Lords, but I fancy he is no more than a Lord amongst Wits."[7]

Reed goes on to report that Chesterfield took his revenge on Johnson by describing him as a "respectable Hottentot" in one of the letters to his natural son. At best Reed's account makes Johnson seem prickly and stubborn and at worst ill-tempered and boorish. This is largely because Lord Chesterfield's letters to the *World* are presented by Reed as an act of generosity, a large-hearted attempt to promote the work of someone who returned his kindness only with contempt. There is not the slightest hint that there may have been an ulterior motive guiding Lord Chesterfield's actions. What may be more surprising, though, is Reed's silence about the most central matter of all. There is, astonishingly, no reference in his account to Johnson's unpublished letter to Chesterfield repudiating his patronage. However, Reed does introduce details that will become familiar parts of the story. The metaphors of dictionary-making as a sea voyage and Lord Chesterfield's letters to the *World* as cock-boats will be heard again and again. We don't know from whom or how Reed got his information, but a good guess would be that David Garrick was the ultimate source, if not the actual source for Reed. Garrick of course knew Johnson well, and was from all we know Johnson's closest confidant at the time of the quarrel. He was beyond dispute a great story-teller, his penchant for gossip is well documented (I, 99; 290, n. 1), and the material was irresistible.

The next significant account to appear was published in the *Universal*

Magazine in August of 1784, some six months before Johnson died. It was signed at the end with an L; we have no other clue to the identity of the author. Whoever L may have been, he had some interesting things to say about the quarrel.

> Chesterfield, at that time, was universally esteemed the Mecaenas of the age; and it was in that character, no doubt, that Dr. Johnson addressed to him the letter before-mentioned. His Lordship endeavoured to be grateful, by recommending that valuable work in two Essays, which, among others, he published in a paper entitled "The World," conducted by Mr. Edward Moore, and his literary friends. Some time after, however, the Doctor took great offence at being refused admittance to Lord Chesterfield; a circumstance, which has been imputed to the mistake of a porter. Just before the Dictionary was published, Mr. Moore expressed his surprise to the great Lexicographer, that he did not intend to dedicate the book to his Lordship. Mr. Johnson answered, that he was under no obligation to any great man whatever, and therefore he should not make him his patron. "Pardon me, Sir," said Moore, "you are certainly obliged to his Lordship, for two elegant papers he has written in favour of your performance." – "You quite mistake the thing," replied the other; "I confess no obligation; I feel my own dignity, Sir; I have made a Commodore Anson's voyage round the whole world of the English language, and, while I am coming into port, with a fair wind, on a fine sunshining day, my Lord Chesterfield sends out two little cockboats to tow me in. I am very sensible of the favour, Mr. Moore, and should be heartily sorry to say an ill-natured thing of that Nobleman; but I cannot help thinking he is a Lord amongst Wits, and a Wit amongst Lords."
>
> The severity of this remark seems never to have been forgotten by the Earl, who, in one of his Letters to his son, thus delineates the Doctor [as the "respectable Hottentot"].[8]

L sketches out the first stage of the relationship between Johnson and Chesterfield in familiar terms. However, his chronology is uncertain. He is by our notions clearly reversing the second and third stages, thus he has Chesterfield publishing the letters in the *World* before Johnson is refused admittance "by a mistake of a porter." The cause of the quarrel becomes then Johnson's pique at an understandable mistake by one of Lord Chesterfield's servants. L adds a valuable new detail to the early accounts by introducing Edward Moore. He has Moore rebuking Johnson for ingratitude, if not for the earlier favors done by Lord Chesterfield when he accepted the dedication of the *Plan*, then for the "two elegant papers" he had recently published in the *World*. L tells us that Moore was the proprietor and publisher of the *World* and therefore an interested party. Moreover, Moore himself had frequently been the object of Lord Chesterfield's patronage and felt obliged to show himself grateful. It is not clear, however, where L's information comes from, since Moore himself died on March 1, 1757, not long after this incident. Moore is not assigned this role in any other account, except the one by Johnson himself. The first sentence of the yet unpublished letter to Lord Chesterfield mentions a recent conversation with the proprietor of the *World* as the reason for writing the letter when he did. The rest of L's account follows what we have seen in Reed's except that the metaphors of the sea voyage and the cock-boats are much elaborated.

The first biography of Johnson written after his death was that by Thomas Tyers, a graduate of Pembroke College, Oxford. Tyers was about fifteen years younger than Johnson, but he had been an acquaintance of Johnson for more than twenty-five years. Tyers's sketch first appeared in the *Gentleman's Magazine*, soon after Johnson's death on December 13, 1784, and it was later reprinted with some additions in pamphlet form in 1785. The account by Tyers is the first to point to Chesterfield's neglect or indifference as the cause of the quarrel. He is also the first to mention that Johnson had written a letter to Lord Chesterfield renouncing his patronage. Tyers characterizes the letter as "written with great acrimony." It is clear enough that Tyers was better informed about what had happened than any of the biographers who had written before him. It seems likely that his chief source of information was Robert Dodsley, though when and how he got the information is clearly a puzzle because Dodsley had died in 1764, long before Tyers came to write this account. Whatever his sources or resources, Tyers's account is still notable for its vagueness about when things happened and what caused what.

> It does not appear that Lord Chesterfield shewed any substantial proofs of approbation to our philologer, for that was the professional title he chose. A small present he would have disdained. Johnson was not of a temper to put up with the affront of disappointment. He revenged himself in a letter to his lordship, written with great acrimony, and renouncing all acceptance of favour. It was handed about, and probably will be published, for *litera scripta manet*. He used to say, he was mistaken in his choice of a patron, for he had simply been endeavouring to gild a rotten post. An endeavour has been made to procure a copy of [the letter to Lord Chesterfield], in order to afford an abstract to the reader, but without success. Mr. Langton, when applied to, thought he could not grant it without a breach of trust. It is in more hands than one; and, perhaps, where secrecy was not enjoined. Johnson took care to send his letter by a safe hand to lord Chesterfield, who shewed it to [Robert] Dodsley. His lordship defended himself very plausibly against the misstatements of the writer, and candidly pointed out some beautiful sentences and happy expressions. It was a long letter (*grandis epistola*) and written with great asperity. It prevented, as Dodsley reported, the patronage of his lordship, and the benefit from a dedication, which he said would have been the promotion of the sale.[9]

Tyers's account has some merits, but it is nevertheless confused and misleading. Since there is no mention in his account of Chesterfield's two essays in the *World*, the motivation for Johnson's letter shrivels into something small and distasteful, little more than mean-spirited bitterness that Lord Chesterfield had failed to be as open-handed as he was somehow supposed to be. On the other hand, Tyers adds a new name to the participants in these events, that of Robert Dodsley. Since Dodsley was to be one of the publishers, he had a commercial interest in the *Dictionary* and therefore in Lord Chesterfield's patronage. He had acted as the original go-between when Johnson was composing the *Plan*. It was Dodsley who reported having seen Johnson's letter lying about when he visited Lord Chesterfield. Dodsley also had ties with those who were operating and publishing in the *World*. He may not have been central to the unfolding events, but he had a part in several of the scenes.

The first edition of William Cooke's biography was published at almost the same time as that of Tyers. The indications are that Cooke was also personally acquainted with Johnson. Among other things he is listed among the original members of the Essex Head Club that Johnson had formed in 1783. Like the other early biographers, Cooke mentions the dedication of the *Plan* to Chesterfield. He then goes on to describe the patron's coolness and neglect after initially encouraging the project, and finally the two letters in the *World* which were intended to make up for the earlier neglect. Cooke reports Johnson's contemptuous remarks about Chesterfield in conversation, repeating the description of the letters to the *World* as "*two little Cock-boats*, vainly sent out to partake the triumphs of a long and dangerous voyage, without risquing the hazards of rocks and quicksands."[10] What may be most noticeable, however, in Cooke's account is his description of the unpublished letter Johnson sent to Chesterfield, a description that makes his account much closer to the facts as we now know them than the account in Tyers.

> Mr. Johnson was not even satisfied with using the shafts of ridicule in conversation, but resented his usage of him in a letter which he wrote his lordship, *insisting on being for ever dismissed his patronage*: this letter I have not seen, but once heard a friend, to whom he read it, repeat some of it from memory; and it seemed to breathe a spirit of independence, that did great honour to the author's mind: for many years Mr. Johnson refused giving a copy of it; but some time before his death, he gave one to Mr. Langton, with an injunction never to publish it until an imperfect copy first appeared, which he judged might be the case, as he had often repeated it to several friends.
>
> Lord Chesterfield, too late, found out the error of neglecting a man of genius, and wanted to court Mr. Johnson back to his patronage, through the mediation of Mr. [Robert] Dodsley – but in vain: Johnson was not to be shaken from his purpose; and they never spoke together afterwards.[11]

There is some progress among the early biographers, but it is fitful at best. Those who came later only occasionally took advantage of what could be learned from those who had written before them, so confusion continues to be the norm. The biography by Joseph Towers, published in 1786, for example, makes no mention of Lord Chesterfield's essays in the *World*, nor is there any reference to Johnson's unpublished letter to Chesterfield, though the information on both these matters was available to him. On the other hand, Towers comes closer than any of the other early biographers to our view of the quarrel when he has Johnson refusing to dedicate the *Dictionary* to Chesterfield, despite the dedication of the *Plan*, because Chesterfield had failed to act the part of a patron.[12]

There are a couple of new twists in the biography by William Mavor, published by James Harrison at the beginning of a 1786 edition of Johnson's *Dictionary*.[13] In it Colley Cibber's name first appears in print. Up until now Johnson had been kept waiting or was rebuffed "by the mistake of a porter"; with the Mavor/Harrison biography Johnson's anger becomes an outraged reaction to public humiliation, to having someone whose name was then synonymous with bad poetry, the very king of the dunces, preferred before him. In this version Johnson also writes a letter to Chesterfield, a letter that renounces his patronage, but he writes the letter because he is incensed at being turned away from Chesterfield's door for the likes of Colley Cibber. Mavor also tells us that Lord Chesterfield tried to soothe Johnson's hurt pride with an apology, and asked Sir Thomas Robinson and Sir Joshua Reynolds to act as go-betweens. Johnson would not of course accept the apology, but this was, according to Mavor, how he first became acquainted with Joshua Reynolds, later one of his closest and most trusted friends. When the apology failed to gain its object, Chesterfield then sent "an essay" to the *World*, in an effort to win him back with praise. But that too proved futile: "Johnson was not to be appeased."[14]

Perhaps it is not so surprising that the accounts of Johnson's quarrel with Lord Chesterfield in the early biographies should be so flawed. Many of them, as Brack and Kelley readily admit, were hasty efforts where information was being gathered to meet a pressing journalistic deadline. Moreover, there is very little evidence that any of the early biographers, with the possible exception of Thomas Tyers, knew Johnson particularly well. William Shaw and Joseph Towers could claim to have been in Johnson's company on occasions, but William Cooke despite having his name on the list of the Essex Head Club remains a shadowy figure, and William Mavor even more so. None of this would be true about the major biographers, and it is only natural to expect more from them as we try to solve the puzzles that surround the quarrel.

Oddly enough, we do not get any help from Hester Thrale Piozzi. There is no mention whatsoever of the quarrel with Chesterfield in the *Anecdotes*. This may not be as surprising as it might seem at first if we consider that the stories that comprise her biographical account deal with a different sphere of Johnson's life. Moreover, the stories that she does tell date for the most part from the time of her and her husband's first meeting with Johnson in January

1765, and that is nearly ten years after the composition of the famous letter. The quarrel with Lord Chesterfield would have been as much a part of Johnson's past to the newly married Mrs. Thrale as his marriage or his years of penury. For all that, though, her silence is disquieting. It is hard to believe that the quarrel was never discussed, or that nothing noteworthy was ever even said about it.

Sir John Hawkins represents quite a different case. Of all of Johnson's numerous London acquaintances it was Hawkins who accepted the task of composing a full-length biography of his friend, one that would account for all parts of Johnson's life. Hawkins was in a particularly good position to do this because he had known Johnson for forty-five years or more, their acquaintance going back at least to the days when they both worked for Cave on the *Gentleman's Magazine.* Moreover, Hawkins's position as one of the executors of Johnson's will gave him unusual access to the papers that Johnson had left behind. For these very substantial reasons Hawkins is generally considered the most serious rival to Boswell's pride of place as a biographer of Johnson. We have every right to expect much of Hawkins, and in fact Donald Greene has told us to prefer him over Boswell,[15] especially and particularly for anything that occurred before May 16, 1763, when Boswell met Johnson for the first time. If that is so, Hawkins's account should be especially worthwhile when it comes to the quarrel with Lord Chesterfield. The quarrel, after all, had occurred well before Boswell had even met Johnson, but at a time when Hawkins was from everything we can gather still very much a part of Johnson's circle of acquaintances.

Hawkins does offer a full account of Johnson's quarrel with Lord Chesterfield, but one that proves to be poorly informed. We find first that Hawkins was attracted to what he took to be the dramatic elements in the story, to the clash, if you will, between the "scholar" and the "courtier," "the one ignorant of the forms and modes of address, the other, to an affected degree, accomplished in both."[16] But before coming to the moment of the clash, Sir John wants to prepare us with a full sketch of Lord Chesterfield. He uses this occasion to let us know his disgust with Chesterfield's fondness for seduction and dissimulation. He also takes time to scold Chesterfield for publicly acknowledging an illegitimate child, an unpardonable breach of propriety from Hawkins's point of view.

Hawkins leads into his account of the quarrel with this transitional sentence, "Such was the person whom Johnson in the simplicity of his heart chose for a patron, and was betrayed to celebrate as the Maecenas of the age; and such was the opinion he had conceived of his skill, his love of eloquence, and his zeal for the interests of learning, that he approached him with the utmost respect, and that he might not err in his manner of expressing it, the style and language of that address which his plan includes are little less than adulatory" (pp. 188–9). This analysis is seriously flawed by most measures.

To describe Johnson as "choosing" Lord Chesterfield as his patron is not consistent with the facts as we know them, and it is not probable on the surface of things. Dedicating the *Plan* to Chesterfield was almost certainly Dodsley's idea. That Johnson went along with Dodsley is understandable, for where else was the funding to come from for a long-term project like a dictionary of the English language? We might also want to question the "simplicity" of Johnson's heart on this matter, never mind the notion that he was almost overcome at the thought of having a patron.

Hawkins's unexacting attitude about the basic facts of what he is recounting leads him into serious errors. According to Hawkins, for example, the quarrrel began when

> Johnson one day made [Lord Chesterfield] a morning visit, and being admitted into an antechamber, was told, that his lordship was engaged with a gentleman, and would see him as soon as the gentleman went. It was not till after an hour's waiting that Johnson discovered that this gentleman was Colley Cibber, which he had no sooner done, than he rushed out of the house with a resolution never to enter it more. (p. 189)

Hawkins next mentions that Johnson "expressed in a letter to his lordship himself his resentment of the affront he had received at his last visit, and concluded it with a formal renunciation forever of his lordship's patronage." All this, according to Hawkins, took place in the year 1747, more than seven years before the letter actually renouncing Lord Chesterfield's patronage would be written and sent.

The implications of what Hawkins is saying are probably worse than his bungled account of the facts. As with William Mavor, Johnson's magnificent letter to Lord Chesterfield is shrunk to the dimensions of the narrow and the small, becoming little more than an expression of Johnson's outrage over being snubbed in favor of Colley Cibber. The two gushing letters to the *World*, we learn, did not provoke the quarrel; they are described as coming after the letter and therefore as an attempt to smooth it over. According to Hawkins, they are an act of generosity on Lord Chesterfield's part, his attempt to pour the soothing ointment of flattery over a smart to ridiculously tender pride. When the letters to the *World* had no apparent effect, Hawkins, like Mavor before him, reports that Chesterfield made further attempts at reconciliation, again sending emissaries to Johnson, one of them "a well known painter," the other Sir Thomas Robinson, a former governor of the Barbadoes. But, as we know, Johnson's stubborn sense of injury would not tolerate any further compromise of his dignity, and he refused the offered apology. Hawkins does add a new detail to Mavor's account by having Johnson threaten to throw Robinson down the stairs.[17] Chesterfield would have his revenge on the upstart Johnson for his boorish behavior when, according to Hawkins, he describes him as a "respectable Hottentot," in one of the letters to his natural son, a passage that Sir John quotes in full.

The matter of tone may not be a question of right or wrong, but Hawkins is not very satisfactory on this account if only for his inconsistency. He can be warmly sympathetic at one moment, only to turn icy and patronizing at the next. So after seeming to applaud Johnson's grit in standing up to Chesterfield, we come upon a startling reversal in tone in the analogy that follows. In it Johnson becomes a gardener's dog that has fallen into a well. Lord Chesterfield becomes a passer-by who has heard the dog's cries for help. The passer-by reaches his hand down into the well to save the drowning dog, only to have his hand bitten by a now maddened dog (p. 193). Is he praising Johnson? Or blaming him? Possibly both, but there appears to be more blame than praise, meaning that Hawkins would now have Johnson lap the hand that two pages earlier he had cheered him for biting. It is for reasons such as this that Hawkins has had so few friends in our times.

What becomes clear when we come to Boswell is that his account of the quarrel differs in major ways from the earlier accounts. He assigns the origins of it, like all the others, to Johnson's dedication of the *Plan* to Lord Chesterfield in 1747. However, he introduces a new detail. He mentions in a note that Johnson was in fact the beneficiary of Lord Chesterfield's patronage on one occasion. He did in fact receive a gift of £10 from Lord Chesterfield when the Earl first accepted the dedication of the *Plan*. We ought not to dismiss a gift of £10 cavalierly. Ten pounds, though a long way from riches, was clearly a significant amount of money for someone in Johnson's circumstances.[18] That is readily apparent when we consider that he received the sum total of five guineas for his translation of Father Lobo's *Voyage* in 1735, ten guineas for his poem *London* in 1737, and fifteen for *The Vanity of Human Wishes* in 1749.

Boswell's next step is to undo the apocryphal story that made Johnson's anger the catalyst for the quarrel. According to that story, Johnson was furious at being kept waiting in Chesterfield's anteroom, but once he discovered that he had been kept waiting while his lordship talked with Colley Cibber his anger exploded and he stormed out of the door. Boswell was eager to discredit this story, seemingly validated by Hawkins, because its thrust, as he clearly recognized, was one that diminished Johnson, making the cause of the quarrel no more than an unintended slight to petty pride. Boswell's ability to discredit this story single-handedly, especially a story that had been so long believed and so widely cherished, underscores his special strength as Johnson's biographer. All the previous biographers, but especially Tyers, Mrs. Thrale, and Hawkins, had spent a great deal of time in Johnson's company. But only Boswell had taken the pains to ask Johnson if the story about Colley Cibber was true. Johnson had assured him on April 7, 1773 that "there was not the least foundation for it." He went on to say, "There never was any particular incident which produced a quarrel between

Lord Chesterfield and him; but that his Lordship's continued neglect was the reason why he resolved to have no connection with him."[19] With the fanciful story about Colley Cibber put aside, we are now prepared to take a more sober view of the quarrel.

The reason for the quarrel, according to Boswell, lay in events that immediately preceded the publication of the *Dictionary*. The appearance of the two papers in the *World* was sufficient indication that Chesterfield still entertained the notion that Johnson would dedicate his *Dictionary* to him. Much has been made about the long gap between the appearance of those two issues of the *World* (November 28, 1754; the other a week later, December 5) and the date of Johnson's letter to Chesterfield (the first week of February 1755). A lapse of six or more weeks, we are told, is simply too great for us to believe that the essays in the *World* were what truly provoked Johnson into writing his letter, that something else must have happened, and the essays in the *World* could only be the pretext.[20]

Such speculation, however, assumes that Johnson read the essays or heard about them soon after they were published.[21] Perhaps, but perhaps not. Though none of the early accounts says so explicitly, most of them seem to suggest that Johnson did not come upon the essays in the *World* on his own. In some of the accounts we are told he was first informed that two essays had appeared in the *World* that were enthusiastically endorsing his forthcoming *Dictionary* and that these essays, though anonymous, were in fact by Lord Chesterfield. Johnson himself mentions being told about the Chesterfield essays by Edward Moore, the proprietor of the *World*, and he was un-doubtedly also told by Robert Dodsley.[22] It is also possible there were others. In fact, the sheer number of voices reporting the news of the recent puffs in the *World* may have been what focused Johnson's attention on what was happening. If we allow that Johnson was likely to have been preoccupied with the final preparations for printing the *Dictionary* and that he did not rush out to read the essays in the *World*, and/or that he may not have realized immediately that their real purpose was a proud lord's indirect bid for a dedication, and/or that he needed some time to think over what he wanted to say and how he wanted to say it, we have an ample number of ways to explain the six- or seven-week delay between the appearance of the essays in the *World* and Johnson's letter to Lord Chesterfield. In short, we have no good reason to suspect or to challenge the cause-and-effect relationship between the essays in the *World* and the letter that Boswell postulates in his account.

If we want to have a better sense of Boswell's value to Johnsonian biography, we can now look at what he contributed to our understanding of the Johnson–Chesterfield quarrel in each of its five stages. Much of what we know as well as what they knew was rooted in the oral tradition, with all the hazards attendant upon that. Moreover, many of the key figures – Edward

Moore, Robert Dodsley, Lord Chesterfield himself – were dead before there was any attempt to produce a written record of the events. Perhaps for that reason all of Johnson's various biographers, including Boswell, seem to have had only a hazy notion of the origins of the relationship between Johnson and Lord Chesterfield. Boswell along with the others traced the origins of the 1755 quarrel back to 1747 and Johnson's decision to dedicate the *Plan* to Chesterfield.[23] However, no one before Boswell mentions the gift of ten pounds, nor does anybody place much emphasis on what is probably the crucial role played by Robert Dodsley in fashioning a relationship between the two. The picture of the motives of the two principals is much more confusing. Most of the early biographers have Johnson more than happy to have a patron, particularly one as distinguished and munificent as Lord Chesterfield was reputed to be, whereas the truth is probably the opposite. If we look back to what Johnson had to say about patrons and patronage in his *Life of Savage* published in 1744, it is clear that he was far from naive about the unhappy side of relationships between authors and patrons.

All of the early biographers report a falling out between the two in the second stage. Some assign the reason for the falling out to a specific incident of apparent rudeness, whereas Boswell maintains that it was "continued neglect," or, more accurately, Chesterfield failing to live up to his reputation as a generous patron. A surprising number of the early biographers seem anxious to exonerate Lord Chesterfield, usually by attributing any seeming coldness on his part to unfortunate "misunderstandings."

The third stage of the quarrel begins with Chesterfield's letters to the *World* in late 1754, and at this point the picture is almost total confusion before Boswell. Virtually all of the early biographers refer to Chesterfield's letters in the *World* in praise of the *Dictionary*, and many of them portray Johnson as an ingrate for what they considered to be an extraordinary act of disinterested kindness. Hawkins and Cooke confuse the picture even more when they describe the letters to the *World* as Chesterfield's attempt to win Johnson back after he had already renounced his patronage.

The fourth stage is of course Boswell's triumph as a biographer. After all, we have the text of the letter Johnson sent to Lord Chesterfield in February of 1775 primarily if not exclusively because of him. When the early biographers had any real picture of what had happened between the two, it was that a letter had been sent. Their guesses at what the letter actually contained were typically wide of the mark. Boswell had first acquired the text of the letter when he persuaded Johnson to dictate a copy to him from memory on June 4, 1781 while they were at Southill in Bedfordshire visiting with John Dilly, elder brother of the Edward and Charles Dilly of the Poultry (IV, 128). In other words, because of Boswell posterity finally had a copy of the text of the famous letter. Still, it was a copy that dated from more than sixteen years after the event.

Some time after dictating this copy to Boswell, Johnson came across a copy he had dictated to Giuseppe Baretti at a much earlier date. We know remarkably little about how this copy came into being, why Johnson would have thought it important to dictate a copy, or even when he did. We do know that Johnson first became acquainted with Baretti some time after he arrived in England in 1750. We do not know exactly when they became acquainted,[24] but it was well before the publication of the *Dictionary* in 1755. It seems likely that Johnson dictated this copy to Baretti soon after he had sent the original to Lord Chesterfield, but it is possible that a substantial amount of time passed before he realized that he should have a copy of what had become a famous letter. In any event, this is the copy that he turned over to Bennet Langton for safe keeping sometime in 1784. When it came time to publish the *Life* Boswell secured this "more authentic" copy from Langton and checked it against the version that had been dictated to him in 1781. He then published the copy given to Langton, first separately in 1790, and then as part of the *Life* in 1791.

The fifth stage, the final and futile attempts to reconcile after the letter, is more curious because there seems to be no satisfactory account of these events. Boswell allows the Rev. William Adams a role in trying to reconcile Johnson and Lord Chesterfield, but Adams is not assigned a role of any moment by anyone else. William Mavor and Sir John Hawkins together provide some interesting information on further efforts by Chesterfield at reconciliation. In the 1950s Sledd and Kolb were willing to credit an un-published letter by John Douglas that claims that Sir Thomas Robinson passed on a message from Chesterfield to Johnson that so melted his heart that he could never be angry at Chesterfield again.[25] Douglas's report is not at all consistent with what Hawkins has to say about Sir Thomas's visit, when far from melting him, Sir Thomas only succeeded in making Johnson furious. On the other hand, Douglas's letter could be referring to an altogether different visit, at a much later time. Moreover, a marked softening of Johnson's anger is consistent with Boswell's observations. He reports that Johnson did mellow toward Chesterfield. That mellowing would also be consistent with his documented reluctance to have the letter to Lord Chesterfield made public. Furthermore, no one any longer believes that the portrait of the respectable Hottentot was Chesterfield's revenge on Johnson, since it is now a matter of record that it was intended to be a portrait of George, Lord Lyttleton (I, 267, n. 2).

The real questions about Boswell's account are a few omissions.[26] He does not tell us how Johnson found out about the essays in the *World*, perhaps because he was counting on our noticing what Johnson had to say in the letter. In any event, he gives no attention to Moore's role in the matter, even though he would have known from the account by L in the *Universal Magazine* that Johnson had learned about the essays and their author from

Moore, not to mention Johnson's own testimony in the text of the letter. Nor does Boswell mention any active role by Robert Dodsley. He restricts Dodsley by and large to the role of dupe to Lord Chesterfield, though Dodsley was clearly an interested party in the unfolding events. Instead of relying on information from or about Moore or Dodsley, Boswell relies on what he was told by William Adams who was in London about the time the letter was sent. Adams seems to have been a reliable source, but it is far from clear how or why his testimony would be superior in this instance to that of either Moore or Dodsley, or their associates.

Boswell also fails to mention that Chesterfield made further attempts to appease Johnson by sending at least two persons as his personal emissaries, identified by Hawkins as Sir Thomas Robinson, a Yorkshire baronet "whose talent was flattery," the other "an eminent painter now living," said by William Mavor to be Sir Joshua Reynolds. Perhaps Boswell was afraid that by dwelling on further attempts at reconciliation he might create some undeserved sympathy for the Earl, or perhaps he was not sure of the accuracy of the information at hand. In any event, he did leave these out of his account, and the omissions are curious. It is also worth mentioning that Boswell was the first to report reservations that the portrait of "the respectable Hottentot" was really Chesterfield's revenge on Johnson, something that is repeated as an unquestionable truth by virtually every biographer who preceded him. Finally, it was Boswell who first pointed out the substitution of "*patron*" for "*garret*" in 1. 160 of *The Vanity of Human Wishes* in all the editions of the poem published after the quarrel.[27]

If we are concerned with what kind of standing we should assign Boswell as a biographer, it is only fair to point out that he did what none of his predecessors had done. He supplied new information about the quarrel that corrected serious errors in the widespread popular version. Secondly, and more importantly, Boswell was the first to put the events of the quarrel in their proper order, and this despite the fact that virtually every biographer before him had emphasized the importance of the sequence of events leading up to the quarrel. Clearly, we must have the correct sequence if we are to see the cause-and-effect relationship between Lord Chesterfield's essays in the *World* and Johnson's letter rejecting his patronage. Thirdly, it is worth noting that Boswell is the only one of the early biographers who leaves us room to make our own judgement. He not only tells us about the essays in the *World*, he provides us with full quotations from them so that we can, if we want, take our own measure of Chesterfield's honeyed words. Lastly, and most obviously, Boswell is the first of Johnson's biographers to supply the text of the letter Johnson actually sent to Chesterfield. It was not handed to him – he worked to obtain it. If there had been no Boswell, the most famous letter in English literature might never have seen the light of day.

Curiously, though, there seem be some who secretly wish that we had never heard of Lord Chesterfield. They hold dear another picture of Johnson, and the Chesterfield episode is at odds with it. If the Johnson one cares about is Johnson the great moral teacher or a religious Johnson, then a Johnson quarreling with an English lord can be distracting or even embarrassing. Nor does the firm and decisive Johnson of the letter to Lord Chesterfield fit well into the picture of Johnson agonistes tortured by self-demand. Perhaps we are not then really talking about biography when we discuss the biography of Johnson; perhaps what we are really talking about is the picture of Johnson we prefer and the one we would like to see others admire. If that is so, the interesting questions become which picture is it that matters and why.

If that is what our discourse is really about, then the Johnson who quarreled with Lord Chesterfield really is part of the phenomenon referred to as "Boswell's Johnson." The account of the quarrel does not come to us solely or exclusively from Boswell, but the account of it that is fixed in our collective memory does. Nor is it hard to see why this Johnson has so long held pride of place. For a Johnson willing to stand up to a proud and somewhat devious English lord is a far more engaging, more inspiring figure than one who gnaws at himself in his diaries and prayers.

What may be more interesting yet is that the individual who brought this Johnson to our attention is not the biographer we might have thought would have done it. In many ways Boswell had led a spoiled, even pampered existence, entitled as he was to all the perquisites that come with wealth and position even when they are on a modest scale. In fact, pride about his aristocratic heritage is one of Boswell's distinguishing marks as a writer. If he had followed only his cultural bias, then, we might have expected him to have identified with the polished and elegant English earl when he found himself entangled in an unpleasant quarrel with a pretentious upstart. But he did not. Boswell identified strongly with the unpolished, inelegant son of a provincial bookseller. Moreover, his personal involvement in the events of the quarrel was authentic and deeply felt.

Undoubtedly there are many reasons for that. Perhaps he was revenging himself for all the slights and snubs he had received from those above him on the social scale. The incident also has unmistakable Oedipal overtones, and it is possible it represented the successful rebellion he yearned for against the tyranny of his own father. Whatever the reasons, it seems clear that he saw there was something more at stake in these events than just their literal meaning. Perhaps that explains why it was so important to him that he get the story right.

NOTES

1 *Life*, v, 130, n. 3. All future references to *Life* will be included in the text.
2 The most notable of these are the attacks by Donald Greene and Richard

Schwartz. Greene has carried on his assault on Boswell's *Life* in many places and by varied means. His most concentrated attack, however, is probably the essay "'Tis a Pretty Book, Mr. Boswell, But – ," originally published in 1978 in the *Georgia Review*, but recently reprinted in *New Questions, New Answers*, pp. 110–42. Richard Schwartz has employed an equal amount of ingenuity in attacking Boswell's *Life*, but the flavor of his arguments is captured best in *Boswell's Johnson: A Preface to the "Life"* (Madison: University of Wisconsin Press, 1978).

3 The evidence for mellowing comes from an unpublished letter by John Douglas. See James H. Sledd and Gwin Kolb, *Dr. Johnson's Dictionary: Essays in the Biography of a Book* (Chicago: University of Chicago Press, 1955), pp. 102–3. Douglas's testimony is corroborated by Boswell's report of an occasion when the Bishop of Salisbury asked Johnson if he would be willing to show the letter, and Johnson's reply was "No, Sir; I have hurt the dog too much already" (*Life*, I, 260, n. 3).

4 Patricia Meyer Spacks, *Gossip* (New York: Knopf, 1985). There need be no doubt that the story of Johnson's quarrel with Lord Chesterfield existed first as gossip and then as legend well before it took written form. A wonderful piece of evidence for this comes in one of Boswell's journals, an incident that occurred in May 12, 1778. Boswell had been visiting with Hugh Hume-Campbell, Lord Marchmont, to urge him to share his personal knowledge of Alexander Pope with Johnson, then writing his life of Pope. Marchmont was clearly skittish about working with Johnson: "'So (said his Lordship) you would put me in a dangerous situation. You know he knocked down Osborne the bookseller.'" When Boswell tempered his proposal to a suggestion that he bring Johnson "to wait on" his Lordship, Marchmont replied: "If he should be kept waiting a little, there might be a quarrel, as with Lord Chesterfield" (*Boswell in Extremes*, p. 336).

5 Cooke's report is consistent with others of how the story got about. We are told, for instance, Johnson repeated it from memory to his friend the Rev. William Adams shortly after it had been sent. "When Dr. Adams first spoke to Dr. Johnson of his letter to Lord Chesterfield there was somebody present. Dr. Johnson took him into the next room and repeated it from beginning to end" (*Corr: Life*, p. 25).

6 These are items nos. 1, 2, and 3 in *The Early Biographers of Samuel Johnson*, ed. O M Brack, Jr. and Robert E. Kelley (Iowa City: University of Iowa Press, 1974), p. 102.

7 From item no. 4 in *The Early Biographers*, pp. 16–17.

8 From item no. 7 in *The Early Biographers*, p. 38.

9 From item no. 9 in *The Early Biographers*, pp. 69–70. This passage as quoted was printed in the biographical sketch by Tyers that appeared in the December 1784 issue of the *Gentleman's Magazine*. However, the text printed in Brack and Kelley continues with additions that appeared only in the pamphlet version that was published six months later in 1785.

10 From item no. 10 in *The Early Biographers*, p. 102.

11 From item no. 10, p. 102.

12 From item no. 12 in *The Early Biographers*, p. 197.

13 J. D. Fleeman pointed out this mistake in the attribution in his review of *The Early Biographers* in *Modern Language Review*, 71 (1976), 138. David Nichol Smith first

identified William Mavor as the actual author of the Harrison biography in the *Bodleian Quarterly Record*, 6 (1931), 259–60.

14 In item no. 14 in *The Early Biographers*, p. 268.

15 Donald Greene, "Reflections on a Literary Anniversary," *Queen's Quarterly*, 70 (1963), 198–208; reprinted in *Twentieth Century Interpretations of Boswell's "Life of Johnson*," ed. James L. Clifford (Englewood Cliffs, N.J.: Prentice-Hall, 1970), pp. 97–103.

16 Sir John Hawkins, *The Life of Samuel Johnson, LL.D.* (1787; rept. New York: Garland, 1974), p. 176. All further citations from Hawkins's *Life* will be from this facsimile edition.

17 Bertram Davis believes that Hawkins too may have had help from the Rev. William Adams. *Johnson before Boswell: A Study of Sir John Hawkins' "Life of Samuel Johnson"* (New Haven: Yale University Press, 1960), p. 46. However, none of the information that sets Boswell's account apart from the others is to be found in Hawkins, not even the Adams story that had been added to the pamphlet version of Tyers's biographical sketch.

18 For an informative discussion of Johnson's earnings shortly after he arrived in London, see Thomas Kaminski, *The Early Career of Samuel Johnson* (New York: Oxford University Press, 1987), pp. 73–6.

19 *Defence*, pp. 168–9.

20 Paul Korshin finds enough evidence in the delay to argue that the letter was really the final result of his growing disgust with Chesterfield's politics. See "The Johnson–Chesterfield Relationship: A New Hypothesis," *PMLA*, 85 (1970), 247–59. Howard Weinbrot has suggested that Johnson's anger was intellectual in character. He found his view of language was hopelessly at odds with the view that he had once expressed in the *Plan*, the same view that informed Chesterfield's essays in *The World*. See "Johnson's *Dictionary* and *The World*: The Papers of Lord Chesterfield and Richard Owen Cambridge," *Philological Quarterly*, 50 (1971), 663–9. Elizabeth Hedrick has expanded considerably on Weinbrot's suggestion in 'Fixing the Language: Johnson, Chesterfield, and *The Plan of a Dictionary*," *ELH*, 55 (1988), 421–2.

21 Johnson's letters, at least as they have come down to us, shed no light on the quarrel. There is not a single reference to the essays in *The World* or to Lord Chesterfield in the letters we have that were written around this time. What letters we do have would seem to indicate that Johnson's major concern at the time was securing a diploma from Oxford that would allow him to have the letters A. M. after his name on the title page of the *Dictonary*.

22 For a recent examination of the information we have on Dodsley, see Lois M. G. Spencer, "Robert Dodsley and the Johnsonian Connection," *New Rambler*, C:18 (1977), 1–16.

23 Sledd and Kolb believe there is evidence that points to an earlier date, that Chesterfield's corrections are to be found in a manuscript copy of an earlier version of the *Plan* called the *Scheme*. That would push back the date of the beginning of their relationship by almost a year. See *Dr. Johnson's Dictionary*, pp. 90, 96–7.

24 There seem to be some differences about when Johnson and Baretti first met. According to Sir James Prior, it would have been as early as the fall of 1751 (I,

223, n. 2). According to Walter Jackson Bate, it was in 1753. *Samuel Johnson* (New York: Harcourt Brace Jovanovich, 1977), p. 333. According to James L. Clifford, it was late in 1752 or early in 1753. *Dictionary Johnson* (New York: McGraw-Hill, 1979), p. 128.

25 Sledd and Kolb, *Dr. Johnson's Dictionary*, pp. 102–3.

26 It is certainly legitimate to wonder what Boswell's revisions might reveal about how he reconstructed the events of the quarrel. Thanks to the generosity of Rachel McClellan, managing editor of the Boswell project at Yale, and to the staff of the Beinecke Library, I have had the opportunity to examine those portions of the manuscript version of the *Life* that are directly relevant to the quarrel. It is my conclusion that Boswell's revisions in this part of the *Life* do not seem to involve matters of substance. For instance, in the manuscript version after he quotes Dodsley's report telling how Chesterfield had pointed out to him the severest passages in the letter and praised their strong expression, we have this sentence: "This unconcerned air, which imposed upon the worthy Dodsley, was certainly nothing but a specimen of that address which he [Lord Chesterfield] inculcated as one of the most essential lessons for the conduct of life." When revising this passage Boswell changed "this unconcerned air" to "this air of indifference," and "a specimen of that address" to "a specimen of that dissimulation." It seems fair enough to describe such changes as stylistic improvements, but I would not characterize them as substantive changes.

27 "Patron" was first substituted for "garret" in a revised text of *The Vanity of Human Wishes* printed in Dodsley's *Collection of Poems*, 1755. See the Hill–Powell edition, I, 264, n. 4.

11

SELF-RESTRAINT AND SELF-DISPLAY
IN THE AUTHORIAL COMMENTS IN THE
LIFE OF JOHNSON

Marlies K. Danziger

Readers of the *Life of Johnson* are immediately aware of Boswell's presence
not only as a participant in scenes and conversations with Johnson but also as
a later self engaged in the process of writing and rethinking his material. His
authorial comments have been deplored as "annoying" and "a continuing
nuisance" for both their content and their tone.[1] But a closer scrutiny of the
text shows that such "Boswellian intrusions after the fact"[2] are not all of the
same kind – that although some indeed consist of unabashed self-display,
others are deliberately reticent. Examples of his self-display are not hard to
find, especially in the notorious passages on slavery and the French
Revolution. But if we focus on less familiar authorial comments, limiting
ourselves to those about his personal and professional life and his opinions as
a Scotsman, we will find a greater moderation in the way he presents himself.
Moreover, by taking into account Boswell's experiences while he was
working on the *Life*, as revealed in his last journals and correspondence, we
may be able to read some of the authorial comments – without ignoring their
shortcomings – with greater understanding and even, in some instances, with
greater sympathy.

In writing and revising the *Life*, Boswell was well aware of the danger of
seeming too intrusive and particularly of including too much about his
personal affairs. The biting attack in a pamphlet by "Verax" on his *Journal
of a Tour to the Hebrides* (1785), ridiculing his "egregious vanity,"[3] and the
comment on his egotism in the *English Review* of November 1785 must have
rankled; he kept both the pamphlet and the review among his papers (now at
Yale University). In the *Tour* he had not hesitated to pay a fulsome tribute to
his wife Margaret for giving up their bedchamber during Johnson's visit –
and, indeed, for marrying him in the first place. And he had made much of
the infant Veronica's gurgling attention to Johnson.[4] Edmond Malone, while
helping Boswell to revise the *Tour*, had objected to this episode, considering
it too personal and trivial; he wished, with their mutual friend John
Courtenay, "that Veronica had been left quietly in her nursery."[5] Malone
had also warned Boswell against letting one thought lead him to another and

called one of Boswell's more far-fetched digressions an "excrescence."[6]

Whether by his own inclination or because of these warnings, Boswell repeatedly made an effort not to intrude his private concerns in the *Life*. Asking his friend Sir William Forbes for copies of Johnson's and Forbes's letters about Boswell's coming to the English Bar, he wrote: "though as they entirely concern myself, I should think I ought not to insert them in my book";[7] and, indeed, he ultimately did not include these letters. In his Dedication to Sir Joshua Reynolds, furthermore, he declares that, having been mistaken for a fool by some of the readers of his *Tour*, he has been "more reserved" in the *Life*, and that although he has told "nothing but the truth," he has not always told "the whole truth" (i, 4). Within the text, when he discusses his family's affairs at some length in connection with the principle of entail, Boswell begins his presentation by explaining that he would not "obtrude [this matter] upon the world" were it not for Johnson's interesting ideas on the subject (ii, 412–13). Eventually, close to the end, Boswell formally states that he will now "relieve the readers of this Work of any farther personal notice of its authour" and hopes they will not consider him "to have obtruded himself too much upon their attention" (iv, 380). Clearly Boswell felt the need to apologize when he shifted his focus away from Johnson and on to himself.

Perhaps it was these qualms that caused Boswell's remarkable self-restraint in his presentation of Margaret Boswell in the *Life*. Although she is discussed in his own and Johnson's letters, Boswell does not mention that while he was working on his draft of the *Life*, he was living through the last stages of her consumption and that he was torn by conflicting emotions: apprehension about her impending death, hope that she would survive the next bout of illness, and guilt about neglecting her. Only once does he allude to her death, which occurred in June 1789.

We can appreciate how great was Boswell's self-control and how reluctant he was to reveal his feelings about Margaret in the *Life* by considering two authorial comments about dying and grief. When he discusses Johnson's *Life of Edward Young*, Boswell expresses his own admiration for "Night Thoughts," particularly for its "power of the *Pathetick*," and singles out one scene that must have touched him personally. But he couches his appreciation in deliberately impersonal terms:

> He who does not feel his nerves shaken, and his heart pierced by many passages in this extraordinary work, particularly by that most affecting one, which describes the gradual torment suffered by the contemplation of an object of affectionate attachment, visibly and certainly decaying into dissolution, must be of a hard and obstinate frame. (iv, 61)[8]

With his highly generalized diction, Boswell suggests his own strong feelings but avoids any direct expression of them. The phrasing may strike modern readers as excessively abstract and elevated, but to Boswell and his readers this experiment in the Johnsonian style would have seemed quite appropriate to the solemn subject.

Some pages later, describing his visit with Johnson to the house in which Young had lived, Boswell records their discussion of Young's melancholy. Johnson declares it a regrettable lack of acceptance of Providence "to be gloomy because he has not obtained as much preferment as he expected...[or] to continue gloomy for the loss of his wife" and adds, "Grief has its time." Boswell, in retrospect differing from Johnson, finds the last remark purely theoretical. "Practically, we know that grief for the loss of a wife may be continued very long, in proportion as affection has been sincere. No man knew this better than Dr. Johnson" (IV, 121). Here again Boswell refrains from revealing his own feelings, the strong pangs of grief he was still experiencing when he revised this passage for the press; as late as March 17, 1791, for instance, he writes in his journal: "It is impossible to describe fully what I suffer...My thoughts are agitated with gloom and regret and tender sensation...The dismal circumstance that I am *never again* to have her cheering and affectionate society in this world is so afflicting that I am amazed how I can for a moment forget it, or ever be in the smallest degree easy."[9] Yet in the Young episode in the *Life* he applies his observation only to Johnson. That his silence about his personal feelings is deliberate is indicated by the fact that he omits the additional detail, recorded in the journal entry he is transcribing, that his visit to Young's house reminds him of the pleasure with which he and Margaret read "Night Thoughts" together.[10]

The one specific reference to his wife's death that Boswell permits himself is very brief indeed. After quoting Johnson's warning, in a letter of January 5, 1782, that losing Margaret would be like losing an anchor and being "tost, without stability, by the waves of life," Boswell adds a poignant footnote: "The truth of this has been proved by sad experience" (IV, 136). Again the personal statement, which sounds as if Boswell were completing to himself the thought that Johnson had begun for him, is expressed only in dignified abstract terms. Later, in a last-minute insertion in his "Additions" to the second edition (published in 1793, two years after the first edition), Boswell slips in an allusion to the spirit of Margaret. Having quoted a prayer of Johnson's pleading for his deceased wife's continued watchfulness over him, Boswell acknowledges that he has had comparable feelings and adds: "I, whom it has pleased GOD to afflict in a similar manner... have certain experience of benignant communication by dreams" (I, 236). Indeed, he experienced several such dreams, most notably one during the night between February 28 and March 1, 1791 in which, as he writes in his journal, Margaret "distinctly pointed out in her own handwriting the propitiation of our Saviour"[11] and thereby broke the spell of an extended depression. Since

Boswell attached great importance to his dreams and took pains to record them, this allusion to Margaret in the *Life*, so oblique that it could easily be overlooked, is another sign of deliberate self-restraint.

What are we to make of these unobtrusive references to Margaret? The very fact that they are there at all suggests that Boswell wanted to express his feelings about her, to leave some mark of her in his work. Yet the brevity of the references suggests his conscious decision not to display those feelings – and at least some of the remarks are all the more poignant for what he leaves unsaid.

Although quite restrained in revealing his thoughts about Margaret's death, Boswell does present one telling anecdote that shows her in her prime. No doubt he could justify its inclusion because it was directly relevant to Johnson, although he plays it down by relegating it to a footnote. Having quoted Johnson's letter of November 27, 1773 in which he astutely acknowledges that Margaret must have been glad to see the last of him after his stay in Edinburgh, Boswell admits that Johnson had been a difficult guest and that Margaret, though she had been attentive, did not much like him:

> She had not that high admiration of him which was felt by most of those who knew him; and what was very natural to a female mind, she thought he had too much influence over her husband. She once in a little warmth, made, with more point than justice, this remark upon that subject: "I have seen many a bear led by a man; but I never before saw a man led by a bear." (II, 269)

While the image Boswell gives of Margaret – her suppressed displeasure and asperity – is clear and vivid, his self-presentation in this passage is not so controlled. The complacent assumption that his wife could be expected to resent a possible rival and the patronizing reference to what is "natural to a female mind" are offset by the touch of pique in his assertion that her quip has "more point [i.e., wit] than justice," and the impression of masculine superiority he seems to be trying to create is deflated by Margaret's punchline, in which the joke is quite as much on him as on Johnson. And yet Boswell is honest enough to present her remark even though it was not to his credit.

Eventually Boswell seems to have had second thoughts about so conscientiously avoiding Margaret's name in the *Life*. In the second edition he identifies the anonymous lady of "admirable good sense and quickness of understanding," whose thoughtful comment about one of Johnson's remarks he quotes in the first edition, as "the late Margaret Montgomerie, my very valuable wife, and the very affectionate mother of my children, who, if they inherit her good qualities, will have no reason to complain of their lot" (III, 160, n. 1). Here the desire explicitly to pay tribute to her at least once seems to have outweighed his desire for reticence. The same pattern of restraint in the first edition and greater expansiveness in the second is apparent in

Boswell's remark about the schooling of his sons (III, 12). Perhaps the success of the first edition made him feel less embarrassed about including such details. Perhaps, too, he felt freer to add a personal touch once Malone and Courtenay were no longer watching him so closely and warning him.[12]

About his general psychological state, the severe depression from which he periodically suffered all his life, Boswell could again be quite restrained in his authorial comments. A good example is his observation on the Prologue Johnson wrote to Goldsmith's *Good-Natured Man* (1768). Boswell finds the opening lines – "Press'd with the load of life, the weary mind / Surveys the general toil of human kind" – characteristic of the "dismal gloom of his [Johnson's] mind" and adds: "which in his case, as in the case of all who are distressed with the same malady of imagination, transfers to others its own feelings" (II, 45). His allusion to others distressed by melancholy, so brief that it, too, might be easily overlooked, is certainly an understatement when read in light of Boswell's own recurring fits of depondency, recorded in detail in his journals.[13]

Among the causes of Boswell's depression were some definite and practical problems – extreme financial difficulties, the end of all hope for a Parliamentary seat after his break with Lord Lonsdale in June 1790, and, with Malone's departure for Ireland in November of same year, the loss of much-needed support and help on the *Life*. About these problems Boswell retains a discreet silence in the text.

On the other hand, he could not resist commenting on another problem – his increasingly evident lack of professional success – when reporting the conversations he and Johnson had about his becoming a London barrister. By the time that Boswell was working on the *Life*, he had given up his Edinburgh practice, and although he was making little effort to attract London clients, he still had some hopes. Even when reviewing his situation in a mood of despondency, he wrote in his journal on May 29, 1790: "Still I dreamed of applying resolutely to the practice of the law, and of having it said, 'He never took fairly to the English bar till he was fifty.'"[14] In at least two authorial comments in the *Life*, however, he expresses doubts about finding merit rewarded by success.

Boswell reveals such doubts after quoting Johnson's vehement refusal to complain about *his* lack of worldly success. Self-deprecatingly, Johnson had asserted that authors had no right to expect recognition and also that the failure of "a man of merit" was probably his own fault. When Boswell objected that barristers "of merit" do not get a practice, Johnson countered that this must be due to a prospective client's failure to recognize the merit but not to any intentional injustice. Having transcribed this exchange from his journal of March 23, 1783,[15] Boswell, after an initial first-person reference, launches into a general reflection:

I cannot help thinking that men of merit, who have no success in life, may be forgiven for *lamenting*, if they are not allowed to *complain*. They may consider it as *hard* that their merit should not have its suitable distinction. Though there is no intentional injustice towards them on the part of the world, their merit not having been perceived, they may yet repine against *fortune*, or *fate*, or by whatever name they choose to call the supposed mythological power of *Destiny*." (IV, 172)

After dwelling on the injustice of not having one's merit recognized, Boswell answers himself with "a consolatory thought" – that by a compensatory balance some people are rewarded with success while others are granted higher satisfactions:

How much harder would it be if the same persons had both all the merit and all the prosperity. Would not this be a miserable distribution for the poor dunces? Would men of merit exchange their intellectual superiority, and the enjoyments arising from it, for external distinction and the pleasures of wealth? If they would not, let them not envy others who are poor where they are rich, a compensation which is made to them. Let them look inwards to be satisfied...(IV, 173)

In his 1783 journal entry Boswell assumes that Johnson is referring to a mutual friend, William Johnson Temple, when he mentions someone who has retired to the country, has written a book or two that no one reads, and complains of neglect. Later, in reworking his material for the *Life*, Boswell must have realized that the shoe fit him as well, and seeks solace in his rationalization.

This passage is just the kind of "excrescence" Malone had warned him against, and it may be no accident that Boswell apparently inserted it shortly before or during January 1791[16] when Malone was temporarily away from London and not available to restrain him. While high-mindedly claiming to prefer merit to worldly success, Boswell seems strangely unaware of how snobbish he sounds as he counts himself among the intellectually superior and assumes that the others are dunces. And his thought about a compensatory balance is certainly facile. Yet is there not also something touching in Boswell's attempt to console himself, as if he were whistling in the dark?

By the time of the second edition, even Boswell's slender hope for success as a barrister was dashed. Although he had taken chambers in the Inner Temple in January 1791, he could not bring himself to spend time in them and gave them up at the end of the second year, and he envied the lawyers he saw with their briefs while he had none.[17] On December 21, 1792 he wrote in his journal: "The delusive hope of *perhaps* getting into some practice at the bar was *now* dead, or at least torpid."[18] It was in this despondent mood that

Boswell added a footnote to a passage describing another conversation with Johnson, on September 20, 1777, about moving to the English Bar. A "very sensible lawyer" had informed Johnson that in London there were many candidates but only a few successful barristers. Johnson's informant had conceded that intelligence, application, and work on a few cases might testify to a barrister's merit and bring clients, but Johnson then added his own warning about the risks (III, 179). In his footnote, written fifteen years later, Boswell acknowledges sadly: "However true the opinion of Dr. Johnson's legal friend may have been some time ago, the same certainty of success cannot now be promised to the same display of merit." Actually, he was assuming that the "very sensible lawyer's" opinion was more encouraging than it had been in its context. Boswell then expresses his discouragement in the impersonal terms in which he liked to couch his feelings: "The reasons, however, of the rapid rise of some, and the disappointment of others equally respectable, are such as it might seem invidious to mention, and would require a longer detail than would be proper in this work." Certainly his understated refusal to complain is more dignified than the earlier self-pity and rationalization.

Boswell's disconcerting habit of stating that he could say more if he would – a rhetorical device he uses several times in the *Life* – may be irritating to modern readers who prefer greater forthrightness. And his formal, highly generalized diction, quite possibly encouraged by Malone,[19] is also no longer to our taste. Yet we can hardly blame Boswell for adopting a formal style when he shifts from the scenes and conversations with Johnson to his own observations, considering that this style was used in his time by Johnson, Reynolds, Gibbon, and Burke, to name only a few.[20] In any case, we can at least understand that Boswell was trying not to present his private experiences directly.

On the other hand, the very fact that Boswell alludes to his professional problems suggests his need to bring his frustrations, too, into his work. In writing about them in the impersonal terms he prefers, he seems to be working through them, consoling himself, and, at least in the last-mentioned passage, trying to come to terms with his disappointment.

As for his authorial comments as a Scotsman – chiefly about his countrymen – Boswell again shows considerable reticence concerning his own unsettling experiences. His sense that Scotland was too narrow and confining, which had driven him to try the English Bar, was strong while he was working on the *Life*. Although he was usually pleased to be in London, he intermittently felt guilty about not being at Auchinleck. And he was subjected to conflicting pressures – from Malone, who advised him to stay in town to work on the *Life*, from Margaret and his brother T. D. Boswell who urged him to return to his profession and estate in Scotland.[21] He realized that his countrymen did not approve of his "partiality to England," but also that in London he was at times not treated with the respect due to a landed Scottish gentleman.[22] From 1788 on, he felt increasingly removed from Scotland, and after Margaret's death he could hardly bear to go to Auchinleck even on a visit. Furthermore, though he retained his strong national pride, he disliked any reminders of Scotland, whether these came from encounters with his countrymen or merely from reading Scottish newspapers.[23] For the most part, however, Boswell does not reveal his increasingly ambivalent feelings about his native land in the *Life*.

In transcribing Johnson's anti-Scottish jokes from his journals to the *Life*, Boswell usually offers no further remarks of his own, and so he appears to accept the role as the loyal representative of Scotland that Johnson usually assigns to him. Yet Boswell gives a glimpse of his more ambivalent feelings when he quotes Johnson's witticism that the pity is not that England is lost but that the Scots have found it – presumably alluding to the many Scotsmen who had risen to prominence in England – and inserts a footnote that emphasizes his deliberate lack of comment: "It would not become me to expatiate on this strong and pointed remark, in which a very great deal of meaning is condensed" (III, 78 and n. 3). Again suggesting he could say more if he wished, he seems to be hinting that, as a Scotsman, he will not speak ill of his countrymen, but at the same time he registers no objection to Johnson's anti-Scottish sentiment.

Boswell is more explicit on a question that had long interested him: what a Scotsman could or should do about his pronunciation. A long digression – truly another "excrescence" – about Thomas Sheridan leads him to Alexander Wedderburn, by then Lord Loughborough, Chief Justice of the Court of Common Pleas, who had benefited from Sheridan's elocution lessons, and Wedderburn's experience gives Boswell the opportunity to indicate that he thoroughly approves of getting rid of coarser accents but that – speaking momentarily as a loyal Scot – he would "heartily despise" any Scotsman who eliminated all Scottish flavor from his speech (I, 386–7).

Boswell's remark gives no hint that he is indulging in tacit self-justification here. We are made aware of this possibility by another conversation about accents in the *Life* in which he mentions that he, too, took elocution lessons early in his career and alludes to the traces of Scottish accent in his own speech (he quotes Johnson's soothing "Sir, your pronunciation is not offensive"). Avoiding any revelation about himself in this second conversation as well, Boswell offers general advice to his countrymen: they should not strive for a perfect "High English" accent because the effort of maintaining this would be unpleasantly noticeable (II, 160). Ironically, while urging others to cultivate their English accent but not to shun a few Scottish inflections, Boswell was making an effort to ensure that his youngest daughter, Betsy, would be free of any Scottish accent whatsoever; to prevent her from losing the English she was acquiring at her boarding school, he allowed her only brief visits to his London house in Great Portland Street, run by a Scottish housekeeper.[24] In his own life he was becoming more of an Anglophile than he reveals in his work; in this instance, though he tells the truth in the *Life*, he does not tell the whole truth.

In several of the authorial comments Boswell gives his opinion – couched yet again in impersonal terms – of his countrymen in England. On this topic, of special interest to him now that he was established in London, his views appear to have changed. Early in the *Life* Boswell takes Wedderburn as an example of what an ambitious Scot can achieve, calling him "an animating encouragement to other gentlemen of North-Britain to try their fortunes in the southern part of the Island" (I, 387). But later Boswell focuses rather on what he considers the obnoxious *arrivistes*. For instance, he suggests that Johnson might have been less prejudiced against the Scots if he had not seen "the worst part of the Scottish nation, the needy adventurers, many of whom he thought were advanced above their merits, by means which he did not approve" and if, instead, he had known "the worthy, sensible, independent gentlemen, who live rationally and hospitably at home" (IV, 169). Further-more, in extolling the advantages of an English education for "Scotch gentlemen of talents and ambition," Boswell writes feelingly about another group:

> I own, indeed, that it is no small misfortune for Scotch gentlemen, who have neither talents nor ambition, to be educated in England, where they may be perhaps distinguished only by a nick-name, lavish their fortune in giving expensive entertainments to those who laugh at them, and saunter about as mere idle insignificant hangers on even upon the foolish great; when if they had been judiciously brought up at home, they might have been comfortable and creditable members of society. (IV, 131–2)

The journals do not provide a key to who in particular is meant, but they are full of references to the crudeness and other shortcomings of the Scotsmen who crossed Boswell's path in London. And no doubt he had plenty of opportunity to observe his countrymen mocked by the Englishmen they were trying to impress.

Although Boswell is quite outspoken here, he does not disclose the personal experiences that prompted his views. Actually, this digression about the advantages and dangers of an English education is a reworking of a journal entry of June 5, 1781 about a conversation with Johnson concerning Boswell's wish to settle in England. In that conversation he reports that Margaret considers an English schooling advantageous for their son, and he himself insists that once in England, he will make sure his son retains his affection for his native place, whereupon Johnson says drily: "That...you could not."[25] Recasting this passage in the *Life*, Boswell makes no mention of Johnson's doubts, focuses on his own point that frequent visits to their home might prevent Scottish gentlemen "from being totally estranged from their native country," and moves on to the sycophantic Scotsmen who have been spoiled by an English education. Avoiding any conclusions about his own estrangement from his native country – and, perhaps understandably, giving no sign that he recognizes himself as a hanger-on in the train of Lord Lonsdale – Boswell yet again depersonalizes his experiences in the *Life*.

But his presentation is not always so impersonal. In one vivid comment, in which Boswell adopts a complex pose of at once distancing himself from his countrymen and maintaining his right to speak as one of them, Boswell reveals himself as conspicuously self-centered. He does so while arguing that Scotsmen need not be offended by Johnson's criticisms of them in his *Journey to the Western Isles*. Without denying Johnson's prejudice against the Scots, Boswell points to extenuating circumstances: that Johnson was no more critical of them than he generally was of his friends, that he was praised by several Scotsmen of unquestioned patriotism, and that the accuracy of his descriptions was corroborated by one of these who subsequently made the same tour. Then comes the undeniable self-display:

> And let me add, that, citizen of the world as I hold myself to be, I have that degree of predilection for my *natale solum*, nay, I have that just sense of the merit of an ancient nation, which has been forever renowned for its valour, which in former times maintained its independence against a powerful neighbour, and in modern times has been equally distinguished for its ingenuity and industry in civilized life, that I should have felt a generous indignation at any injustice done to it. (II, 306)

That Boswell was fond of seeing himself as a cosmopolitan is evident from the fact that he already uses this image in the *Tour to the Hebrides*. There he declares, "I am, I flatter myself, completely a citizen of the world," and he maintains that his own experience of having travelled widely abroad enables him to discount the narrow-minded contempt for Scotland shown by the English, including Johnson (V, 20). With a significant change of focus, Boswell uses the same self-image in the *Life* to defend Johnson's view of Scotland – yet another sign of Boswell's shifting allegiance.

Considered in isolation, this passage with its formal diction and elevated tone certainly sounds self-important as well as patronizing towards the Scots. Yet in the context of Boswell's life, his statement is not just empty boasting. Boswell did have intense feelings about his native soil – feelings that led him to purchase the estate of Knockroon, once part of the Auchinleck lands, in the fall of 1790 even though he had to go heavily into debt to acquire it.[26] Furthermore, compared with the patriotic Scotsmen he mentioned, Boswell was indeed a man of the world, someone who had travelled widely on the continent and now moved in London society with

Reynolds, Malone, Courtenay, Windham, the Wartons, and other prominent people of the day. Nor is the self-presentation gratuitous here, for in the build-up of his argument, Boswell is creating a rhetorical emphasis for an important point. He is suggesting that not only Scotsmen but someone with a broader perspective could recognize that Johnson was not basically hostile to the Scots he met on his tour. Significantly, Boswell follows his own remark with that of no less an authority than Sir Joshua Reynolds, who knew Johnson well and who confirmed his general critical bent. Boswell, in his eagerness to defend Johnson, may not have been aware of how snobbish he sounds in this passage, but his self-presentation is not inaccurate.

This citizen-of-the-world passage is, however, an exception; most of the authorial comments about Scotland – and they are remarkably few in view of the importance of the subject to Boswell – avoid such personal display. Still, all the remarks we have considered are revealing. That Boswell should take it for granted that the Scots in England would make an effort to overcome their native accent and that he should look down on numbers of his countrymen suggests how detached he was becoming from Scotland while writing the *Life*. At the same time, the very fact that he could present himself as a loyal Scot at one point and insist on being a cosmopolitan at another suggests how much he lived in two worlds, not fully at home in either.

Summing up, we can conclude that although in some of his authorial comments in the *Life* Boswell indeed indulges in the self-display to which a few of his contemporaries as well as modern critics have objected, in many more he takes the trouble to recast his personal experiences into more generalized observations. Although these may sound overly formal to twentieth-century readers, we can hardly blame Boswell for adopting a style that was practiced by some of the most respected writers of his day. In any case, such passages become more meaningful and, in some instances, more touching when one knows the full extent of the personal experiences behind them. Nor has Boswell been given sufficient credit for those comments, especially about matters close to him, in which he gives only glimpses of his feelings with poignant brevity.

Readers who are interested in the *Life of Johnson* primarily as a biography of Johnson will argue that Boswell's authorial comments "after the fact" should not have been included in the first place, and that they are merely a sign of Boswell's self-indulgence. On the other hand, those of us who consider the double focus on Boswell as well as Johnson one of the strengths of the *Life of Johnson* may find that these comments have their own interest in revealing an older, sadder Boswell trying to come to terms with personal loss, professional disappointment, and his feelings as a displaced Scotsman.

NOTES

1 Leopold Damrosch, "*The Life of Johnson*: An Anti-Theory," *Eighteenth-Century Studies*, 6 (1973), 499–500; see also Donald Greene, "'Tis a Pretty Book, Mr.

Boswell, But – ," in *New Questions, New Answers*, p. 123, and Frederick A. Pottle, "The Adequacy as Biography of Boswell's *Life of Johnson*," in *New Questions, New Answers*, p. 158.

2 Paul K. Alkon, "Boswell's Control of Aesthetic Distance," in *James Boswell's "Life of Samuel Johnson*," ed. Harold Bloom (New York: Chelsea House Publishers, 1986), p. 44. Alkon is, however, less critical of Boswell as narrator than his phrase suggests. See also David L. Passler, *Time, Form, and Style in Boswell's Life of Johnson* (New Haven: Yale University Press, 1971), pp. 6–9.

3 *Remarks on the Journal of a Tour to the Hebrides* (1785), pp. 13–19.

4 *Life*, V, 24–6. All references to *Life* subsequently included in the text.

5 Malone to Boswell, October 5, 1783, *Corr: Garrick, Burke, Malone*, p. 200. Boswell's praise of Margaret for changing her bedchamber is also mocked in the *English Review* of November 1785.

6 Malone to Boswell, October 19, 1785, *Corr: Garrick, Burke, Malone*, p. 229.

7 Boswell to Forbes, May 8, 1787, Fettercairn Papers, Acc. 4796/87, quoted by kind permission of the Trustees of the National Library of Scotland.

8 Hill identifies the episode as the death of Narcissa in the third "Night Thoughts" and suggests the association with the dying Margaret (IV, 61, n. 1).

9 *Great Biographer*, p. 136.

10 Journal of June 2, 1718, *Laird*, p. 373.

11 *Great Biographer*, p. 131.

12 Malone's restraining influence is noted by Peter S. Baker, "Introduction: Malone," *Corr: Garrick, Burke, Malone*, pp. 179–80, Courtenay's influence is suggested by his advice to Boswell to tone down his criticism of Mrs. Piozzi (see Boswell's journal of February 22, 1791, *Great Biographer*, p. 127).

13 *English Experiment*, pp. 93–6, 146–9, 151–5, 165–99, 196–201; *Great Biographer*, pp. 61–2, 64–6, 69–79, 116–27.

14 *Great Biographer*, p. 56.

15 *Applause*, pp. 79–80.

16 A footnote in the first edition gives the date.

17 *Great Biographer*, pp. 117, 139 and n. 5, 194.

18 *Great Biographer*, p. 208.

19 Baker, "Introduction," p. 175.

20 James R. Sutherland, *On English Prose* (Toronto: University of Toronto Press, 1957), pp. 78–80.

21 *English Experiment*, pp. 123, 133, 138, 140, 147, 154, 190–1.

22 *English Experiment*, pp. 124, 196–7.

23 *English Experiment*, pp. 60, 68, 121, 124, 194, 268; *Great Biographer*, pp. 16, 95, 122, 191, 205.

24 Journal of July 28, 1790, *Great Biographer*, p. 97.

25 *Laird*, p. 337.

26 Brady, *Later Years*, p. 415.

12

JOHNSON'S CONVERSATION IN
BOSWELL'S *LIFE OF JOHNSON*

Paul J. Korshin

I

Samuel Johnson's conversation is the best known of any figure in literary history, so well known that we seldom ask any more what the term actually means with regard to his life and literary career. Conversation, obviously, in the sense of the interchange of speech between people, must refer first to Johnson's real talk with real people from the end of his infancy to the day of his death. These speeches are lost, irretrievably, for he lived at a time before the existence of mechanical means for reproducing the human voice. We may know that Johnson's voice was sonorous, that he spoke with a pronounced Staffordshire accent, that he had a "bow-wow" method of speaking, but we cannot know how he sounded. Johnson's conversation refers next to the verbal exchanges which Johnson himself created for the characters in his literary works to speak: of this body of speeches we know a great deal although, to be sure, it is fictional rather than real and, because these exchanges never took place, their status is not in doubt. The third meaning of Johnson's conversation, which refers to what other people who talked with or listened to him record him as saying, is open to great uncertainty, for a large number of his contemporaries made some effort to recall, in writing, what he said on various occasions. This category of Johnson's conversation is complicated: it includes what some of his contemporaries called "wit and wisdom," what others described as his "sayings," and what still others called his "talk." Indeed, sometimes a single observer of Johnson uses all three of these terms more or less interchangeably, so that distinctions among these subcategories of conversation blur.

The most famous and most copious recorder of Johnson's conversation, his biographer James Boswell, used all of these terms over a period of about thirty years of observing and writing about Johnson and, of course, Boswell emphatically described Johnson's verbal exchanges as "conversation" as well. On the title page of his *Life of Samuel Johnson* (1791), Boswell describes his work as "comprehending...A Series of His Epistolary Correspondence and Conversations with Many Eminent Persons," among other rarities which – he hoped – would make his biography better than all its predecessors. The "Eminent Persons" include a number of people of varying degrees of eminence; Boswell himself is the most frequent person to appear in his own pages. We all know the result of Boswell's ambitious efforts: not only has his *Life* taken precedence over all its competitors, but his versions of Johnson's conversation have become the undisputed voice of Johnson. Boswell himself insists on his accuracy as a recorder of Johnson's speech and, in years when he failed to meet with Johnson, specifically mentions his disappointment, as he does in his narrative for 1770: "During this year there was a total cessation of all correspondence between Dr. Johnson and me...and as I was not in London, I had no opportunity of enjoying his company and recording his conversation."[1] This statement has many analogues in the *Life*, and we can understand the importance of the theme for Boswell, for he assures us in his opening pages that the conversation of a learned man will best display his character. Hence the uniqueness of the *Life*:

> What I consider as the peculiar value of the following work, is, the quantity that it contains of Johnson's conversation; which is universally acknowledged to have been eminently instructive and entertaining; and of which the specimens that I have given upon a former occasion, have been received with so much approbation, that I have good grounds for supposing that the world will not be indifferent to more ample communications of a similar nature. (I, 31)

Boswell's interest in making some record of Johnson's conversation started soon after their first meeting, or many years before he had any thought of writing his friend's biography and making its "peculiar value" the presentation of those records. Hence we cannot expect to find complete consistency in the kind of records that Boswell kept of Johnson's talk. We can see how Boswell changed his methods of noting down his meetings with Johnson by comparing the records that survive from the early years, say from 1763 to the early 1770s, with those from the mid- and late 1770s, of which the best example is certainly the portion of his diary for September 1777, the section that students of Boswell call his "Ashbourne Journal" because it records his visit with Johnson at the home of the Rev. John Taylor at Ashbourne, from September 14–24, 1777. I think we should first try to understand the development of Boswell's reporting of Johnson's talk.

II

Since Boswell's journals from his early meetings with Johnson did not appear in print until the mid-twentieth century, let me begin instead with

Boswell's first major publication, his *Account of Corsica* (1768). During his visit with General Paoli, Boswell reports that "I gave [him] the character of my revered friend Mr. Samuel Johnson" and "I repeated to [him] several of Mr. Johnson's sayings, so remarkable for strong sense and original humour. I now recollect these two":

> When I told Mr. Johnson that a certain author affected in conversation to maintain, that there was no distinction between virtue and vice, he said, "Why Sir, if the fellow does not think as he speaks, he is lying; and I see not what honour he can propose to himself from having the character of a lyar. But if he really does think that there is no distinction between virtue and vice, why Sir, when he leaves our houses, let us count our spoons."
>
> Of modern infidels and innovatours, he said, "Sir, these are all vain men, and will gratify themselves at any expence. Truth will not afford sufficient food to their vanity; so they have betaken themselves to errour. Truth Sir, is a cow which will yield such people no more milk, and so they are gone to milk the bull."[2]

Paoli, Boswell tells us, was "delighted with the sayings of Mr. Johnson," as well he might have been. Boswell was very pleased with them, too, for he introduces both of these pieces of talk in almost exactly the same words in the *Life*. He assigns the first (the "count the spoons" *bon mot*) to July 14, 1763 (I, 432). The second appears as part of an attack on Hume on July 21, 1763 (I, 444). This saying, however much "strong sense and original humour" Boswell thought it contained, is more of a problem. We can find other sources for it, since "To milk a bull" appears at least as early as Erasmus's *Adagia*, and there are a number of recorded uses of the phrase and its implications in the sixteenth and seventeenth centuries, where "to milk the bull" is taken to mean "a thyng veraie absurd and contrary to Reason."[3] Were Johnson's sayings, as Boswell calls them in his *Account of Corsica*, so hackneyed as to consist of proverbial statements? Did Boswell, after citing this saying in 1768 as "original," ever discover its true proverbial source? Or was he simply inventing a Johnsonian saying for his earliest work, knowing that there was absolutely no way that anyone could gainsay his accuracy? Of course we cannot tell the truth now, but there must be a certain suspicion about Boswell's reliability as a reporter.

It is worth noting, too, that at least at this early stage Boswell did not regard Johnson's talk as "conversation," as he would later call it; these examples of Johnson's intellect are "sayings," showing that he originally thought of Johnson as embodying the older maxim-like tradition of talk. Perhaps he did not realize how telling a description this was, but another perception may be useful here. We may find it in an essay by the late Truman Capote, in a collection called "Conversational Portraits." Here Capote, in an essay entitled "Nocturnal Turnings," creates the following exchange:

Q: Do you consider conversation an art?
A: A dying one, yes. Most of the renowned conversationalists – Samuel Johnson, Oscar Wilde, Whistler, Jean Cocteau, Lady Astor, Lady Cunard, Alice Roosevelt Longworth – are monologuists, not conversationalists. A conversation is a dialogue, not a monologue. That's why there are so few good conversations: due to scarcity, two intelligent talkers seldom meet.[4]

Capote's observation perfectly describes the problem that Boswell faced from the start in his recording of Johnson's talk: Johnson tends to be a monologuist, not a conversationalist. It was possible to disguise this quality, to an extent, in Boswell's first major attempt to present Johnson as talker, his *Journal of a Tour to the Hebrides*, by using captions for each speaker in an exchange, as a dramatist would do in writing dialogue. But this device ought not to disguise the essential fact that the vast majority of exchanges between Johnson and another person are actually occasions where someone asks a brief question and Johnson presents a "saying" in reply. The key to ascertaining whether genuine dialogue or conversation takes place is whether the exchange includes more than one statement on each side of the dialogue. Beginning with the *Tour*, there are occasions when Boswell does print real dialogue, true Johnsonian conversation, but these incidents represent a minority, a very small minority, of Johnson's talk. Hence the conversational exchanges which he includes in the *Life* are relatively few in number: I have counted about fifty of them in all.

All the other examples of Johnson's colloquial speech that Boswell presents fall into the *bons mots* tradition. Boswell or another speaker makes a statement, Johnson responds with a brilliant, even crushing *bon mot*, and the matter is settled. Every Johnsonian, every reader of the *Life* will have his or her favorites, and there are hundreds of clever sayings to choose from. On Scotland: "I do indeed come from Scotland, but I cannot help it." "That, Sir, I find, is what a great many of your countrymen cannot help" (I, 392). On Christopher Smart's exercise in the madhouse: "[to Charles Burney] He has partly as much exercise as he used to have, for he digs in the garden. Indeed, before his confinement, he used for exercise to walk to the alehouse; but he was *carried* back again" (I, 397). On Fielding: "Will you not allow, Sir, that he draws very natural pictures of human life?" "Why, Sir, it is of very low life. Richardson used to say, that had he not known who Fielding was, he should have believed he was an ostler" (II, 174). This kind of anthologizing of Johnson's sayings is not a new practice: admirers of his conversation have been compiling such collections, most of them drawn exclusively from Boswell's *Life*, for nearly two hundred years. I will return to this phenomenon later in this essay, but for the present I would merely note the paradox, which I have discussed before, of compiling an anthology from a work which is itself a vast anthology, for such, indeed, is the *Life*.[5] The *bons mots* tradition is a very respectable one, presenting, as it does, the Johnson whom many admirers find most memorable, but it also presents Johnson as monologuist rather than as conversationalist. Nor is there anything innovative about it – this tradition, which recalls the *Adagia* and other similar collections of proverbs, maxims, and sayings, was already venerable and even overdone by the time Boswell began to compose his biography.

How did Boswell assemble Johnson's conversations? Fortunately, we know a great deal about the composition of the *Life*. His method in the *Tour to the Hebrides* had been uncomplicated. He had spent every day for nearly three successive months in Johnson's company and had taken careful notes in small memorandum books which he later transcribed into the narrative form of his diary, much of which is preserved in the *Private Papers*. Since he had almost no distractions, either social or amorous, during the three months of the tour, he tended to make his records punctually. But the composition of the *Life* presented enormous difficulties, in comparison with the earlier *Tour*. As we are well aware by now, he had spent a maximum of 425 days – inclusive of the months of the *Tour* – in Johnson's company during the twenty-one years from their first meeting until Johnson's death.[6] Boswell never mastered the techniques of shorthand (there were many popular, competing systems available in the last half of the eighteenth century) – he tells us so himself. On April 10, 1778, he tried to take down a passage from Robertson's *History of America* that Johnson slowly dictated to him but, as he acknowledges, "it was found that I had it very imperfectly" (III, 270). And we know, too, that Boswell did not habitually take notes while Johnson spoke, except for occasions when Johnson specifically dictated something to him. After all, Boswell takes part in virtually all of the conversations he records in the *Life*, so he could hardly have been taking notes assiduously throughout.[7] The evidence of Boswell's diaries and private papers suggests that he did take notes on his meetings with Johnson, usually in a fragmentary form in a small notebook, some time after the end of the conversation. Boswell himself is inadvertently misleading about this practice: on one occasion, he says that he made his memoranda every evening, but elsewhere he makes it clear that he is summarizing conversations that took place three, four, or even more days ago. It is hardly surprising, therefore, that so many of Johnson's "conversations" in the *Life* consist of mere snippets of talk, Johnsonian sayings rather than genuine conversations. From the brief memoranda, Boswell worked up the longer encounters that we find in the *Private Papers*, and from these accounts he assembled the conversations that appear in the *Life* itself. A thorough comparison of the longer conversations in the *Life* with their earlier form in the volumes of the *Private Papers* reveals that Boswell almost always transfers the earlier long form of a conversation to the *Life* without significant changes. Naturally, our basis for comparison is limited, for what Geoffrey Scott printed in the *Private Papers* is just the fragmentary survivals of Boswell's diaries.

The vital link in the transmission of Johnson's conversations from drawing-room and tavern to the pages of Boswell's biography, then, must be Boswell's memory, which would appear to have been miraculous. Or at least, Boswell's admirers, when they have paused to consider this transmission, have generally decided that his memory was prodigious. Was it? We know, of course, that the trained memory of a professional actor or actress, a trained lecturer, or a poet like the bardic oral poets of primitive cultures can indeed be extraordinary. But the trained memorizer profits from repeating the same speeches many times. Boswell's advocates simply assume that he had a one-time memory so strong and accurate that he could perfectly recall Johnson's elaborate sayings and complicated dialogues several days after hearing or taking part in them. One can speculate endlessly about this skill at memorizing. It is better, I think, for us to consider a curious paradox inherent in Boswell's writings about Johnson. This paradox is that, while Boswell had no difficulty reconstructing Johnson's sayings and dialogue when he wrote the *Tour to the Hebrides*, the greater time-span of a memoir of Johnson's entire life, combined with his much more miscellaneous collections for this longer span, imposed upon his entire endeavor an indelible tincture of inaccuracy. Moreover, we can have no doubt that Boswell knew of this shortcoming, inherent as it was in his work. He could disguise it, to an extent, by insisting on his own complete reliability while, at the same time, derogating that of other writers about Johnson like Sir John Hawkins and Hester Piozzi. But there is another consideration that is relevant here, especially in view of Boswell's own experience in legal trials. He knew, as did every legal professional in the late eighteenth century, that the testimony of witnesses, especially that of eyewitnesses, could be shaky. So, I suggest, Boswell knew that his own memory was far from perfect and, rather than attempt to disguise it completely, he chose rather to refer openly to it. On literally scores of occasions, he tells us that he failed to record any part of Johnson's conversation for days or even weeks while he was in London; he mentions that something "has escaped my memory" or says "I forget," "I do not recollect," or another apologetic phrase; he mentions how difficult he found it to record Johnson's talk accurately.[8] Yet at the same time that Boswell allows us to doubt his accuracy and his memory, he takes pains to assure us that he is trustworthy: "I must, again and again, intreat of my readers not to suppose that my imperfect record of conversation contains the whole of what was said by Johnson, or other eminent persons who lived with him. What I have preserved, however, has the value of the most perfect authenticity" (II, 350). This strong, even astounding, statement, from the narrative for April 1775, appears in a portion of the *Life* that is especially rich in detail, famous Johnsonian sayings, and alarming lacunae, entire weeks when Boswell recorded nothing or remembered nothing. An *apologia* of this sort must have a purpose, something I can only surmise now, but it is fair to say that one does not defend oneself unless one suspects that there is a need to do so. Hence, at this point in his narrative, I would guess that Boswell was sensitive about his lapses and decided to reassure his public that, gaps and lapses of memory notwithstanding, the conversations that he does present are not simply authentic, they are *superlatively* perfect, "of the most perfect authenticity."

III

Now, Boswell is not the only person who kept records of Johnson's sayings or conversation, he is just the one who published the most copious such accounts. We know that there are many other records of what Johnson said on different occasions, usually collected without regard to time and place of the conversation. Boswell himself prints a large sampling of this kind of sayings in the *Life*, most conspicuously the two large collections for the years 1770 and 1780, when "there was a total cessation of all correspondence between Dr. Johnson and me" (II, 116–33; IV, 1–34). The first such collection, which Boswell acquired from the Rev. William Maxwell, he passes on without any comment about the method of transmission, except to mention that Maxwell had been "for many years the social friend of Johnson, who spoke of him with a very kind regard" (II, 116). Presumably someone for whom Johnson had such kind regard is absolutely reliable, but Boswell does not tell us anything more. As for the second body of *collectanea*, which he obtained from Bennet Langton, Boswell is more explicit: "The authenticity of every article is unquestionable. For the expression, I, who wrote them down in his [i.e. Langton's] presence, am partly responsible" (IV, 2). The inconsistency between the treatment of these two collections of second-hand sayings is astonishing. Langton had known Johnson for longer than Boswell had, the authenticity of his recollections was irreproachable, yet Boswell admits that he is "partly responsible" for the "expression" or, to put it differently, for putting Langton's recollections into what he deemed appropriate Johnson-like diction. Maxwell had not known Johnson anywhere near so well as Langton had, but Boswell does not admit to having edited or rephrased *his* recollections. A close survey of both collections shows, in fact, that they are quite similar stylistically, so either the Rev. Maxwell had a splendid ear for Johnson's cadences or Boswell silently rephrased his collection of sayings so that they fitted the mould that he had decided upon for Johnson. I would not make too much of a single inconsistency in a work so long as the *Life*; despite the editorial attentions of such an astute scholar as Edmond Malone, Boswell composed his biography over a period of almost four years, so oversights are inevitable. Yet these two observers and recorders of Johnson's sayings, whose collections were accessible to Boswell in their entirety, still needed his editorial attentions to make their accounts of the conversation acceptable to him. What is the situation with collections of sayings over which he had no control?

The most notable such collection is that of Mrs. Thrale or, as she was known by the time she published her *Anecdotes of the Late Samuel Johnson, LL. D. during the last twenty years of his life* (1786), Hester Lynch Piozzi. Mrs. Piozzi had kept records of Johnson's sayings since her first meeting with him in 1764 and, of course, we know that she spent more time with him than did any other memoirist or biographer. Her records vary in quality and depth, but she was a keen observer with first-class literary gifts. As we can see from the various diaries she kept, such as the journal of her journey to France with Johnson in autumn 1775 and the large collection now known as *Thraliana* (an odd title, since for the bulk of the time that she kept this journal she was Mrs. Piozzi, not Mrs. Thrale), the bulk of the Johnsonian material appearing in these places ultimately found its way into her *Anecdotes*.[9] Nor was Mrs. Piozzi merely an observer or, like Boswell, mainly an interrogator of Johnson; conversation was something she excelled at. As Burney noted, she "had no passion but for conversation, in which her eminence was justly her pride."[10] Like Boswell, Mrs. Piozzi recorded not Johnson's conversations but his sayings – he is almost always a monologuist in her *Anecdotes* – but, unlike Boswell, she does not make any pretense about conversations with eminent persons. She presents Johnson's sayings on a great variety of subjects as just what they are, with no attempt to glorify them:

> To recollect... and to repeat the sayings of Dr. Johnson, is almost all that can be done by writers of his life; as his life, at least since my acquaintance with him, consisted in little else than talking, when he was not absolutely employed in some serious piece of work; and whatever work he did, seemed so much below his powers of performance, that he appeared the idlest of human beings; ever musing till he was called out to converse, and conversing till the fatigue of his friends, or the promptitude of his own temper to take offence, consigned him back again to silent meditation.[11]

Mrs. Piozzi gives us no laments about the weakness of her memory or her failure to record Johnson's sayings; since she is not writing his life in a chronological sequence, she had no worries about gaps in her story. Nor does she display much concern about how accurate her recollections of Johnson are. She tells us that she would not take notes on his conversation, since she regards this activity as "something I never practised myself, nor approved of in another. There is something so ill-bred, and so inclining to treachery in this conduct..."[12] Hence we have to rely on Mrs. Piozzi's memory, although, unlike that of Boswell, no one has ever made any great claims for its prodigiousness. With these potential shortcomings in mind, the specimens of Johnson's conversation and sayings that appear in the *Anecdotes* are different from those that Boswell gives in several ways. First, Mrs. Piozzi uses indirect statement more often than Boswell does, so we are deprived much of the time of Johnson's colloquial style. Second, the Johnson whom we see in her *Anecdotes* speaks almost exclusively without the elaborate rhetorical periods or polysyllabic embellishments familiar from Boswell's specimens of his talk. Mrs. Piozzi's Johnson is a more informal person than Boswell's figure and, consequently, his sayings are less impressive, less quotable than those that Boswell presents. Of course, the compilers of dictionaries of quotations have generally not been keen to harvest exemplars of Johnson's sayings from authors other than Boswell, so my criterion of a saying's being more or less quotable is obviously subjective. Third, Mrs. Piozzi almost never takes Johnson's comments down from dictation, but on the one occasion when she does so, the resulting statement sounds exactly like Johnson's writings or like the legal opinions that Johnson dictated to Boswell.[13]

Mrs. Piozzi was not obsessed with making Johnson sound, in his talk, as if he were the author of *The Rambler* or *Rasselas*, so the figure whom we hear discoursing in her *Anecdotes* is a relatively informal man. The sayings that she recollects are often rather humble: "A man who cannot get to heaven in a green coat, will not find his way thither sooner in a grey one"; "Poverty is *hic et ubique*...and if you do shut the jade out of the door, she will always contrive in some manner to poke her pale lean face in at the window"; "One can scarcely help wishing, while one fondles a baby, that it may never live to become a man; for it is *so* probable that when he becomes a man, he should be sure to end up in a scoundrel."[14] There is an occasional somewhat longer conversation in the *Anecdotes*, and these, too, are less studied, less philosophical than those that we find in Boswell. For example, Johnson and Mrs. Piozzi have a discussion about a clergyman who preaches in the City: Johnson asks, "What was the subject, Madam?" "Friendship, Sir." "Why, now, is it not strange that a wise man, like our dear little Evans, should take it in his head to preach on such a subject, in a place where no one can be thinking of it?" "Why, what are they thinking upon, Sir?" "Why, the men are thinking on their money I suppose, and the women are thinking of their mops."[15] The conversation is informal and, indeed, not especially memorable but, then, this extract is consistent with what Mrs. Piozzi hoped to present, a picture of Johnson that would be sufficiently credible to those who had never met him to make him recognizable. That her figure of Johnson is so informal, compared with the portrait that Boswell gives, does not necessarily mean that Boswell distorted Johnson's sayings to make them sound elaborate and periodical; Mrs. Piozzi simply presents him in a more natural pose, without any tinge of literary style. Her apology suggests as much: "I am well aware that I do not, and cannot give each expression of Dr. Johnson with all its force or all its neatness; but I have done my best to record such of his maxims, and repeat such of his sentiments, as may give to those who knew him not, a just edge of his character and manner of thinking."[16] Elsewhere she tells her readers that Johnson was not intentionally pompous, but that he only used large words when little ones would not express his purpose. Her anecdotes would have a second life, in a way, or at least those of them that Boswell appropriates for use in his own biography, rephrasing them to make them sound like *his* version of Johnson. And, of course, Boswell made good use of the factual material that Mrs. Piozzi had collected from Johnson about his youth and early friendships in London. Her presentations of Johnson's conversation are still recognizably Johnsonian, still sententious and witty, but a good deal less philosophical and ironical.

There are few observers of Johnson closer to him than Mrs. Piozzi was, and few specimens of his conversation of a length sufficient to permit analysis appear in the many memoirs which Wright collected in his *Johnsoniana* (1835) and which George Birkbeck Hill reprinted (and augmented) in his *Johnsonian Miscellanies*. There is just one significant exception, the diary of the Irish clergyman Rev. Thomas Campbell, who met and observed Johnson on a number of occasions in April 1775. Campbell's diary does not have the polished quality of Mrs. Piozzi's *Anecdotes* or Boswell's *Life*, a circumstance that is hardly surprising in view of the fact that Campbell never intended to publish it. By good fortune, Boswell himself was present at three of the dinners where Campbell spoke to Johnson, so it is possible to compare the two men's recollections of the talk that took place. On April 1, 1775, the first meeting Campbell had with Boswell, over dinner at the Thrales', with Johnson not present, there was a great deal of discussion of Johnson's conversation: "His bon mots were retailed in such plenty that they like a surfeit c^d not lye upon my memory."[17] Nevertheless, Campbell manages to recall a number of anecdotes, some of which Boswell would later use in the *Life*, others of which appear to be apocryphal. The most interesting – and scandalous – of them is worth mentioning for the intricate train of hearsay that it presents:

> – Murphy gave it (on Garricks authority) that when it was asked what was the greatest pleasure, Johnson answered f—g & the second was drinking. And therefore he wondered why there were not more drunkards, for all could drink tho' all could not f—k. But Garrick is his most intimate friend – They came to London together – & he is very correct both in his conduct & language.

Arthur Murphy, then, who was present at dinner at the Thrales', retells this story (with Mrs. Thrale out of the room, presumably), naming Garrick, who was not present, as the source for it.

Clifford has little patience with this account, pointing out with some exasperation that it is "second or third hand gossip about something which occurred long before [which] cannot be considered trustworthy evidence."[18]

Without doubt Clifford is correct: an anecdote based on such makeshift evidence, that is, hearsay, has just a remote chance of being true, and we should not credit it as something that Johnson actually said. What is interesting about the anecdote is not whether it is true, but rather that Campbell scrupulously identifies the train of witnesses who attest to it, so it is possible for us to see how dubious the story actually is. Campbell, as I said above, was not writing his diary for publication. Yet this anecdote, probably apocryphal, is precisely the kind of story or saying that Boswell habitually includes in the *Life* with the train of witnesses omitted so that the saying appears to be something he heard Johnson speak. Many of the most famous sayings in the *Life* fit this pattern: Boswell does not state that Johnson delivered them during a conversation, he simply introduces them as part of the sayings for a given day with the observation that Johnson "also" made this comment. So Johnson's remark about a woman's preaching appears with the telltale marks of hearsay on July 31, 1763 (I, 463); his famous statement about patriotism ("Patriotism is the last refuge of a scoundrel," II, 348) suddenly appears, apropos of nothing, on April 7, 1775; and his toast "to the next insurrection of the negroes in the West Indies" mysteriously appears as part of a conversation on September 23, 1777 (III, 200). In Campbell's version of an untrustworthy story, we can see that it is hearsay because Campbell describes the circuitous route by which the saying comes to him; but when Boswell gives us such dubious sayings, he seldom if ever leaves on the identifying tag.

Campbell's records of his meetings with Johnson, limited though they are, help us to perceive a quality of his conversation which Boswell's far more extensive records seldom reveal. This is Johnson's jocular, bantering tone (often at Boswell's expense) which makes so many of his best sayings seem like punchlines rather than *sententiae*. On April 8, 1775, Campbell was again in Johnson's presence, once more at the Thrales', where there are several revealing conversations. Here is the first:

> He seems fond of Boswell, & yet he is always abusing the Scots before him, by way of joke – talking of their nationality – he said they were not singular – The negros and Jews being so too. – Boswell lamented there was no good map of Scotland. There never can be a good map of Scotland, says the Doctor sententiously. This excited Boswell to ask wherefore. Why Sir to measure land a man must go over it; but who c^d think of going over Scotland?[19]

Campbell was amused by the exchange, but this is one joke on himself that Boswell does not bother to include in his diary or the pages of the *Life*. The undertheme of abuse continues; later in the evening, there is a comparison between David Garrick and Spranger Barry. Johnson and Mrs. Thrale get into an exchange about the two actors, with Mrs. Thrale recalling some comments of Arthur Murphy:

Murphy [i.e., Mrs. Thrale] standing up for Barry, Johnson said that he was fit for nothing but to stand at an auction room door with his pole &c – Murphy said that Garrick w^d do the business as well & pick the people's pockets at the same time. – Johnson admitted the fact but said Murphy spoke nonsense for that peoples pockets were not picked at the door, but in the room &c &c... It was a case decided here, that there was no harm & much pleasure in laughing at our absent friends – And I own if the character is not damaged I can see no injury done.[20]

Boswell does refer to this conversation, but without mentioning the two actors or the principle of harmless laughter about absent friends; instead, he manages to derogate Mrs. Thrale and completely to alter the nature of Johnson's remarks (II, 349). The incident is certainly minor, except that it appears on the same page of the *Life* on which Boswell assures us of his "most perfect authenticity." And, once again, Campbell's sparse notes about his meetings with Johnson show us a much less oratorical, more informal talker than we are accustomed to encounter in Boswell's biography. Campbell, as I mentioned, had no intention of becoming Johnson's biographer – he was merely an interested observer with no ulterior motives – and he was new to Johnson. Boswell had been chatting to Johnson for years and, as he would attest when he began to compose his biography, "when my mind was, as it were, *strongly impregnated with the Johnson æther*, I could, with much more facility and exactness, carry in my memory and commit to paper the exuberant variety of his wit and wisdom" (I, 421). As I have suggested, Boswell's memory was far less capacious than he suggests here, but there is indeed more to the story than he implies here.

IV

The other witnesses to Johnson's conversation, then, while their testimony is fragmentary, give us a hint that he did not necessarily sound exactly the way he does in Boswell's version. Boswell did more than merely rephrase and alter Johnson's talk; he invented it as well. The discovery of his diaries – his working papers – permitted scholars to see how impressive a feat these inventions were. We know of occasions where Boswell's surviving diary entry consists of no more than thirty words but from it he constructed tremendously circumstantial accounts of many hundreds of words for the *Life*.[21] How did Boswell do it? As Frederick A. Pottle observed nearly half a century ago, "I have no doubt that the pages of the *Life are* an imaginative reconstruction, but I wish to differentiate his controlled use of the imagination from the free imaginative interplay that results in fiction."[22] To be sure, as Pottle makes clear, Boswell is not like Sir Walter Scott, who merely invents imaginary conversations; the conversations that Boswell imaginatively reconstructs are not fictional; they actually happened. In a similar way, the speeches that Johnson wrote for members of Parliament and which the *Gentleman's Magazine* published as "Debates in the Senate of Magna Lilliputia" actually happened, too, just not in the way that Johnson invented them. No members of the Lords or Commons were ever recorded as objecting to the invention of their speeches; in the same way, few if any of the people whose conversations Boswell created for the *Life* are known to have complained about their accuracy. It is very flattering, after all, to be quoted in print. It is a fact that the finished *Life* is substantially the same as Boswell's narrative diaries, but, in R. W. Chapman's words, "the Boswellian record was never a verbatim report."[23] Boswell undoubtedly did remember, more or less accurately, what people, especially Johnson, had said on a given occasion, especially when he made notes about the conversation later. Everyone's memory is capable of almost total recall of some events and conversations. And when Boswell's memory was not strong enough to recall a conversation in detail, there was "*the Johnsonian æther*" to fall back on. No one has ever tried to explain what Boswell means by this phrase, which he introduces into the *Life* for July 1763. To understand what Boswell meant by it, we have to look at the history of his biography in the century after his death.

The first and most important assistance that Boswell received with the *Life* was from Edmond Malone. We cannot be certain of exactly what changes in the drafts of the work are his responsibility, but Boswell readily acknowledges his superior knowledge of Johnson, giving him the cognomen of "*Johnsonianissimus*."[24] Like Boswell, Malone had legal training, but (unlike Boswell) he was especially skilled in working with the intricacies of evidence, as we know from his superb Shakespearean studies, especially his analyses of the Ireland Shakespeare forgeries.[25] We know that Malone's keen eye for Johnsonian detail was responsible for Boswell's altering or deleting many passages and many examples of Johnson's talk that he deemed somehow un-Johnsonian. Hence even before the *Life* appeared, Boswell and his advisor worked diligently to change Johnson's utterances so that they fitted the man's received personality and style. Boswell's great reputation for accuracy not only owes a great deal to Malone's assistance; it is also due to the sheer multiplicity of detail that he presents. According to probability theory – a major eighteenth-century development in mathematics – the more times one tries to achieve a certain event, the greater is the probability that one will attain it. Fortuitously, Boswell reports on much more of Johnson's life and conversation than did any other contemporary writer. Hence Boswell's original audience quickly accepted the great mass of detail that the *Life* incorporates simply because there was so much of it that it *seemed* plausible. Another phenomenon of the first years of the history of the *Life* is the anthologizing of Boswell, a practice which I mentioned earlier. The first of these collections appeared the same year as the first edition of the *Life* –

The Witticisms, Anecdotes, Jests, and Sayings of Dr. Johnson, by the obviously pseudonymous "J. Merry," and before the end of the decade we have the publication of Stephen Jones's *Dr. Johnson's Table Talk* (1798), another collection of aphorisms and sayings extracted from Boswell. By 1807, Jones's publisher added a second volume of table-talk from the *Life* and, during the first thirty years of the nineteenth century, these extracts from Boswell enjoyed considerable popularity, with an entirely new selection appearing every decade or so. In 1820, the first collection to be entitled *Johnsoniana* was published, yet another selection of extracts "from Boswell's Life of the Great Lexicographer and Moralist"; this collection also occupied Volume 16 in a publisher's series called "The English Prose Writers," thus blending together for the first time Johnson the writer and Boswell the recorder of Johnson's conversation. Insensibly, the Boswellian record of Johnson's talk, which we have seen to be of such uncertain accuracy that even Boswell has to remind his original audience of his untrustworthy memory, becomes, through the facts of nineteenth-century publishing history, identical with the canon of Johnson's prose writings.

Another publishing process parallels the anthologizing of Boswell – the annotating of the *Life*, a cottage industry that consumed nineteenth-century literary men and women and their audiences and that furnished the reading public with several dozen different editions (and several hundred printings) of Boswell's work. I cannot discuss all of them – and, in any case, most of them are too unoriginal to merit attention – but several editors stand out as especially impressive. The first, obviously, is John Wilson Croker, whose five-volume edition Macaulay disparaged so thoroughly in the *Edinburgh Review* (September 1831) that we now tend to dismiss it as worthless. Croker's edition is worthy of modern scrutiny for a number of reasons. He was the first to include the *Tour to the Hebrides* as part of the *Life*; he prints numerous selections from Johnson's own writings that Boswell did not include; he runs long sections from other biographies to fill up Boswell's lacunae; and he is the first editor to begin the fashion of adding scholia as appendices. Croker admired Mrs. Piozzi's statement that Johnson's life was mainly conversation, and adds enthusiastically, "and that conversation was watched and recorded from night to night and from hour to hour with zealous attention and unceasing diligence."[26] That Croker allows himself to get carried away by his praise for Boswell is a truism; but Macaulay's famous phillipic against the work relates not to Croker's editorial efforts but to his disgust at Boswell's littleness and infamy. Johnson emerges from Boswell's biography as an extraordinary character, Macaulay proposes, because he was such a great man himself:

Johnson, as Mr. Burke most justly observed, appears far greater in Boswell's books than in his own. His conversation appears to have been quite equal to his writings in matter, and far superior to them in manner. When he talked, he clothed his wit and his sense in forcible and natural expressions. As soon as he took his pen in hand to write for the public, his style became systematically vicious...The reputation of those writings, which he probably expected to be immortal, is every day fading; while those peculiarities of manner and that careless table-talk the memory of which, he probably thought, would die with him, are likely to be remembered as long as the English language is spoken in any quarter of the globe.[27]

The transformation is complete: conversation becomes, nay, *exceeds* the writings as the authentic record of Johnson's genius.

Croker's annotating of Boswell was so thorough, especially with respect to discovering the names of people whom Boswell mentions but does not identify, that later editors of the *Life* can add little except more Johnsoniana. Further scholia are always possible. Hence when Percy Fitzgerald proposed a new edition of the *Life* in 1874, he could pose as a purifier of the text from the needless accretions of Croker and his successors.[28] Fitzgerald may have been critical of Croker, but he, too, was completely under Boswell's spell so far as Johnson's talk is concerned. Years later, in his own anthology of the best of Boswell, he would ask how Boswell "contrived to report Johnson's talk so accurately, how his memory served him so well."[29] Fitzgerald, thoroughly biased though he was in Boswell's favor, hits it right: Boswell had a gift of "visualization" which enabled him to see things as Johnson would have seen them, so that he was able to supply the very words and phrases that Johnson *would* have used: "Therefore though Johnson did not use the exact words and phrases, [Boswell] supplied a truly Johnsonian version..."[30] Fitzgerald clearly had made a convert of himself to the cause of Boswell's genius but, paradoxically, he is still capable of astonishing perceptions. He was the first editor to compare the text of the two editions of the *Life* that appeared during Boswell's lifetime; thus he remarks on how much Boswell managed to *improve* Johnson's conversation between the first and second editions![31] If the accuracy of Boswell's recollection was an issue, then one would have thought that his first memory would not require later emendation. But Fitzgerald's most telling remarks about Boswell do not appear in his edition of the *Life*; they are part of his reaction to the edition of G. Birkbeck Hill.

Hill spent twelve years, from 1875 to 1887, on his edition and, of course, it is the only one of the nineteenth-century editions that is still in print (contained in its entirety within L. F. Powell's contemporary revision). Hill's effort deserves full-length treatment, so I will do no more than touch upon a few of its qualities in this essay. Hill was a miscellaneous writer and editor with wide antiquarian interests who read more widely than any previous editors had done. But he spent most of the twelve years of work on his edition either on the Riviera or Lac Leman (whence he dated his preface), suffering from indifferent health. Since the Croker school of editors had already identified most of the miscellaneous Johnsoniana that we associate with the *Life*, there was not a great deal of this sort of editing for Hill to do, although he adds his share of scholia. And, since he was separated from a research library during his years of preparing his edition, his principal contribution had to be limited to annotating Boswell's text with respect to a limited number of memoirs, periodicals (the *Gentleman's Magazine* in particular), and Johnson's own writings. So Hill's greatest contribution was to search for parallels between the opinions that Johnson voices in his conversations and statements that he made in his own writings. Hence Hill, in hundreds of notes, does something that no Johnsonian had done in the previous century: he locates places in Johnson's own writings where he said something similar to his colloquialisms. All of these identifications still appear in the revised Hill–Powell edition. Hill never realized that he had come upon the key to Boswell's imaginative reconstruction (to use Pottle's term) of Johnson's conversation, for he was convinced that Boswell's versions were absolutely correct. And that key is simple: Boswell also had made himself familiar with Johnson's writings and, whenever he did not have a full statement in his diary of Johnson's views, he constructed one very ably and convincingly by paraphrasing Johnson's own opinions as he had expressed them in his works. Much of Johnson's conversation, as we find it in the *Life*, is undoubtedly authentic. But on the many occasions when we find that Boswell presents Johnson as giving an especially long and complicated comment, the kind for which there is seldom any corresponding entry in his diaries, I think that Boswell must have drawn upon his quite thorough knowledge of Johnson's major writings to furnish himself with appropriate Johnson-like views. This practice also helps explain why so much of Johnson's talk in Boswell's versions sounds so much more oratorical than does the talk in Mrs. Thrale's *Anecdotes* or Campbell's *Diary*. Hill was so thorough that he spotted occasional discrepancies in Boswell's presentations of Johnson. There is such a case in the miscellaneous assortment of sayings that Boswell inserts into his narrative for 1783 (IV, 176–98) – any miscellany in the *Life* is always cause for suspicion. This is the statement Boswell says he made to Sir William Scott lamenting the ending of public executions at Tyburn (IV, 188). In this anecdote, Johnson's favoring of public executions is so strong that Boswell himself, a strong advocate, expresses perfect agreement. But Hill's knowledge of Johnson's writings is superior to Boswell's, for in a note he adds the following comment: "We may compare with this 'loose talk' Johnson's real opinion, as set forth in *The Rambler*, No. 114," and proceeds to quote at length from that landmark essay against capital punishment.[32] Hill is such a believer in the accuracy of Boswell's reporting, even in the accuracy of Boswell's hearsay, that he prefers to make a distinction between Johnson's "loose talk" and his "real opinion," implying that Johnson was capable of appearing in conversation with views exactly the opposite of his expressed written opinion.

The success of Hill's edition of the *Life* was large, despite the persistent attacks, over the next two decades, of Percy Fitzgerald in a variety of publications. Fitzgerald criticized – with good reason – some of Hill's tendentious and tangential annotation, the silly table of Johnson's contemporaries that appears as a foldout frontispiece to Volume VI, and the inspired nonsense of Hill's lexicon of Johnson's sayings, "Dicta Philosophi."[33] But public opinion, or at least, literary opinion seems to have sided with Hill. Fitzgerald ridiculed one of the newspaper reviews of Hill, which included the curious paean, "*Six volumes of solid happiness!*"[34] and he correctly noted that Hill's concordance of Johnson's sayings included a good many by other people. Notwithstanding his efforts, Hill had brought about an important advance in Johnsonian studies: he solidified beyond doubt Macaulay's assertion that Johnson's talk would outlive his writings by actually treating the two as the same thing. He was quick to have his Oxford publishers capitalize on their now standard edition of Boswell – the next year he had them bring out an anthology of his own. Hill's *Wit and Wisdom of Samuel Johnson* (1888) is not just another abridgement of Boswell. It is the first harvest of Johnson's sayings from the *Life* that also contains quotations from Johnson's writings: for the first time, we have published evidence, and from an undoubted Johnsonian authority, that Johnson's conversation was the same thing as his writings.[35] It seems strange that anyone should regard Boswell's biography of Johnson as simply an extension of his works, as a Boswellian composition equivalent to one of Johnson's writings, but this conclusion is the logical result of Macaulay's admiration for the "careless table-talk" and of a century of dedicated editing without any serious doubts about Boswell's credibility as a reporter. The effects of this nineteenth-century evaluation of Johnson's conversation have affected our estimation of Johnson ever since.

V

This old-fashioned and, I think, incorrect evaluation of Johnson's conversation has had mixed consequences. Ever since Macaulay's review of Croker's edition of Boswell, there has existed the view that Boswell made Johnson a great writer. By no means has modern revisionism of Boswell's role in creating Johnson's conversation extirpated this belief: as recently as 1987, Alvin Kernan still could assert that "it was and is [Boswell's] biography, more than any other document, that made Johnson the great author of the age of print."[36] The *Life* does contain, on a very large scale, a redaction of what Boswell meant to be Johnson's own words, but the redaction, as I have argued, is not an accurate one. Moreover, even if the conversations were accurate, they would still consist entirely of Johnson's words that emphatically were not meant for print.[37] On the other hand, the notion that Boswell's *Life* made Johnson a great writer, if we readjust it slightly to reflect literary realities, does have real value, for there can be no doubt that the artistry of the *Life* did make Boswell a great writer. Macaulay may have been exaggerating somewhat (he was wont to do so) when he trumpeted that Boswell was the first of biographers, that he had no second, that his competitors were not even worthy of mention, that "Eclipse is first, and the rest nowhere."[38] But there can be no question that Boswell's imaginative reconstructions, his partial inventions, of the conversation of the most famous man of letters of his century are without parallel. I have deliberately emphasized how inventive Boswell is, but of course there are places in the *Life* where he must have set down what Johnson said with greater veracity than he shows in his creative sections. The strange phenomenon of the *Life* (to paraphrase Macaulay) is that it has created for its subject, Samuel Johnson, a dimension that most literary men and women have never possessed. This is the dimension of talk, of endlessly brilliant and effortless sayings that awaken a chord in every intelligence. Johnson, through the agency of Boswell, may be quoted correctly in literary reviews or misquoted ridiculously by politicians (I have in mind a recent instance by the Bush White House[39]), but in some way even the misquotation is still Johnson, and the imitation convincing evidence of an unexpected literacy. We might hope for more. But Johnson is surely, thanks in part to Boswell, the most widely quoted – and misquoted – writer of English prose in history: it is hard to improve on that.

NOTES

1 *Life*, II, 116. All further references to *Life* will appear parenthetically in the text.
2 *Account of Corsica*, pp. 334–5.
3 See Morris Palmer Tilley, *A Dictionary of the Proverbs in England in the Sixteenth and Seventeenth Centuries* (Ann Arbor: University of Michigan Press, 1950), p. 70.
4 "Nocturnal Turnings, or How Siamese Twins Have Sex," in *Music for Chameleons* (New York: New American Library, 1981), p. 255.
5 See "The Paradox of Johnsonian Studies," in *Johnson After Two Hundred Years*, ed. Paul J. Korshin (Philadelphia: University of Pennsylvania Press, 1986), pp. xi–xiii. The *Life*, as an anthologgy, consists of Boswell's own narrative, Johnson's own writings, which he quotes at length, hundreds of Johnson's letters, the legal opinions Johnson dictated for Boswell, and other Johnsonian documents.
6 Donald Greene, "'Tis a Pretty Book, Mr. Boswell, But – ," in *New Questions, New Answers*, pp. 132–42, gives a statistical appendix that enumerates the actual days on which Boswell passed any time in Johnson's company. As Greene notes (p. 134), it is certain, from the evidence of the *Life* itself, that there were 327 days on which Boswell had some contact with Johnson, but a generous form of "extrapolation" has permitted some scholars to raise this total to 425.

7 Percy Fitzgerald, *Boswell's Autobiography* (London: Chatto & Windus, 1912), p. 216, first noted that Boswell's part in the conversations he records tends to preclude his also recording them, but does not offer an explanation.

8 Louis Baldwin, in "The Conversation in Boswell's *Life of Johnson*," *Journal of English and Germanic Philology*, 51 (1952), 493–4, lists many of the places where Boswell apologizes for his lapses of memory. But Baldwin, whose doubts about Boswell's memory are the most detailed of any twentieth-century scholar, ultimately concludes that Boswell's figure of Johnson is reliable: "in the bulk of the conversation, if not all of it, the Dr. Johnson of the *Life* is quoting the real Dr. Johnson practically verbatim" (p. 506).

9 For example, the only fragment of Johnson's conversation that she preserved from her journey to France (*The French Journals of Mrs. Thrale and Doctor Johnson*, ed. Moses Tyson and Henry Guppy [Manchester: Manchester University Press, 1932], p. 131), Johnson's clever *mot* on performing Shakespeare's *Henry V* in a French theater, appears in the *Anecdotes*, as do virtually all of the colloquial comments from *Thraliana*.

10 See *Memoirs of Dr. Burney*, ed. Madame d'Arblay, 3 vols. (London, 1832), II, 76.

11 *Anecdotes* (London, 1786), p. 23.

12 *Anecdotes*, p. 44.

13 See *Anecdotes*, pp. 42–3.

14 See *Anecdotes*, pp. 110, 255, 273.

15 *Anecdotes*, pp. 154–5.

16 *Anecdotes*, p. 268.

17 *Dr. Campbell's "Diary" of a Visit to England in 1775*, ed. James L. Clifford, introd. S. C. Roberts (Cambridge: Cambridge University Press, 1947), p. 68.

18 See *Dr. Campbell's "Diary,"* p. 68 and note 114, pp. 125–6. Johnson certainly was capable of discussing sexual matters in public; Mrs. Thrale reports one such instance. "The other Day speaking of his Negroe Francis; I observed that he was very well-looking, for a Black a moor; Oh Madam says he Francis has carried the Empire of Cupid farther than many Men; When he was in Lincolnshire seven Years ago, he made Hay as I was informed, with so much Dexterity that a female Hay Maker followed him to London for Love." See *Thraliana: The Diary of Mrs. Hester Lynch Thrale*, ed. Katharine C. Balderston, 2 vols. (Oxford: Clarendon Press, 1942), I, 175.

19 *Dr. Campbell's "Diary,"* p. 76.

20 *Dr. Campbell's "Diary,"* pp. 77–8.

21 A good example is the account of an evening's conversation at Lord Mansfield's on April 11, 1773; see *The Private Papers of James Boswell from Malahide Castle*, ed. Geoffrey Scott and F. A. Pottle, 18 vols. (privately printed, 1928–34), VI, 107–11.

22 See "The Power of Memory in Boswell and Scott," in *Essays on the Eighteenth Century presented to David Nichol Smith in Honour of his Seventieth Birthday* (Oxford: Clarendon Press, 1945), p. 185.

23 See "The Making of the *Life of Johnson*," in his *Johnsonian and Other Essays and Reviews* (Oxford: Clarendon Press, 1953), p. 34.

24 See *Letters*, II, 381.

25 S. Schoenbaum, *Shakespeare's Lives* (Oxford: Clarendon Press, 1970), pp.

221–33, discusses Malone's evidentiary skills. A more thorough assessment of Malone's role in the making of Boswell's *Life* will be possible upon the completion of Peter Martin's biographical and critical study of Malone.

26 *The Life of Samuel Johnson, LL. D.*, ed. John Wilson Croker, 5 vols. (London, 1831), I, xxv. Croker adds, "But in recording conversations [Boswell] is unrivalled; that he was eminently accurate in substance, we have the evidence of all his contemporaries; but he is also in a high degree characteristic–dramatic" (I, xxix).

27 Thomas Babington Macaulay, *Critical and Historical Essays, contributed to the Edinburgh Review*, 3 vols. (London, 1843), I, 404, 407.

28 See *The Life of Samuel Johnson, LL. D.*, ed. Percy Fitzgerald, 3 vols. (London, 1874), I, x–xi.

29 See *Gems from Boswell. Being a Selection of the Most Effective Scenes and Characters in the Life of Johnson and the Tour to the Hebrides*, ed. Percy Fitzgerald (The Bibelots, Vol. 23) (London, 1907), p. vii.

30 *Gems from Boswell*, p. vii.

31 See *Croker's Boswell and Boswell. Studies in the "Life of Johnson"* (London, 1880), pp. 219–34. Fitzgerald was especially impressed with "A woman's preaching was like 'a dog walking on his *hinder* legs,' which now stands 'hind'" (p. 277).

32 *Boswell's Life of Johnson*, ed. G. Birkbeck Hill, 6 vols. (Oxford: Clarendon Press, 1887), IV, 188–9.

33 See Fitzgerald, *Editing à la Mode. An Examination of Dr. Birkbeck Hill's new edition of "Boswell's Life of Johnson"* (London, 1891), pp. 1–7, 32; *Life of James Boswell*, 2 vols. (London, 1891), II, 256–73, 281–4; and *A Critical Examination of Dr. G. Birkbeck Hill's "Johnsonian" Editions issued by the Clarendon Press, Oxford* (London, 1897), pp. 1–4, 12.

34 *A Critical Examination*, p. 1.

35 See *Wit and Wisdom of Samuel Johnson*, ed. George Birkbeck Hill (Oxford: Clarendon Press, 1888), esp. Hill's introduction.

36 See *Printing Technology, Letters & Samuel Johnson* (Princeton: Princeton University Press, 1987), p. 46.

37 I owe this astute perception to Isobel Grundy's review of Kernan's *Printing Technology, Letters & Samuel Johnson* in *The Age of Johnson*, 3 (1990), 456.

38 *Critical and Historical Essays*, II, 374.

39 See *The New York Times*, May 18, 1989, p. A-10: "'The media is responding to Gorbachev the way people responded to Doctor Johnson's famous dancing dog,' one senior Administration official said. 'It isn't how he dances, it is the fact that he dances at all.'"

13

REMEMBERING THE HERO IN BOSWELL'S
LIFE OF JOHNSON
Donna Heiland

> The Doctor's bones must be acknowledged to be the bones of a giant, or there
> would be poor picking, after their having furnished *Caledonian haggis*, and a
> dish of *Italian Macaroni*, besides slices innumerable cut off *from the body* [by]
> Magazine mongers, anecdote merchants and rhyme stringers.[1]

This vision of cannibalistic writers steadily carving away at the body of
Samuel Johnson indicates clearly "the Doctor's" fate in the years following
his death. Most immediately, it gives the reader a sense of the grimly
competitive "industry" that grew up around the figure of Johnson. At least
seven accounts of Johnson's life had been published even before his death in
1784, and at that point, production increased dramatically. Two new
biographies of Johnson came out that very month, one in the *Gentleman's
Magazine* and one in the *European Magazine*. 1785 saw the publication of
William Cook's *Life of Samuel Johnson* and William Shaw's *Memoirs of
Samuel Johnson*, as well as Boswell's own *Tour to the Hebrides*, with its
announcement of a full-scale life of Johnson to follow. In 1786 appeared
Joseph Towers's "Essay" on Johnson,[2] and the first of two major texts that
would stand in opposition to Boswell's work: Mrs. Piozzi's *Anecdotes of the
Late Dr. Samuel Johnson*, which Boswell attacked in print,[3] making good on a
promise he had made to Malone, to "trim her *recitativo* and all her *airs*."[4] It
was when Sir John Hawkins's "official" biography of Johnson appeared in
1787, however, that Boswell really asserted himself, not simply disparaging
the work of his rivals (though he did that too), but mapping out where his
own work stood in relation to these others. He ran an advertisement in the
newspaper, informing his potential readers that his work was in a state of
"great Forwardness," having been delayed so that he could have the benefit
of earlier writing about Johnson, from which he had hoped "to obtain much
Information." He now found himself "disappointed in that Expectation,"
and went on to urge his readers "not [to] permit unfavourable Impressions to
be made on their Minds, whether by the light Effusions of Carelessness and
Pique, or the ponderous Labours of solemn Inaccuracy and dark unchari-

table Conjecture," thus setting his work up against that of both Mrs. Piozzi and Hawkins.[5] The life of Johnson at this point was not just the subject of a book, or the focus of a tribute, but – as Pat Rogers has observed – "an ongoing controversy...People who had not been specially interested in Johnson during his lifetime were now fully aware of the wrangles between Boswell, Hawkins, and Piozzi."[6]

The battle for Samuel Johnson was thus well under way by the time Boswell published the *Life* in 1791, and must be in part responsible for the above image of Johnson as a giant corpse on which others feed, but historical context alone does not explain the almost lurid specificity of the image. These writers prey on Johnson's body, consuming it like vampires or ghouls, and further, seem to transform it into something new and strange – metonymies of themselves, perhaps; Boswell makes "Caledonian haggis" of his hero, while Mrs. Piozzi turns him into "Italian macaroni." Whichever way one reads the image, however, it asks the same question: what is the relationship between the living and the dead, or more particularly, between the biographer and his/her subject? How was Johnson regarded after he died? At stake here are questions of literary authority (who has it?), of personal identity (where does it reside? in what does it consist?), and of the relationship between them, questions that the *Life of Johnson* takes up in terms startlingly similar to those set forth in my epigraph.

The question of Boswell's relationship to London dominates the prefatory material of the *Life*, where Boswell takes pains to establish his literary credentials. He is the writer who "know[s] very well what [he is] about" when he portrays himself as the butt of Johnson's jokes.[7] He is the writer who likens his work to the *Odyssey* on the grounds that "[a]midst a thousand entertaining and instructive episodes the HERO is never long out of sight...and HE, in the whole course of the History, is exhibited by the Author for the best advantage of his readers" (I, 12). This simile casts Johnson as Odysseus almost by accident; the real credit here goes to Boswell, whose deft management of his narrative rivals Homer's. Boswell claims control over the formal aspects of the *Life* without hesitation, then. His relationship with Johnson is a somewhat trickier subject, however, and Boswell reserves any substantive discussion of it for the narrative proper, where it is introduced in the first line.

That opening line is well known: "To write the Life of him who excelled all mankind in writing the lives of others, and who, whether we consider his extraordinary endowments, or his various works, has been equalled by few in any age, is an arduous, and may be reckoned in me a presumptuous task" (I, 25). Boswell portrays himself and Johnson as authors, suggesting their status as peers even as he gives what may seem a *pro forma* nod at his own limited abilities. That self-qualification comes to seem more than a polite gesture as the text proceeds, however, and Boswell draws an increasingly limited picture of his authorial role. He is not an author in the way Johnson was. He has not written this life single-handedly, but has acted as editor to the many writers who have contributed to it, adding narrative to "explain, connect, and supply" gaps in stories told by others (I, 29). He mediates various presentations of Johnson (his own included), shaping and controlling a text that is not entirely his production.

Boswell has begun self-consciously to minimize his role in the *Life*, then, partly out of deference to Johnson's greater literary authority, partly out of deference to the various people whose work he has incorporated into the *Life*, and finally, partly out of deference to his readers. His well-known decision to write the *Life* in "scenes" – "interweaving what [Johnson] privately wrote, and said, and thought" – is made specifically for the benefit of the reader, who he hopes will thus be enabled to "live o'er" the various stages of Johnson's life with him (I, 30).[8] According to Boswell, at least, everyone matters more than he himself does, and this stance is pushed to an extreme when he comes to the account of Johnson's return to London in the fall of 1784, announcing that he will now bow out of the *Life*, and intrude on his reader no longer.

Having recounted the final incidents in his own relationship with Johnson, Boswell writes:

> I now relieve the readers of this Work from any farther personal notice of its author, who if he should be thought to have obtruded himself too much upon their attention, requests them to consider the peculiar plan of his biographical undertaking. (IV, 380)

Clearly, Boswell makes this move because he was not in London during Johnson's final illness, and so will no longer figure in the narrative of the *Life*. No long-term reader of Boswell could fail to doubt his ability to stick to this resolution, however, and that skepticism is justified. As Patricia Spacks has observed, Boswell is just as visible in the pages following this statement as in those preceding; first-person pronouns crop up in the very next paragraph, and regularly thereafter.[9] If this statement does not signal Boswell's actual exit from the text, then, it is important to examine why Boswell says it does. What does he have to gain by claiming to disappear in this way, and why does he do it at this point in the narrative?

Some answers to these questions have already been proposed. William Dowling reads Boswell's withdrawal from the text as indicating "the public significance of Johnson's death"; further, says Dowling, Boswell thus objectifies and enlarges his own vision of Johnson, establishing his perspective as "the perspective of an age." These statements are helpful, yet they ignore the fact that Boswell is still in the narrative. Spacks, on the other hand, proceeds from her recognition of Boswell's continuing presence in the text to argue that the "impossibility of his disappearing" from it indicates his centrality to the story. She goes on to say that "[a]t the narrative's heart lies Boswell's discovery of his own power in an asymmetrical relationship with an overwhelmingly powerful man."[10] These remarks, too, are helpful, but still leave one wondering about Boswell's reason for disavowing his presence in the text. What one wants is an approach that tries to understand the logic of the contradiction within the text, the logic that allows – perhaps calls for – Boswell to be a presence in the text, even while he is purportedly absent from it. It is with this task in mind that I'd like to turn to a close reading of the final movement of the *Life*, and observe that, while Boswell may not actually disappear from the text, the moment at which he claims to do so marks a significant change in the way he presents his material. The relatively straightforward chronological narrative of Johnson's life is complicated, as Boswell begins to devote as much attention to the footnotes as to the main line of the narrative.

To this point in the *Life*, the footnotes have primarily addressed issues relevant to the writing of the *Life*: they have glossed or expanded on particular points; they have acknowledged contributions and reviewed alternative versions of specific anecdotes; at times they have even developed into a running commentary, as Boswell systematically denounced Anna Seward, Mrs. Piozzi, and Sir John Hawkins. From the point at which Boswell claims to exit the text, however, the character of the notes changes. Even a quick glance reveals that they get longer and longer, threatening to push the main text right off the page. A more sustained reading suggests that, although some of the old wrangling still goes on, the notes in general are no longer adjuncts to specific points in the main text. Instead, they tell a story of their own, developing an image of Johnson that is not found elsewhere in the *Life*.[11]

The first of these unusually long footnotes appears only four sentences after Boswell has "relieved" his audience of his presence. Even in the final stages of illness, Boswell writes, Johnson's "love of literature did not fail" (IV, 381). A footnote offers the reader a catalog of works – given by Johnson to Bennet Langton, who in turn gave it to the King (and to Boswell) – of works Johnson had conceived but never written. This list is followed by a statement about the "facility" of Johnson's literary talent, introduced by a poem that clearly echoes "The Vanity of Human Wishes"; the first two lines read, "While through life's maze he sent a piercing view, / His mind expansive to the object grew."[12] This unacknowledged borrowing leads to a list of works that Johnson probably wrote but never acknowledged, beginning with sermons that others "were to preach...as their own," and ending with a denial of the claim that Johnson wrote "a Dedication to both Houses of Parliament of a book entitled 'The Evangelical History Harmonized.'" Even in this last piece, however, Boswell finds "several sentences constructed upon the model of those of Johnson." This point leads to a discussion of imitators of Johnson's style – "[e]ven our newspaper writers aspire to it" – and Boswell concludes by promising to publish an edition of Johnson's poems (IV, 381–4). The note runs on for approximately three pages in all editions in which Boswell had a hand, with a scant two or three lines of the main narrative heading the majority of those pages.[13]

This survey of Johnson's aims and influence suggests that an understanding of Johnson's authority, even identity, as a writer rests on a recognition of the range and impact of his thought. And almost as soon as this footnote ends, several pages in the main narrative – "exhibiting specimens of various sorts of imitations of Johnson's style" – extend the discussion of imitators begun in the note preceding, and at the same time make explicit these questions of authority and identity (IV, 385).[14] Of particular interest are the four passages from "serious imitators of Johnson's style." All of them take power as their subject, and are so arranged that they move from a portrait of man as a being whose power over "inferiour creatures" is "one of [his] noblest prerogatives," through two discussions of how misguided a "love of power" can be, to a consideration of language, the primacy of the rules by which it is governed, and by which one's own desire to change or improve it should also be governed (IV, 388–90). Each imitation of Johnson offers a narrower vision of the extent of human power than the one preceding. Yet the longer the list grows, the more forcefully Johnson's own power over others – and so his superiority to the rest of mankind – are affirmed.

This much is easily comprehensible, and the interlude moves to its conclusion, with Boswell saying that he thinks "the most perfect imitation of Johnson is a professed one, entitled 'A Criticism on Gray's Elegy in a Country Church-Yard'...[which] has not only the peculiarities of Johnson's style, but that very species of literary discussion and illustration for which he was eminent." Remarkably, however, Boswell does not include this imitation in his text. "Having already quoted so much from others," he writes, "I shall refer the curious to this performance, with an assurance of much entertainment" (IV, 392). Clearly, in a book as long as the *Life of Johnson*, well over a thousand pages in most editions, another paragraph or two would not have mattered much. Perhaps Boswell is afraid of another artist's representation of Johnson, one that may be more authentic than his own. This reading has an element of truth to it, and it is one to which I will return. Its limitation, however, is that it considers only what Boswell omitted from his text, and not what he included. For while he does suppress the "Criticism on Gray's 'Elegy,'" he does not suppress mention of it altogether; rather, he points to it as a work other than his own that will give the reader access to Johnson. By naming this and other such texts within the *Life*, Boswell manifests an explicit confidence in the face of other Johnsonians that he surely intends to take precedence over any unstated anxiety. Each of their narratives can be seen in the context of his all-encompassing vision of

Johnson, yet that vision does not seek to assimilate those narratives, but rather, directs the reader to them.[15] As had his earlier listing of Johnson's works (projected, published, and to be collected), Boswell's list of stylistic imitators of Johnson looks toward a literature outside the *Life*, suggesting that Boswell's subject is making its way into the world at large.

This suggestion is soon reinforced, with the appearance of still another "catalog," again a footnote and again of unusual length. This one is Johnson's will, reprinted in full over two, three, or nearly four pages, in major eighteenth-century editions of the *Life*, and rendered roughly half as long again by the commentary following (IV, 402–5).[16] This representation of the dispersal of Johnson's worldly goods follows logically on the heels of the preceding accounts of his literary projects, writing style, even ideas having been claimed by the public. And the closing pages of the biography carry this process of dispersal further still.

The announcement of Johnson's death is followed very quickly by a footnote that does all it can to sugggest that art has worked to counteract nature, to keep Johnson alive in memorial form at least. The note begins with Boswell recalling for the reader the fact that Johnson had enjoyed many tributes from his contemporaries, and then moves on to "reckon the extraordinary zeal of...artists to extend and perpetuate [Johnson's] image." Boswell cites "a bust by Mr. Nollekins" and the casts made from it; paintings of Johnson by Reynolds and others; eighteen engravings made from Johnson's portrait; and finally, "seals" and "copper pieces" with Johnson's head figured on them, the latter of which Boswell says "pass current as half-pence [in Birmingham], and in the neighbouring parts of the country" (IV, 421–2).[17]

This footnote climaxes the pattern described here, and the task now is to synthesize the details. What exactly does this series of passages depict? The answer is twofold.

First of all, the group of passages in question – an initial footnote, a portion of the main narrative generated thereby, and two further notes – begins by considering what Johnson might have produced, proceeds to review the literary and material legacies he did leave, and concludes by surveying what others have made of him. An attempt is thus made to anatomize the nature of Johnson's greatness, and to acknowledge the various forms in which that greatness manifested itself. Further, each of the passages in question repeats that effort to anatomize Johnson's achievement, tracing the path of his fame, his progress through the world. Stories of works he might have written passed from Johnson to Langton to the King to Boswell; imitations of Johnson's style abound; his personal fortune is distributed among his friends. And the final note discussed above, with its enumeration of the forms in which Johnson's image was to be found scattered across England, focuses attention on the fact that what has been depicted in this whole series of footnotes is equivalent to the dissemination of Johnson's body.

Cultural analogues for such a phenomenon include the Dionysian ritual of *sparagmos* – in which a sacrificial body often identified with the god is torn to pieces, and then consumed, in the separate ritual of *omophagia* – as well as the Christian counterpart to these two rituals, the celebration of the Eucharist. And such analogues are useful in understanding Boswell's representation of Johnson after death. The man whom Boswell "worshipped" while alive, the man for whom he felt a seemingly religious "reverence," "veneration," and "enthusiasm" (I, 384; II, 13, 229; III, 331), is in fact best seen as a divinity whose body is divided among and consumed by his followers after his death. He might be called a "body god."[18] Recent criticism has suggested that the greatness of Boswell's Johnson lay at least partly in his physical presence, and my reading agrees with and extends this observation.[19] By the end of the *Life*, Johnson has become the lifeblood of the culture he himself helped to create, a kind of host body off which others feed.

Even as the *Life* images this fragmenting and scattering of Johnson's body, it at the same time represents and so repeats the process it describes. The text itself becomes increasingly fragmented, both in terms of its typographic and its narrative line, as the footnotes become ever more dominant. By the end of the *Life*, one is reading about Johnson in discontinuous chunks, and this is a mode of reading for which the work gives an explicit rationale. According to the theory of biography developed in the early pages of the *Life*, "the boy is the man in miniature" – Johnson at three is the "infant Hercules of toryism" (I, 38, 47). The narrative is not developmental, but moves through a series of scenes, anecdotes, and so on that conveys a single image of Johnson. Thus, any one of Boswell's representations of Johnson is as complete and as valid as any other; each is a metonymy of the whole man. By this logic, the *Life* and each piece of it are to be seen in the same way – as metonymies of the hero. And whether one reads and remembers the whole text, or – as most readers do – only a favorite part of it, that mode of reading is sanctioned by the text itself. For the reader to single out any one scene, anecdote or other piece of the text is to signal that, on one level, Boswell has done what he set out to do, and "*Johnsonised* the land" (I, 13).

If Boswell encourages the fragmentation of the *Life* on the one hand, however, on the other he makes sure that his text, and its subject, will always be reconstituted by the reader as well. To read about Boswell's Johnson is inevitably an "endlesse work," for the biography never comes to a full stop. As Boswell himself announces, the *Life* ends with essentially the same portrait of Johnson as that which opened the *Tour to the Hebrides*; the end of the biography thus sends the reader back to the beginning of the earlier work, and asks that he or she begin reading all over again. Boswell thus guarantees that Johnson will rise again, but also that he will have control over that resurrection, and over all those representations of Johnson's body listed in the passages discussed above – representations distinct from, but at the same time subsumed, epitomized, and even completed by his own.

That is one reading of the pattern described above, a reading that sees in the end of the book the identification of Johnson as a divine figure, celebrated by a priestly Boswell and offered to a sympathetic reader.[20] It is a satisfying pattern to discover – ongoing, self-generating, and so perfectly closed – or so it seems. A second look reveals trouble in paradise, however, first within this neatly closed figure, and finally of a sort to challenge the stability of the figure itself.

In portraying Johnson as a "body god," Boswell inevitably endows him with the paradoxical status common to all such divinities. He at once has power over and is subservient to the disciples who celebrate him; he is at one and the same time an ideal and sacrificial victim, a standard of moral and even material worth (virtually "coin of the realm") and one whose value is determined by his culture.[21] The paradox inherent in the concept of divinity incarnate is the epitome, or perhaps the ultimate extension, of the familiar dichotomy in Boswell's portrayal of his subject.[22] Boswell reveres Johnson, and at the same time manipulates him continually. He makes Johnson an icon of an age, and at the same time takes care to expose the "shade" of his character (I, 30). If the footnotes studied here suggest a reading of Johnson as divine, then the text running above those notes makes clear that he was also painfully human.[23] And even as his subject emerges as a contradiction in terms, so Boswell himself appears as one whose status in the text vacillates. He is and is not present in the text (and now the problem of his presence in absence begins to have at least a context, if not a motive); he does and does not have authority over Johnson, over his readers, over rival Johnsonians. That the hierarchical relationship between god and priest is reversible indicates the fragility of the pattern of death and resurrection described above; neither Johnson's authority nor Boswell's servility is absolute. And readers and rival Johnsonians have the power to break that structure altogether, taking advantage of the uncertain distribution of power to make their own bid for control of the text, and Johnson.

Of these two groups, the readers have an obvious potential to truncate the textual mechanism Boswell has set in motion. If they do not read the text, his intention to "Johnsonise the land" will undoubtedly be thwarted. The real danger, however, comes from the rival Johnsonians, all those other authors, artists, engravers, and so on who not only people the footnotes, but also comprise the industry that Boswell sought to control before he even began to write the *Life*. Boswell is the one who incorporated them into his text, and yet – as I suggested earlier – in so doing, he invoked a wider world, one that might not be entirely in his control.

Taking these remarks as a starting point, and looking again at the way this final movement of the *Life* proceeds, it is now possible to see that the series of notes represents not only the dispersal of Johnson's body in the world at large, but the parasitical activity of the world at large, of all those imitators, engravers, painters, and poets that Boswell lists, who prey on that body to produce their own work. Here, the image of Johnson as a host body off which his survivors feed provides the obvious model for reading. Both Boswell and those artists he refers to are parasites on Johnson, though one suspects that Boswell himself would like to escape this label. This may be part of his purpose in gradually effacing himself from his own text, completing the process shortly before the point when Johnson dies and the biographers go to work. By not being there, he is not guilty. He is not one of the ghouls preying on Johnson; if anything, he is trying to put his hero back together again.

Boswell, of course, cannot avoid his role of parasite. In his work, he does prey on Johnson, and many others as well, but even as he does so, he is in turn able to claim authority over all those artists and writers whose work he names in the footnotes. They are so portrayed that they appear to be parasites on him – or on his book.[24] Those footnotes that creep up the page are feeding off the body of Boswell's text, a body that thus begins to replace Johnson's body as the central figure in the narrative. And yet, just as parasites can destroy the host body, the footnotes of the text threaten to take over the center, as I noted earlier; Boswell's rivals demand more of the reader's attention than does Boswell himself, thus undermining Boswell's authority even as he asserts it. And the footnotes do seem to win at last, with the final note of the first edition, one not yet discussed in this essay.

In this note, Boswell is meditating on the impossibility of finding "a perfect resemblance of Johnson" (IV, 428), though he does find that "parts of [Johnson's] character" have been "admirably expressed" by others. The examples he cites are not men, but specific biographies of men. The note thus evolves into a meditation on biographical method, as Boswell discusses Clarendon's portrait of Lord Falkland, noted for his "wit...judgement... fancy...[and] ratiocination," and then Bayle's account of Menage, noted for his conversation. The final sentence of the note tells us that the contributors to *Menagiana* "were not obliged to rectify what they had heard [Menage] say; for, in so doing, they had not been faithful historians of his conversations," and this statement – an oblique justification of Boswell's own method – is literally the last word on literary practice in the *Life of Johnson* (IV, 429). The parasite – the other or alien within the text – thus seems to be the voice of authority, making Boswell's authority seem secondary, derived; and so the host–parasite relationship turns yet again, as Boswell comes to seem the one preying on other writers.

Only on returning to the main narrative does one see that the host–

parasite relationship reverses itself one last time. In the closing pages of the *Life*, Boswell preys on his own work; one recalls that he presents readers with a final portrait of Johnson that is a revision of his own earlier portrait of Johnson in the *Tour to the Hebrides*. Any idea of Johnson's body distinct from its representation in the *Life* really has disappeared, then; the body of the text is the only body left, and Boswell himself is both host and parasite. Where Boswell began by defining his writing in comparison with Johnson's, he ends by defining his writing in comparison with his own writing. He has become his own standard of value, and his literary authority is thus, for a moment, assured.

This assurance of authority will vanish as soon as the cycle of reading initiated by the return to the *Hebrides* begins again, yet even as it is achieved, that assurance is significantly qualified. Boswell's insistence on the self-referentiality of his vision of Johnson emphasizes that this Johnson is his own creation, embodying but a single perspective on the man who existed outside the *Life*. And so one is led to ask whether the host–parasite relationship overturns the pattern of death and regeneration described earlier, a pattern that purports to describe Johnson's fate beyond the world of the *Life* even as it tries to control that fate. Is Johnson's body finally sacrificed to the body of the text? Yes and no. These two paradigms are themselves finally related as host and parasite, for each implies the existence of the other. Boswell's perception of Johnson as a god whose body is dispersed throughout the world implies the existence of the parasites that claim it. Conversely, the parasites need a body on which to prey. The Doctor's bones are the bones of a giant, and it is thanks to Boswell, and all the rest of those magazine mongers, anecdote merchants, and rhyme stringers – parasites every one – that this is so.

NOTES

A version of this essay was read at a meeting of the New York Eighteenth-Century Seminar, and my thanks go to those who were present – particularly Kenneth Craven – for responses which sharpened and broadened my thinking.

1 The passage is from an unidentified source, quoted in Mary Hyde, *The Impossible Friendship* (Cambridge: Harvard University Press, 1972), p. 116.

2 Robert E. Kelly and O M Brack, Jr., *Samuel Johnson's Early Biographers* (Iowa: University of Iowa Press), pp. 121–4 give further details on these early accounts of Johnson's life.

3 A full account of Boswell's attack on Mrs. Piozzi's *Anecdotes* appears in Hyde, *The Impossible Friendship*, pp. 106–15.

4 James Boswell to Edmond Malone, March 31, 1786, *Corr: Garrick, Burke, Malone*, p. 314.

5 St. James's Chronicle, May 12–15, 1787, partly quoted in Hyde, *The Impossible Friendship*, p. 120.

6 Pat Rogers, "Introduction" to James Boswell, *Life of Johnson*, ed. R. W. Chapman, rev. J. D. Fleeman (Oxford: Oxford University Press, 1980), p. xxvi.

7 *Life*, 1, 3. References to this edition will appear within the body of the essay.

8 Boswell recorded his decision "to write Dr. Johnson's life in scenes" in his journal for October 12, 1780. See *Laird*, p. 260.

9 Patricia Meyer Spacks makes this point as part of a longer discussion of the ways in which Boswell continues to "obtrude" on his audience. See *Gossip* (New York: Alfred A. Knopf, 1985), p. 102.

10 See William Dowling, *The Boswellian Hero* (Athens: University of Georgia Press, 1979), p. 172, and *Language and Logos in Boswell's Life of Johnson* (Princeton: Princeton University Press, 1981), pp. 162–3. For Spacks's discussion, see *Gossip*, pp. 102–3.

11 This point is most obvious if one examines the first or second edition (published in 1791 and 1793 respectively). The third edition (1799) is the final authority for my purposes, incorporating Boswell's final changes and additions to his text; beginning with the third edition, however, the notes of Boswell's editors make it at least initially difficult to distinguish clearly the shape of the original text. My decision to use the Hill–Powell edition of the *Life* as my primary text stems first of all from the fact that it is based on the 1799 edition, secondly from the fact that it indicates clearly those notes which Boswell authorized, and thirdly from the fact that it is a text to which most readers will have access. On the few occasions when a reference to this edition alone is not enough to make my point, I direct the reader specifically to the earlier editions.

12 The lines of verse are from John Courtenay's *Poetical Review of the Literary and Moral Character of the Late Samuel Johnson, LL.D.* (Dublin, 1786).

13 See the first three editions of the *Life*:

James Boswell, *The Life of Samuel Johnson, LL.D.*, 2 vols. (London, 1791), II, 557–60; hereafter cited as *Life*, 1791.

James Boswell, *The Life of Samuel Johnson, LL.D.*, 2nd ed, 3 vols. (London, 1793), III, 656–60; hereafter cited as *Life*, 1793. There were two major emendations to the note in this edition; the list of works attributed to Johnson on the basis of internal evidence was shortened, while the discussion of stylistic imitators was lengthened.

James Boswell, *The Life of Samuel Johnson, LL.D.*, 3rd ed., 4 vols. (London, 1799), IV, 405–9; hereafter cited as *Life*, 1799.

14 My reading counters that of Donald J. Newman, who argues that the pages devoted to Johnson's imitators "work against the flow of his narrative." While he sees their placing as an inexplicably bad artistic choice, however, his speculation that they may represent "Boswell's unconscious resistance to reliving the pain of his loss seven years earlier," his desire to "cut himself off" from Johnson's death, moves closer to the reading I am developing here. See p. 67 of "The Death Scene and the Art of Suspense," in *New Questions, New Answers*, pp. 53–72.

15 *Cf.* Dowling's point that quotation in the *Life* does not assimilate the work quoted, but rather invokes the "entire world" of the work in question (*Language and Logos*, pp. 41–2).

16 See *Life*, 1791, II, 572–3 for the will and codicil, and II, 574–5 for the commentary; *Life*, 1793, III, 681–4 for the will and codicil, and III, 684–6 for the commentary; *Life*, 1799, IV, 429–32 for the will and codicil, and IV, 432–4 for the commentary. In the Hill–Powell edition, the will and codicil run from IV, 402–4, and Boswell's commentary from IV, 404–5.

17 In the Hill–Powell edition of the *Life*, Johnson's death occurs at IV, 417, and the details up to and including the funeral continue to IV, 421, where the footnote in question begins. This note grew progressively longer; the first edition lists only seventeen engravings of Johnson (*Life*, 1791, IV, 581); the second lists eighteen (*Life*, 1793, III, 700–2); the third adds the references to the seals and coins (*Life*, 1799, IV, 449–51).

18 Thanks to Ellen Martin for suggesting the phrase "body god." Rituals of tearing apart and consuming a sacrificial body of course occur in many cultures, and have been discussed extensively in the literature of several disciplines. For a critical survey of major work on this subject, see pp. 24–35 of Marcel Detienne, "Pratiques culinaires et esprit de sacrifice," in Marcel Detienne and Jean-Pierre Vernant, *La Cuisine du sacrifice en pays grec* (Paris: Gallimard, 1979), pp. 7–35. Pages 30–1 comment specifically on the connections between Dionysian ritual and the celebration of the Eucharist. For a specifically literary contextualization of this subject, see Maggie Kilgour, *From Communion to Cannibalism: An Anatomy of Metaphors of Incorporation* (Princeton: Princeton University Press, 1990).

19 See Fredric V. Bogel, *Literature and Insubstantiality in Later Eighteenth-Century England* (Princeton: Princeton University Press, 1984), pp. 173–94, as well as his essay, "Did You Once See Johnson Plain?" in *New Questions, New Answers*, pp. 73–93. See also *William Dowling, The Boswellian Hero* (Athens: University of Georgia Press, 1979), p. 141, and *Language and Logos*, pp. 66–103. Dowling's earlier work coincides nicely with mine, specifically asserting the importance of Johnson's presence. We continue to agree, insofar as his later work locates that presence in concrete representations of Johnson, not looking farther for an essence or reality behind the appearance. But when *Language and Logos* suggests that the body is a trivial manifestation of that presence, which is to be found in Johnson's speech – if anywhere – we part company.

20 For a suggestive context in which to place Boswell's efforts to ensure the continuing presence of Johnson in the world, and in the lives of his readers, see Max Weber, "The Routinization of Charisma," in *Economy and Society: An Outline of Interpretive Sociology*, trans. Ephraim Fischaff *et al.* ed. Guenther Roth and Claus Wittich, 2 vols. (1968, rpt. Berkeley: University of California Press, 1978), I, 246–54. Thanks to Michael Suarez, S.J., for this reference.

21 For a more general discussion of the paradoxical nature of sacred beings, and of their relationships with their worshippers, see Emile Durkheim, *The Elementary Forms of the Religious Life*, trans. Joseph Ward Swain (1915; New York: Macmillan–Free Press, 1965), pp. 385–8.

22 For different reading of antithetical relations in the *Life*, see *Language and Logos*, pp. 3–65.

23 On the portrait of Johnson that emerges in the narrative running above the footnotes discussed in this essay, see Newman, "The Death Scene and the Art of

Suspense." This is the most recent in a series of discussions of the dying Johnson as a Christian hero.

24 In this paragraph and what follows, I am indebted to J. Hillis Miller's discussion of the host–parasite relationship. See "The Critic as Host," in *Deconstruction and Criticism: Harold Bloom, Paul DeMan, Jacques Derrida, Geoffrey H. Hartman, J. Hillis Miller* (New York: Seabury Press, 1979), pp. 218–53.

14

TRUTH AND ARTIFICE IN BOSWELL'S
LIFE OF JOHNSON
Greg Clingham

I

Boswell was ever-protective of Johnson's reputation and concerned to establish what he considered the truth about the great moralist.[1] On March 16, 1776 Boswell pointed out to Johnson that he had been misrepresented in a volume of Johnsoniana just published, and suggested that Johnson disavow the publication lest it damage his reputation. Boswell's identification with Johnson seems to have been so strong that to Johnson's unequivocal "I shall give myself no trouble about the matter," Boswell could not help thinking of Johnson's elevated character and how worried he, Boswell, would be if he were in Johnson's place (*Life*, II, 432–3). Perhaps by way of explaining his position, Johnson tells a story about telling stories:

> The value of every story depends on its being true. A story is a picture either of an individual or of human nature in general: if it be false, it is a picture of nothing. For instance: suppose a man should tell that Johnson, before setting out for Italy, as he had to cross the Alps, sat down to make himself wings. This many people would believe; but it would be a picture of nothing...[Langton] used to think a story, a story, till I shewed him that truth was essential to it. (*Life*, II, 433–4)

The "truth" of Johnson's absurd little anecdote is obviously other than the traveller's literal intention or capacity to fly over the Alps. Boswell takes this opportunity to moralize about the "importance of strict and scrupulous veracity" and to affirm that Johnson's conversation reflected "veracity" on the slightest occasions; for example, in the anecdote Johnson tells of being mistaken for a night-watchman: "A gentlewoman...begged I would give her my arm to assist her in crossing the street, which I accordingly did; upon which she offered me a shilling, supposing me to be the watchman. I perceived that she was somewhat in liquor" (II, 434). "This," Boswell says, "if told by most people, would have been thought an invention; when told by Johnson, it was believed by his friends as much as if they had seen what passed."

Why should this be so? Obviously, Boswell is pointing out Johnson's integrity and trustworthiness, which feature largely in his portrayal of Johnson's character in the *Life*. But there is nothing intrinsically *un*inventive about Johnson's anecdote; yet it is accepted by Boswell as if he had seen it happen, and, therefore, as if it were *not* a story. While Boswell responds imaginatively to Johnson's story – there is something eloquently revealing of human nature, though incongruous, about an old lady mistaking the grand moralist for a working man – he accounts for its effect by invoking a notion of truth implying a correspondence between Johnson's words and independently existing and personally verifiable facts. That is, although Boswell is recounting a moment in which Johnson demonstrates that by his powers of story-telling, he is larger than the publicly received image of his character identified with his printed conversations and *bons mots* – "I shall give myself no trouble about the matter" – Boswell *values* that experience by claiming historical veridicality for it. Coming in a work in which the skillful use of "fictional" means to dramatize and portray a historical personage is conspicuous, Boswell's inclination to blur the distinction between Johnson's story-telling and unmediated historical fact is central to the nature of his biography.

That blurring is expressed in the prefatory material to the first and second editions, and in the opening pages of the *Life*. Boswell makes two related points in these pages: that the *Life* will constitute a monument to the memory of Johnson – specifically, that Johnson "will be seen as he really was," "will be seen...more completely than any man who has ever yet lived," by means of a "scrupulous authenticity" (I, 30, 8); and that the *Life* will embalm Johnson in a kind of mausoleum.[2] In the early pages Boswell takes issue with the factual accuracy and the jaundiced tone of the biographies of Johnson by Sir John Hawkins and Mrs. Thrale-Piozzi, and proposes that his method of dramatizing Johnson through his letters, conversation, and the points of view of various contemporaries is the most "perfect mode of writing any man's life" (I, 29–30). In the light of what we now know of the care with which Boswell shaped his portrait of Johnson, and the creative consciousness which informs the work, it is noticeable in the opening pages, and in the repeated assurances throughout the *Life* that the Johnson we are being given is "authentic," that Boswell underplays what might be seen as an inauthenticating artifice. In his depiction of the character of Pascal Paoli in *An Account of Corsica* (1768) Boswell earnestly asserts the truthfulness of his work by eliminating the idea of artifice and emphasizing the authenticity of what he presents:

> as I have related his [Paoli's] remarkable sayings, I declare upon honour, that I
> have neither added nor diminished; nay so scrupulous have I been, that I
> would not make the smallest variation even when my friends thought it would

be an improvement. I know with how much pleasure we read what is perfectly authentick. (p. xiii)

Whatever Boswell does with Paoli, we have come to know that he did not, and could not, simply transcribe Johnson's conversation.[3] However, he does everything possible to suggest that the portrait of Johnson he presents *has* existed independently of his efforts, and that his creative shaping only reveals the authenticity of Johnson's character. This attitude implicitly attributes a historical, *a priori* factual status to Boswell's portrait of Johnson.

However, the discrepancy between Boswell's practice and his claims is ontologically interesting – different, for example, from the principle espoused by Pope when he wrote that "Men must be taught as if you taught them not; / And Things *unknown* propos'd as Things forgot" (*Essay on Criticism*, 574–5); and different, too, from a mere rhetorical strategy designed to present a certain literary image of Johnson. However artful Boswell is in presenting Johnson, he seems to believe, or needs to give the impression of believing, that the rhetorical, metaphoric presence of Johnson is real and historical. This attitude reflects a distrust of language and biography which Boswell had already articulated in an essay "On Diversion," in the *London Magazine* (subsequently published as *The Hypochondriack*) in October 1779. In this essay Boswell differentiates the biographical portraits of Xenophon from fiction:

> Of the many valuable records of human nature which have been preserved from remote antiquity through a series of ages down to the time in which we live, there is none which pleases me more than the character of Agesilaus, as drawn by Xenophon. In all the writings of Xenophon there is a beautiful simplicity which is not only agreeable in its manner, but also materially estimable for its being a certain indication of truth; so that while we read, we can trust with salutary confidence to the information which is communicated to us. Instances of excellence of whatever kind will not do us essential good if we know or even suspect that they are but the fictions of imagination: but if we are assured that they are real, we may hope to attain to what others of our species have actually been. Horace in enumerating the various instructions which may be derived from Homer, observes,
>
> > "Quid virtus et quid sapientia possit
> > "Utile proposuit nobis exemplar Ulyssen."
> > "What virtue and what wisdom join'd may reach,
> > "He makes Ulysses' great example teach."
>
> But, as Homer's work is a poem, to the truth of which we cannot give credit, his character of Ulysses can operate only as exciting high ideas of human excellence; whereas Xenophon's character of Agesilaus affords us the encouragement of knowing that such excellence has indeed existed. (*Hypochondriack*, I, 299–300)

The distinction Boswell sees between a "historical" character, such as Agesilaus, and a "fictional" one, such as Ulysses, is that the "truth" of the former can be "credited," and can therefore be the basis of moral emulation and influence. The "truth" of Agesilaus lies in the assurance that he is "real," and is set over against the "fictions of imagination." Now, although the works of Xenophon and Homer are generically different – biography as opposed to epic – there is no way in which Boswell can verify the factual reality of Xenophon's Agesilaus any more than he can falsify that of Homer's Ulysses; indeed, he implicitly recognizes this by basing his conviction of the reality and the truth of Agesilaus on Xenophon's "beautiful simplicity" and "agreeable...manner" of writing. In other words, Xenophon writes so convincingly that we feel the truth of his portrayal, and so "we can trust with salutary confidence to the information which is communicated to us." Homer, however, also writes well, but because his characters are poetic and not historical Boswell is unprepared to "trust...[himself] to the information" being communicated.

Boswell's point of view is didactic and his historical understanding implicitly exemplary.[4] He also clearly needs, emotionally and morally, the assurance that the past is real, and that it exists prior to the literary structure which makes it present, mediates it to his experience. The importance of Xenophon's Agesilaus lies in this assurance, yet Boswell cannot account for that assurance of historical reality other than by focusing on Xenophon's artifice. It is a conviction of, or desire for, *a priori* historical reality ambiguously related to the biographer's artifice which Boswell seems to have in mind when he so frequently mentions "authenticity" in the *Life of Johnson*.

But "authenticity" is not truth. Boswell's emphasis on communicated "information" in the *Hypochondriack* essay, and on the accuracy of essential detail in the *Life*, suggests the claim to originality, authority, and a legal status inherent in the historical meanings of "authentic" (see *OED*). However, while Boswell cannot believe in the truth of Homer's Ulysses because he has not existed historically, Johnson, by contrast, takes Homer's characters as the standard of general nature by which to approximate the human truth of Shakespeare's drama: "the poems of Homer we yet know not to transcend the common limits of human intelligence, but by remarking, that nation after nation, and century after century, has been able to do little more than transpose his incidents, new name his characters, and paraphrase his sentiments."[5] There is a tension between authenticity and truth in Boswell's invocation of *Rambler* 60 in the early pages of the *Life* to justify the kind of portrait of Johnson he creates. Boswell is at one with the *Rambler* essay in presenting the light and shade of Johnson's character; in drawing on his personal knowledge and experience; and in his sensitivity to the significant, personal, and domestic particulars of behavior through which the biographer "can portray a living acquaintance."[6] Boswell quotes a large part of *Rambler* 60, but omits a passage in which Johnson goes beyond the question of the authenticity of the details of the life of a biographical subject, and speaks instead of biography's capacity to draw on and appeal to general human experience by virtue of its kinship with poetry and drama:

> All joy or sorrow for the happiness or calamities of others is produced by an act of imagination, that realises the event however fictitious, or approximates it however remote, by placing us, for a time, in the condition of him whose fortune we contemplate; so that we feel, while the deception lasts, whatever motions would be excited by the same good or evil happening to ourselves.
>
> Our passions are therefore more strongly moved, in proportion as we can more readily adopt the pains and pleasures proposed to our minds, by recognising them as at once our own, or considering them as naturally incident to our state of life. (I, 318–19)

The sympathetic experience described here is no different in kind from that described in the "Preface" to Shakespeare or being brought to bear by Johnson on the poetry of Donne and Cowley when he finds their writing "not successful in representing or moving the affections." For "As they were wholly employed on something unexpected and surprising they had no regard to that uniformity of sentiment, which enables us to conceive and to excite the pains and the pleasures of other minds."[7] In *Rambler* 60 Johnson suggests that a biographer fulfills his purpose in proportion to his capacity to write creatively; he may be able to conceive the pains and pleasures of other minds, but he must also excite them. Many biographers, Johnson notes (in a passage partly quoted by Boswell), "imagine themselves writing a life when they exhibit a chronological series of actions and preferments," while only a few can "portray a living acquaintance, except by his most prominent and observable particularities, and the grosser features of his mind."[8]

Boswell is celebrated for having surpassed a mere chronological structure in the *Life* and for giving us a "living acquaintance" in his portrait of Johnson. But the question is, how much and what kind of truth does Boswell's "living acquaintance" encompass? If Johnson's discussion of biography in *Rambler* 60 points to the dramatic evocation and revelation of the subject's character through the biographer's art and his possession of nature which characterize the *Lives of the Poets*, then, despite associating himself with Johnson's position on biography early in the *Life*, Boswell seems to shun the idea of the dialectical interdependence of biographical artifice and truth.[9] What then is Boswell's relation to his subject, what does Boswell's "monument" signify, his "mausoleum" contain? How much truth about – truth *of* – Johnson does Boswell reveal in the *Life*?

II

The question of truth rather than authenticity is one that modern criticism of the *Life* has not asked, and its silence on this issue reflects Boswell's susceptibilities and the tension at the heart of his biography. My interest in this issue does not concern Boswell's assiduity as a researcher, nor the extent of his genius or memory, nor, strictly speaking, his method of "translating" his notes and memoranda into his journal entries and into the scenes in the *Life* – all of which have been widely discussed.[10] I am interested in *what* Boswell makes and *what* that portrait tells us about Johnson and about Boswell.

Boswell scholars can be divided into two main groups: the first, including William Siebenschuh, Ralph Rader, William Dowling, and Fredric Bogel, takes Boswell's dramatic artifice and fictional techniques for granted, and discusses the *Life* as self-contained, self-consistent, and self-reflexive.[11] The second group, including Frederick Pottle, Frank Brady, Geoffrey Scott, and Marshall Waingrow, shares the first group's admiration for Boswell's dramatizing powers, but also claims that he is factually accurate and authentic.[12] Like Pottle, Waingrow, and Scott, James Clifford invokes Boswell's "supreme gift of dramatization" in order to defend him against questions of his factual accuracy.[13]

Ralph Rader's "Literary Form in Factual Narrative: The Example of Boswell's *Johnson*" has come to be regarded as seminal in arguing for the intrinsic merit of Boswell's fictionalized presentation of Johnson's life and character. He acknowledges that by themselves the accuracy and narrative coherence of Boswell's account do not constitute his strength. Following Boswell's own statements about his intentions – and concurring with most critics who have written on the *Life* – Rader finds the conversations and "scenes" of greatest interest, particularly because their place in the narrative facilitates the presentation of the "essence" of Johnson's character (p. 28).[14] To make the character of Johnson the subject of the book, Boswell was not required to adhere to strict factual accuracy: "He gives not the whole of Johnson's words but the essence of them, preserving only the spirit and, we may add, the effect of Johnson's talk and the atmosphere of the moment as the listeners felt it" (p. 28). Rader argues that Boswell was "creating an objective correlative of a grand emotive idea," so that we might "feel that admiration and reverence which is the natural emotive consequence of full empathetic perception of the character" (p. 27). Boswell's image of Johnson, drawn from a myriad of fragments and particulars, unifies the *Life*, and Boswell's art lifts the image of Johnson out of the constrictions and obscurity of his quotidian, historical world for us to encounter now. Despite local differences, this ideal, transcendental conception of Boswell's artistic creation is the basis of Bogel's argument that Boswell has created a "hero of presence," of Dowling's argument that Boswell has created a hero of the ordinary, and the general sense that Boswell's art and his ubiquitous sensibility have conveyed the truth about the thinker and Christian he so admired.[15]

The main challenge to these views has hitherto come from Donald Greene, who has simply but tellingly pointed out that, unified as Boswell's portrait of Johnson might be, it is sometimes starkly at odds with that which we have about Johnson from other sources (including Johnson's auto-biographical fragments). Indeed, the detailed comparison of Boswell with other biographers of Johnson (both contemporary and modern) has hardly occurred to Boswellians.[16] Perhaps Boswell's very success in convincing readers that the conversations portray Johnson exactly as he was ought to necessitate some skepticism on the part of the reader.

Rader, however, defends his position theoretically. In order to account for Boswell's power of representation he proposes a distinction between factual and fictional works; and he argues that while biography and history might be art, they could only become literature – which the *Life* is – by possessing certain ideal properties:

> Literature in general is, in Coleridge's phrase, that species of composition which proposes pleasure rather than truth as its immediate object. The purely literary artist is free to invent, dispose, weigh, and vivify his or her materials as a means to the greatest intensity of effect, whereas the immediate object of the biographer or historian cannot be effect but fidelity to truth...Factual narratives in order to compass a literary effect must raise their subjects constructively out of the past and represent them to the imagination as concrete, self-intelligible causes of emotion...(p. 25)

This notion of the difference between the "purely literary artist" and the historian or biographer – which is shared by virtually all Boswellians – effectively cuts the ground from under the feet of the biographer. If the biographer writes creatively and profoundly, and successfully conveys the character of his subject and any general human understanding to his reader and to posterity – as Johnson in *Rambler* 60 suggests he must – then, according to Rader, he must be writing something other than biography. The biographer who writes with great literary skill and effectiveness must be either more than a biographer or less than an artist. This generic distinction – which the reader engaged in the act of reading good biography experiences as untrue – suggests an identification between fact and truth. Because confined to the historical and (more dubiously) the material world, fact and truth are then seen as discontinuous from the world of the imagination, which, because of its ideal properties, is untainted by life. This essentially ideal and transcendental notion of art necessarily separates the "effectiveness" *in* the work from the experience *of* the world in its variousness – and leaves "self-intelligibility" and self-referentiality as the tenuous props on which Boswell's portrait of Johnson rests. Seeing Boswell's art as isolated from the experience of the world is fertile ground on which to argue (as Bogel, Dowling, Siebenschuh, and Rader all do) that Boswell presents Johnson's character as transcendent and heroic, and that this is the obvious and most satisfying way of seeing Johnson. Boswellian criticism almost never attempts to establish a correspondence between image, word, and object – between what Boswell says and what Johnson is – assuming that because Boswell says it, Johnson must be it. Johnson's heroism then is the *result of* Boswell's art, which has lifted him out of the supposed materiality of the historical world, which would otherwise have hidden his character from us forever. The deconstructive skepticism of Bogel and Dowling, in this respect, makes no difference to the outcome of their critiques. It is in the elevation above, or idealism within the material world, that Rader, Bogel, and Dowling find the "image" of Johnson which operates as a potent moral, intellectual, and spiritual symbol for successive readers.

The split, in historiographical–biographical theory, between imagination/art and fact/truth – also characteristic of criticism of the *Life* – has, to some extent, been closed by the accounts of historical narrative by Hayden White, Louis Mink, and Paul Ricoeur.[17] But Boswellians respond to the association of truth and fact with a material conception of the historical world – such as that implied by Rader – in one of two ways. Some, such as Bogel, Siebenschuh, and Dowling, adopt the complete skepticism of deconstruction in response to the possibility of being held accountable to a world independent of the text, and argue that not only character but fact and all semblance of an independent reality and logos are linguistically created. Because fact does not lie beyond the text it cannot be invoked as a standard by which Boswell's accuracy can be measured. Because "unmediated presence" – the presence of the "real," hence historical Johnson – is impossible in biography and other linguistic structures, Bogel concludes that truth itself is illusory, a *mere* fiction.

Other scholars, such as Pottle, Brady, Waingrow, and Clifford, adhere to Rader's position but nevertheless believe that Boswell's art is compatible with historical fact. The differences between these two groups are best summed up by Donald Greene. He scrutinizes Boswell's factual accuracy, personal obtrusiveness, and artifice, and asks us to reconsider the truth – as opposed to self-consistency – of Boswell's portrait of Johnson, and suggests that comparison of Boswell with other sources will be important in that process. But though unsympathetic to Boswell, Greene is still unable to make his objections to the more theoretical accounts tell, because he implicitly shares the views of Rader, Bogel, Pottle, and Brady about the nature of art and the differences between it and biography. He is right to challenge Pottle's idea that Boswell's is "literary biography" because it is "not content merely to provide information," yet his argument that the existence of "literariness" in biography is simply a "plea to legitimize falsification by biographers" is obviously inaccurate: "'Imaginative literature' is one thing, biography and history are another. They have a different end, which is most simply stated by the use of a somewhat old-fashioned term, the discovery of the truth."[18]

This mutually exclusive opposition between fiction and the imagination on the one hand, and truth and history on the other, squeezes out truth as a significant concept, as it does the possibility of the *experience* of life which Johnson associated with the finest literature. He wrote of Shakespeare's drama, for example, that "just representations of general nature" facilitated a "repose" of mind on the "stability of truth" ("Preface," I, 61–2). But those Boswellians who divide imagination and truth, and literature and life, are echoing a tension in Boswell's perception of Johnson, and thereby implicitly defining an aspect of Boswell that is fundamentally at odds with Johnson's deepest intuitions about life and art. A serious attempt to understand Johnson (or Boswell, for that matter) biographically or critically could not afford to overlook Johnson's position. For unlike the Coleridge invoked by Rader to illustrate Boswell, Johnson discovers the pleasure of art to have knowledge of life as the content of its form. Although the mind and the world are different – and thinking, language, experience, and truth are not the same (as Johnson's Preface to the *Dictionary*, and many of his other works, make clear) – the literature of general nature discovers an at-oneness of mind and world, in which the *experience* is one of being in momentary possession of a common experience of the human heart, located in history, and larger and more impersonally real than the demands of the ego. Johnson understands that art can structure our quotidian experience so that the truth emerging from the encounter between language and reality has phenomenological independence. As Raymond Tallis remarks, "It is only in judgements on experience, formulated in statements which can then be asserted as facts or told as stories, that reality acquires the status of being in some sense true."[19] That is, a story (literary art) is either a picture of individual or of general human nature (the experience of general nature), or it is nothing (mere reality). True wit, Johnson says, is "at once natural and new," and "that which though not obvious is, upon its first production, acknowledged to be just..."[20]

Boswell tries to confer phenomenological independence on his idea of Johnson: his narrative technique of removing himself as an instrument of mediation between the past and the present (a bridge which will need to be crossed creatively if reality and fact are to become experience and truth), and substituting various narrative personae sometimes described as manipulative,[21] claims the status of unconstructed reality for the artistic image he offers. Boswell has a *need* to claim authenticity for his construction – that this is actually how it was, in the past. That claim assures him of its (and his) unassailability and independence. Bogel argues that Boswell's claim "is not really a critical assertion about the character of the historical order...[but] an investment of faith in the ability to break through the mediacy of one's own life, an ability that Johnson, in his moments of heroic presence, seems to demonstrate."[22] But, in addition, Boswell's is a claim to independence which is fictional in that it accompanies a sense of potential dissolution and insubstantiality, a constant doubt for Boswell that the more he asserted or contrived its reality, the more likely it was to reveal itself as illusory. Hence Boswell's inescapable effort and conscientiousness to incarnate the image he imagined. But this left him caught within the confines of his own self, unable either to comprehend or imagine the truth of the general nature that was the touchstone of Johnson's writing and his character.

III

Boswell's effort to fashion a self while authenticating Johnson – the strengths, the limits, and the contours of his biographical portrayal – manifests itself in his self-absorbed, conscientious involvement. Underlying his dramatic skill and observation of detail is an *idea* of Johnson which governs everything that happens in the *Life*, and which, concomitantly, never leaves Johnson free to reveal himself. This may be seen, for example, in the scenes in which Johnson, Boswell, and others discuss the fear of death. Boswell is constantly pushing Johnson to a decisiveness out of keeping with the inscrutable nature of the subject, in order to satisfy his, Boswell's, own need for certainty: "I ventured to ask him whether, although the words of some texts of Scripture seemed strong in support of the dreadful doctrine of an eternity of punishment, we might not hope that the denunciation was figurative, and would not literally be executed" (III, 200).

Boswell's inclination to fix the extent and nature of judgement hereafter (significantly, by invoking the metaphoric nature of language) predisposes him to miss the subtlety and the substance of the mixture of hope and reasonableness which Johnson offers on the question of the terrors of the future:

> Hope is necessary in every condition. The miseries of poverty, of sickness, of captivity, would, without this comfort, be insupportable; nor does it appear that the happiest lot of terrestrial existence can set us above the want of this general blessing...Hope is, indeed, very fallacious, and promises what it seldom gives; but its promises are more valuable than the gifts of fortune...(*Rambler* 67, I, 354)

Johnson's wisdom lies in neither completely believing nor disbelieving in hope. He is skeptical about it, but ready to turn back into himself, to be skeptical of his skepticism, an action whereby his doubt is transformed into the knowledge that hope is essential to go on actively living and being the self that comes with engagement with the world from that centre – a place (not theoretical or imaginary), a space of in-betweenness. Unlike Hume, whom Boswell liked to place in opposition to Johnson – perhaps as representatives of two unassimilated facets of himself – Johnson establishes a position between skepticism and certainty, in which the strength and the weakness of hope form the limits of what it is to be human. Johnson inculcates that knowledge – the limits of the mind that he *finds* in stretching the mind to its limits – in the very syntax of his style, locating a consciousness feelingly between the general and particular, uncovering levels of experience in the self.[23] This is a truth of the mind, reflected in Johnson's style, also expressed in Johnson's behavior, and becoming part of his character.

But skillful as Boswell's portrayal of Johnson's behavior is, it misses the complex, layered comprehensiveness of Johnson's thought and presence, and therefore misses some truth about Johnson. The famous meeting with Wilkes is an example in kind (III, 64–79). The episode is accepted as an example of Boswell's dramatic skill and ability to persuade us to see exactly and clearly the image of Johnson he wishes to convey; as William Siebenschuh says, "We make whatever details we see in our minds conform to the heroic image of Johnson to which our assent has cumulatively been gained. We see, in part, what we have been made to want to see."[24] And, indeed, the episode is a masterly miniature comic drama, in which, as Ralph Rader sophisticatedly discusses, Boswell creates suspense, heightens tension, introduces several potential difficulties, and finally resolves the episode in a comic conclusion in which Johnson and Wilkes are in harmony and, momentarily, set over against a sacrificial Boswell.[25] Boswell has brought about their harmony and shares a knowledge of Scotland with them that, consequently, separates the three from the rest of the company: "Upon this topick [the barrenness of Scotland] he and Mr. Wilkes could perfectly assimilate; here was a bond of union between them, and I was conscious that as both of them had visited Caledonia, both were fully satisfied of the strange narrow ignorance of those who imagine that it is a land of famine" (III, 77). It is indeed a vivid episode; we feel as if we have been present with Boswell as he witnessed the events.

But the truth of the episode is something other than the vividness of the portrayal: it does not lie in the "fact" that Johnson and Wilkes met at Edward Dilly's home in 1776; nor does it lie in the internal plausibility of Boswell's account. The truth about Johnson in this episode will be something other than Boswell's "idea" of Johnson's character, and Boswell's dramatic prose will have to persuade us to feel that the complexity and richness of character portrayed is how Johnson actually was, independently of this constructed scene – though, of course, this experience of something general and capable of being conveyed to us from beyond the text could only come to us through the text.

It is striking that both Rader and Siebenschuh treat Boswell's prose rhetorically, while nevertheless taking his attitudes, and the judgements of Johnson that they imply, as given. There is no question that what Boswell sees as Johnson's awkwardness and prejudice are given facts, which need to be accepted so that Boswell can artistically depict Johnson transcending his own small-mindedness. Yet these "facts" are themselves the object of Boswell's perception and intellectual make-up. Because Boswellian criticism usually offers no independent sense of how Johnson's mind works – such a sense as one would get from Johnson's works, for example – Boswell's attitudes are taken as being accurately descriptive of Johnson's. Because Boswell can conceive of Johnson's opposition to Wilkes's politics only as a kind of eccentric prejudice to be spirited away by an ingenious trick, we tend to inquire no further into the moral meaning of the episode.

The moral meaning of the episode is located in two areas other than the vividness of the portrayal. The first is in Boswell's clever conduct, the details of which he is keen to present for the reader's appreciation. If what Boswell tells us about Johnson's character in the episode is going to carry any moral weight, his conduct will have to bear the same scrutiny as one friend's behavior towards another. No matter how generously Johnson is finally depicted as behaving, Boswell has nevertheless portrayed him as being manipulated and deceived, as being smaller than Boswell's understanding of his own nature and the situation as a whole, as being a means to Boswell's deliberate, self-aggrandizing performance. Though some readers might not enjoy seeing Johnson cut down to size, Johnson's limitations are not the issue here. For Boswell's deceit and manipulation are directly at odds with friendship, and they make Boswell the centre of attention (in his consciousness and ours), even though it is Johnson at whom we are smiling.

The second aspect of the episode in which its moral meaning is evident is in the dramatic pleasure it conveys. How generous and expansive is the pleasure we feel? How much of ourselves do we discover, as if for the first time, in discovering Johnson to be as Boswell depicts? Is the mind, in Johnson's description of the effect of Shakespeare's drama, able to repose upon the stability of truth? My sense is that the pleasure of Boswell's scene is strictly circumscribed and controlled. The narrator's consciousness is so clearly defined and so separate from the participants in the action and from the reader, that the reader is aware of watching a spectacle, and is unable to make the imaginative and human connection with the scene that Johnson desiderates as essential to imaginative literature of all kinds: "The reflection that strikes the heart is not, that the evils before us are real evils, but that they are evils to which we ourselves may be exposed" ("Preface," I, 78). We do not for a moment feel that we would act like Johnson, nor that there is anything of ourselves in this man, grand as he might be.

Boswell constructs an image of a man towards whom he is at once reverent and controlling:

> I am now to record a very curious incident...which I am persuaded will, with the liberal-minded, be much to his [Johnson's] credit.

> They [Johnson and Wilkes] had even attacked one another with some asperity in their writings; yet I lived in habits of friendship with both. I could fully relish the excellence of each; for I have ever delighted in that intellectual chymistry, which can separate good qualities from evil in the same person.

> Notwithstanding the high veneration which I entertained for Dr. Johnson, I was sensible that he was sometimes a little actuated by the spirit of contradiction... (III, 64–6)

And so on. But Boswell's self-consciousness and his distinctive shaping presence, even when he absents himself as a narrator, make it impossible for reflection to strike the heart, whatever might happen to the eyes and head. What Johnson says of Dryden's comic drama is true of Boswell's:

> the mirth which he excites will perhaps not be found so much to arise from any original humour, or peculiarity of character nicely distinguished and diligently pursued, as from incidents and circumstances, artifices and surprises; from jests of action rather than of sentiment.[26]

Just as Johnson implicitly compares Shakespeare's drama with Dryden's in order to bring out Shakespeare's nature and to suggest the kind of pleasure his drama offers,[27] so we might compare Boswell's with, for example, Shakespeare's Falstaff, and Johnson's response to that creation, in order to discover the thinness of the pleasure in Boswell's portrayal of Johnson in the meeting with Wilkes. The scenes in *Henry IV*, Part I, in which Falstaff's cowardice and bravado are detected, and in which he and Hal take turns to impersonate the King (II.iv, 113–485) – scenes which Johnson thought "supremely comick"[28] – suggest the good humor that Johnson found Falstaff to epitomize. In *Rambler* 72 Johnson calls good humor "a habit of being pleased," or "the act or emanation of a mind at leisure to regard the gratification of another" (IV, 13). It can usually be called into being only by those who do not explicitly claim our admiration or respect and so, confessing or revealing their frail and foolish humanity, make it possible for us to forego the assertion of our individuality and specialness. "We are most inclined to love when we have nothing to fear" (*Rambler* 72, II, 15). It is Falstaff's good humor which "contains" the apparently contradictory responses Johnson has to him:

> But Falstaff, unimitated, unimitable Falstaff, how shall I describe thee? Thou compound of sense and vice; of sense which may be admired but not esteemed, of vice which may be despised, but hardly detested. Falstaff is a character loaded with faults, and with those faults which naturally produce

contempt. He is a thief, and a glutton, a coward, and a boaster, always ready to cheat the weak, and prey upon the poor; to terrify the timorous and insult the defenceless. At once obsequious and malignant, he satirises in their absence those whom he lives by flattering... Yet the man thus corrupt, thus despicable, makes himself necessary to the prince that despises him, by the most pleasing of all qualities, perpetual gaiety, by an unfailing power of exciting laughter, which is the more freely indulged, as his wit is not of the splendid or ambitious kind, but consists in easy escapes and sallies of levity, which make sport but raise no envy...[29]

"The generosity of this," as G. F. Parker remarks, "lies in the way that our knowledge of Falstaff is felt to be a kind of self-discovery: if it is our contempt for Falstaff that allows us to enjoy him in the first place, that enjoyment tells us something about ourselves which overturns our sense of superiority even as we come to feel it – hence the fine discriminations of 'admired but not esteemed...despised, but hardly detested'" (pp. 48–9). Our sense of separateness *and* solidarity with a character who combines such powerfully different qualities, such despicable and such lovable qualities, is a mark of the expansion of self that Shakespeare's drama occasions, and the easy pleasure that Johnson's prose expresses is a celebration of the common humanity that he finds there.

Johnson is a man for whom we commonly do not feel the contempt that Falstaff arouses (though isn't there a kind of contemptuousness in Boswell's predatoriness in the Wilkes episode? – "I exulted as much as a fortune-hunter who has got an heiress into a post-chaise with him to set out for Gretna-Green" [III, 68]). Boswell's portrait, however, gives us none of the density and the complexity of feeling, or the resulting pleasure, or love – and, therefore, no sense of self-discovery that comes with self-acceptance – that Johnson finds and exhibits in writing of Falstaff.[30] How much love do we feel for Johnson when depicted in the midst of his embarrassment at being caught out? We may compare Shakespeare and Boswell:

PRINCE: What trick, what device, what starting hole canst thou now find out to hide thee from this open and apparent shame?
POINS: Come, let's hear, Jack. What trick hast thou now?
FALSTAFF: By the Lord, I knew ye as well as he that made ye. Why, hear you, masters. Was it for me to kill the heir apparent? (*Henry IV*, Pt. I; II. iv, 263–70)

When we entered Mr. Dilly's drawing room, he [Johnson] found himself in the midst of a company he did not know. I kept myself snug and silent, watching how he would conduct himself. I observed him whispering to Mr. Dilly, "Who is that gentleman, Sir?" – "Mr. Arthur Lee." – JOHNSON. "Too, too, too," (under his breath,) which was one of his habitual mutterings... "And who is the gentleman in lace?" – "Mr. Wilkes, Sir." This information confounded him still more; he had some difficulty to restrain himself, and taking up a book, sat down upon a window-seat and read, or at least kept his eye upon it intently for some time, till he composed himself. His feelings, I dare say, were aukward enough. But he no doubt recollected his having rated me for supposing that he could be at all disconcerted by any company, and he, therefore, resolutely set himself to behave quite as an easy man of the world...(III, 68)

Johnson's expansiveness and humor – which he may or may not have indulged more fully on the occasion as it actually happened in 1776 – were aspects of his personality, and components of his understanding of general nature, to which Boswell was not drawn. This is clear in comparing Boswell's description of Johnson's tale of Bet Flint with Fanny Burney's. This is a moment when Johnson displays Falstaffian humor. Boswell's very brief scene registers the impropriety of the connection between Johnson and Bet Flint, and places Johnson above the lady:

He gave us an entertaining account of *Bet Flint*, a woman of the town, who, with some eccentrick talents and much effrontery, forced herself upon his acquaintance. (IV, 103)

Burney, by contrast, conveys the warmth and human contact Johnson apparently expressed when he told his tale in her hearing, and which the young diarist thought "would have made you die with laughing, his manner is so peculiar, and enforces his humor so originally." While Boswell has Johnson tell a tale of Bet Flint's vices and eccentricities ("I used to say of her that she was generally slut and drunkard; occasionally, whore and thief," IV, 103), Burney – without eliminating any aspect of Bet Flint's notoriety – conveys a sense of Johnson relishing the woman's humanity: "Oh, I loved Bet Flint!"[31]

This suggests that Boswell evades Johnson's good humor, and so misses an essential truth of his nature, because – in the words of *Rambler* 72 – his "mind is not at leisure to regard the gratification of another"; Boswell's own gratification is uppermost because his own idea of Johnson is so important to him. "We are most inclined to love when we have nothing to fear"; but because Boswell revered rather than loved Johnson, perhaps feared that his needs were too great to be upheld by the ordinary man in the hero whose life he writes, his portrayal constantly claims our admiration and notice. According to *Rambler* 72, the search for admiration – in effect, narcissism – destroys good humor, and imprisons us within our individual selves. Boswell's self-consciousness in the *Life*, I suggest, is directly related to his search for certainty, and hence to a need to control in matters in which certainty and control are impossible. There are many instances in the *Life* in which Johnson is called upon to reassure Boswell of his affection. Writing of the anxiety brought about by the fear of a future which we cannot *certainly* know will be bad, Johnson remarks, penetratingly, that "anxiety of this kind is nearly of the same nature with jealousy in love" (*Rambler* 29, I, 160). It would be an obvious (though not nugatory) psychoanalytical truth to observe that Boswell's reverence and idealization of Johnson has at its roots a need to be loved by his father, just as it would to note that the spiritual and teleological certainty of Calvinism is being displaced on to men of public authority and articulation (Paoli, Rousseau, Hume, Johnson), but at the same time having its horrors cemented into place by finding the ideals of those men untranslatable into practice, the uncertainties of the future unable to be fixed in thought or language. Like William Dubin, in Bernard Malamud's *Dubin's Lives*, Boswell sometimes gives the impression that "You write muckspout lives because you fear you have no life to live."[32] But in making his portrait of Johnson, and playing himself off against this man whom Boswell had invested with all his own ideals, the biographer is trying to articulate himself, to make real a life too often given to fictionalizing. In other words, in the absence of the love of God and of the father, he is trying to love himself. It is sadly ironic, therefore, that the effort to keep Johnson present in biography and via memory, as a guarantor of Boswell's own empowerment, is conducted in a prose which inevitably undercuts its own aims. It is a prose which encourages an inwardness and illusion of self-sufficiency, and, unlike Johnson's *Rambler* style – constantly moving between different levels of experience and from inside to outside, and outside to inside – Boswell's builds into itself a smoothness and privacy which closes it to falsification, and therefore to confirmation, subtly evading not only the challenge to its propositions but even the thought of challenge. It is significant that Rader turns to Coleridge to define the pleasure of Boswell's prose; but Coleridge also quoted Sir John Davies's view of the soul to illustrate the substancelessness of that experience:

> Doubtless this could not be, but that she turns
> Bodies to spirit by sublimation strange,
> As fire converts to fire the things it burns,
> As we our food into our nature change.[33]

Despite the many "factual" features of the *Life* – conversations, reports, letters, narration, action – Boswell's account of Johnson remains internal and unrealized, constantly striving and constantly failing to make Johnson present in the way Boswell desired. *Pace* Sir John Davies, Johnson is the food that feeds and is transformed by Boswell's nature from other into self.[34] Boswell's psychic undernourishment, his symbiotic identification with Johnson – as if Johnson were both father and mother – means that he is unable to let Johnson die, and unable fundamentally to countenance and accept the possibility of his own death. The death of the father, and absence of the mother, threaten death of the ego.

IV

The last five months of Johnson's life, from Boswell's last leave-taking to Johnson's death, comprise about 100 pages in the Hill–Powell edition. In these pages Boswell *twice* goes over the approach to Johnson's death, on both occasions (the first comprising pages 337–98 of Volume IV, the second pages 398–419) marking significant last events (such as Johnson's last visit to Lichfield) and specific periods before Johnson's death (e.g., "About eight or ten days before his death...," "three or four days only before his death..."). This double attempt at recording and accepting Johnson's death is emotionally interesting. The entire section is, understandably, elegiac – a tone covering feelings Boswell described as "most difficult and dangerous" (IV, 398).[35] The first part of this section opens with an especially poignant depiction of the last parting of Johnson and Boswell, in which Boswell's view is consciously retrospective, feelingly aware of the distance between now and then, and therefore adding significance to that past moment:

> He asked me whether I would go with him to his house; I declined it, from an apprehension that my spirits would sink. We bade adieu to each other affectionately in the carriage. When he had got down upon the foot-pavement, he called out, "Fare you well"; and without looking back, sprung away with a kind of pathetick briskness, if I may use that expression, which seemed to indicate a struggle to conceal uneasiness, and impressed me with a foreboding of our long, long separation. (IV, 339)

The struggle and uneasiness, of course, are Boswell's, and the pain and foreboding of June 30, 1784 are being assimilated and perhaps accepted by the recollection of 1791.

But the transformation takes an unusual turn, for after defending Johnson's moral integrity, once again, against any possibility of his being misunderstood by the public, and after recording (at the end of the second part of this large concluding section) the dignity of Johnson's last moments, Boswell mentions Johnson's burial in a tone of condescension and aggressive independence:

> A few days before his death, he had asked Sir John Hawkins, as one of his executors, where he should be buried; and on being answered "Doubtless, in Westminster-Abbey," seemed to feel a satisfaction, very natural to a Poet; and indeed, in my opinion, very natural to every man of any imagination, who has no family sepulchre in which he can be laid with his fathers. (IV, 419)

Boswell has that family sepulchre, though the painful identification with and exaggerated independence from Johnson that run on together, and mark the concluding pages of the *Life*, suggest that his sepulchre was empty of fathers.

One of the powers of love lies in its capacity both to recall and to undo the past – in psychoanalytical terms, to find in the beloved both stimulation to recall one's earliest experiences, and a desire to have him or her compensate for all the earliest emotional and psychic deprivations. But Boswell's reverence for Johnson points to his difficulty in completely accepting Johnson's death. Incapacity to accept is in fact related to the difficulty in recalling Johnson. Acceptance presupposes a self – a love of self which accepts its limits, its feelings, its own potential death. Paradoxically, acceptance would also be the clearest expression of Boswell's love for Johnson the man, and so the condition on which he, Johnson, could be recalled, and Boswell-as-biographer be defined. Boswell's difficulty in letting Johnson go, then, is proportionate to the difficulty in recalling him. The great spiritual and ontological significance that he places on Johnson's presence, so fully discussed in modern criticism, is another way of noting Boswell's fixation on the body which psychically accompanies the related struggle for selfhood and for independence:

> I tell every body it [the *Life*] will be an Egyptian Pyramid in which there will be a compleat mummy of Johnson that Literary Monarch. (Letter to Anna Seward, April 30, 1785)

> it is my design in writing the Life of that Great and Good Man, to put as it were into a Mausoleum all the precious remains that I can gather. (Letter to Joseph Cooper Walker, July 1, 1785)[36]

Consequently some essential part of Johnson's character escapes recall.

Although Boswell's portrait may be authentic, its truth is not commensurate. Johnson knows that language and experience are not identical, but that the relation of the one to the other can connect human experience to a reality apparently beyond the power of mere words. He knows that the only way a man can be made present after death is through the transformation of the ego and the channelling of memory. The *Lives of the Poets* do not suffer from the ineffectiveness characteristic of the *Life*. Strictly speaking Johnson has no idea of the poets whose lives he depicts, and he has no need to identify with them emotionally. While he accepts the man's mortality as part of nature – a debt owed – and treats the significant events of his life on their own terms in one section of the work, and discusses the man's poetry on its terms in another section of the work, the character of the man – what might be described as the man's truth – is not striven for, but is allowed to come into focus in the encounter between life and work which the structure of the *Lives*, and the transforming love of Johnson's thought, effect. Hence, the character of Pope or Dryden or Milton in the *Lives* is not felt to be personal in any narrow sense (despite, for example, Johnson's antagonism to Milton the man) – even while these characters have come into being as a result of personal statements of judgement and experience by Johnson at every stage. For in Johnson's capacity to see life and art as continuous though different, within the framework of general nature, he discovers the human revelatory powers of literature represented by the works of the poets who form his subject. This is a more significant difference between Johnson and Boswell than has been noticed. The integral presence of an "independent" aspect of a man's life in the *Lives*, in which the poet speaks for his own deepest intuitions and understanding of life through his art, gives a sense of permanence and truth to Johnson's portraits. The story Johnson tells of the lives of his poets is not likely to veer off into fiction, partly because the poet has contributed, in the most profound and impersonal way, to the telling of his own story. We do not have the historical Dryden (or Pope or Milton) before us, but what Johnson's fictional account of their lives has discovered is felt to be true for these individual poets, because true for humanity in general. "A story is a picture either of an individual or of human nature in general" – of an individual *because* of human nature in general. That general truth is facilitated by the active inclusion of the poet's works in the structure of Johnson's thought. It is the absence of such a structure that makes the *Life of Savage* the most Boswellian of Johnson's biographies, depriving it of the creative tension we find in the *Lives*, and making it more obviously a fiction, an allegory for the struggles and moral passion of Johnson's own life.

But it never seriously occurs to Boswell that what, in the nineteenth century, Hallam Tennyson found true of his father may also be so for Boswell's relation to his spiritual father: "besides the letters of my father and of his friends there are his poems, and in these we must look for the innermost sanctuary of his being. For my own part, I feel strongly that no biographer could so truly give him as he gives himself in his own works."[37] Johnson's works are not integral to Boswell's portrait of Johnson, because their indeterminacy and their experiential range and depth leave them beyond Boswell's capacity to control, willfully to make his own image. His critical comments on Johnson's works are commonplace: indeed, mummification would find Johnson's thought as embodied in his own language too resistant to assimilation. Fine as Boswell's final character of Johnson is, it cannot carry the weight of Johnson's character as articulated through his own writing:

> In proportion to the native vigour of the mind, the contradictory qualities will be the more prominent, and more difficult to be adjusted...
>
> As he was general and unconfined in his studies...he had accumulated a vast and various collection of learning and knowledge, which was so arranged in his mind as to be ever in readiness to be brought forth. But his superiority over other learned men consisted chiefly in what may be called the art of thinking, the art of using his mind...(IV, 426, 427–8)

These sentiments require Johnson's writing – the substance of his experience in his thought and his syntax – to reveal the meaning and the truth they aim to convey. For it is only in his writing, at a point at which mind meets world, and the individual self and general nature become one, that the "contradictory qualities" will be seen to be more than authentic eccentricities, to constitute more than the contours of one individual mind. Johnson will then be demonstrating the "art of using his mind." Boswell knew that "In biography there can be no question that he [Johnson] excelled, beyond all who have attempted that species of composition" (I, 256).

Yet Boswell could not enlist Johnson's achievement in support of his own major undertaking. He thought he had to do it alone, and therefore maintained a reverent posture in place of the love he sought and needed. The *Life* ends on this note and, literally, with this word: "Such was SAMUEL JOHNSON, a man whose talents, acquirements, and virtues, were so extraordinary, that the more his character is considered, the more he will be regarded by the present age, and by posterity, with admiration and reverence" (IV, 430). For the reader who follows Boswell's rhetorical and emotional trajectory, the declaration which ends the *Life* is accurate: according to Boswell's design, Johnson will be admired and revered. But Boswell's fate is more problematic. In contrast to Johnson's attitude towards Boswell – an inextricable mixture of love, friendly exasperation, and clear judgement – we tend either to valorize the peculiarities and eccentricities of Boswell's sensibility, or to judge him harshly for them and for the art to which they gave rise. Both modern attitudes indicate a reluctance to recognize those same human weaknesses in ourselves. Boswell – so good at playing the clown – is an ideal sacrifice for our unacknowledged and unassimilated self-fashioning anxieties. But perhaps it is this aspect of the *Life* which appeals above all to modern readers – the unbroken circle of psychological striving for realization and the constant threat of dissolution.

NOTES

1 I should like to thank the editors of *English* for permission to adapt parts of my review article, "Boswell and Literary Biography," *English*, 36 (1987), 168–78. I wish to thank Yale University Press for permission to quote from the *Complete Works* of Samuel Johnson (individual texts cited in full below). All references to *Life* are included in the text.

2 *Corr: Life*, pp. 96, 111–12, 146. Boswell wishes to capture the moral and linguistic impressiveness of Pascal Paoli by resorting to the same imagery: "This uttered with the fine open Italian pronunciation, and the graceful dignity of his manner, was very noble. I wished to have a statue of him taken at that moment" (*Account of Corsica*, p. 297).

3 See Frederick A. Pottle, "The *Life of Johnson*: Art and Authenticity," in *Twentieth-Century Interpretations of Boswell's Life of Johnson*, ed. James L. Clifford (Englewood Cliffs: Prentice-Hall, 1970), pp. 66–73 (this work subsequently cited as *Twentieth-Century Interpretations*); Geoffrey Scott, "The Making of the

Life of Johnson as Shown in Boswell's First Notes," in *Twentieth-Century Interpretations*, pp. 27–39; Marshall Waingrow, *Corr: Life*, pp. xxi–li; William R. Siebenschuh, "Boswell's Second Crop of Memory: A New Look at the Role of Memory in the Making of the *Life*," in *New Questions, New Answers*, pp. 94–109.

4 Boswell's thought is similar to Bolingbroke's historiography (*Letters on the Study and Use of History*, 1752) in proposing, first, a tension between the instructive and the affective aspects of history, and, then (in Boswell's *Life* and in Bolingbroke's *Letters*, Nos. 5–8), in accepting that the moral force of history (the authenticity of character, in Boswell's terminology) need have no foundation in fact. *Cf.* D. J. Womersley, "Lord Bolingbroke and Eighteenth-Century Historiography," *The Eighteenth Century: Theory and Interpretation*, 28 (1987), 217–34.

5 "Preface to Shakespeare," *Johnson on Shakespeare*, ed. Arthur Sherbo, introduction by Bertrand H. Bronson, 2 vols. (New Haven and London: Yale University Press, 1968), I, 60. (This work is subsequently cited as "Preface" and, for other works in the edition, as *Johnson on Shakespeare*.) For further discussion of Johnson on Homer see Greg Clingham, "Johnson, Homeric Scholarship, and 'the Passes of the Mind,'" in *The Age of Johnson*, ed. Paul J. Korshin, III (New York: AMS Press, 1990), pp. 113–70.

6 *The Rambler*, ed. W. J. Bate and Albrecht B. Strauss, 3 vols. (New Haven: Yale University Press, 1969), I, 318. (Cited subsequently as *Rambler*, and page numbers included in text.)

7 *The Lives of the English Poets*, ed. G. B. Hill, 3 vols. (Oxford: Clarendon Press, 1905), "Life of Cowley," I, 20.

8 The first phrase comes from *Idler* 84, *The Idler and The Adventurer*, ed. W. J. Bate, John M. Bullitt and L. F. Powell (New Haven: Yale University Press, 1963), p. 262; the second phrase, quoted by Boswell, comes from *Rambler* 60, p. 323.

9 Maximillian E. Novak notes that Boswell's manner is closer to the realistic novels of Defoe and Richardson than to Johnson's *Lives*; see "James Boswell's *Life of Johnson*," in *The Biographer's Art: New Essays*, ed. Jeffrey Meyers (London: Macmillan, 1989), p. 50.

10 See the works by Pottle, Scott, and Waingrow cited in note 3; Clifford's introduction to *Twentieth-Century Interpretations*; and *Later Years*, pp. 331–2.

11 William R. Siebenschuh, *Fictional Techniques and Factual Works* (Athens: University of Georgia Press, 1983), chapters 3 and 4; Ralph R. Rader, "Literary Form in Factual Narrative: The Example of Boswell's *Johnson*," in *New Questions, New Answers*, pp. 25–52 (also published in *Essays in Eighteenth-Century Biography*, edited with an introduction by Philip B. Daghlian [Bloomington: Indiana University Press, 1968], pp. 3–42); William C. Dowling, *The Boswellian Hero* (Athens: University of Georgia Press, 1979); Fredric V. Bogel, *Literature and Insubstantiality in Later Eighteenth-Century England* (Princeton: Princeton University Press, 1984), pp. 173–90, and "'Did you once see Johnson plain?': Reflections on Boswell's *Life* and the state of Eighteenth-Century Studies," in *New Questions, New Answers*, pp. 73–93. By using the word "group" of these and other Boswell Scholars I do not wish to imply that there is any conscious collaboration.

12 See notes 3 and 11, and *Later Years*, pp. 423–39.

13 *Twentieth-Century Interpretations*, p. 10.

14 *New Questions, New Answers*, p. 28 (I subsequently cite page numbers in the text). The quotations from Rader and Greene (below) reprinted with permission from the University of Georgia Press (Copyright 1985).

15 Brady, for example, thinks that the *Life* is unified by Boswell's sensibility (*Later Years*, pp. 442–3).

16 See Donald Greene, "'Tis a Pretty Book, Mr. Boswell, But – ," and "Boswell's *Life* as 'Literary Biography,'" both in *New Questions, New Answers*, pp. 110–46 and 161–71. See also Greene's "The Uses of Autobiography in the Eighteenth Century," in *Essays in Eighteenth-Century Biography*, pp. 43–66.

17 See Hayden White, *Tropics of Discourse* (Baltimore: Johns Hopkins University Press, 1978) and *The Content of the Form* (Baltimore: Johns Hopkins University Press, 1987); Louis O. Mink, *Historical Understanding*, ed. Brian Fay, Eugene O. Golob, and Richard T. Vann (Ithaca: Cornell University Press, 1987); and Paul Ricoeur, *Time and Narrative*, trans. K. McLaughlin and D. Pellauer, 2 vols. (Chicago: Chicago University Press, 1984–6).

18 "'Tis a Pretty Book, Mr. Boswell, But – ," in *New Questions, New Answers*, p. 129.

19 "As if there could be such things as true stories," *The Cambridge Quarterly*, 15 (1986), 103. For an extended discussion of Johnson and general nature, see G. F. Parker, *Johnson's Shakespeare* (Oxford: Clarendon Press, 1989); and Clingham, "Johnson, Homeric Scholarship, and the 'passes of the mind,'" *passim*.

20 "Life of Cowley," *Lives*, I, 20, par. 55.

21 See, for example, Paul K. Alkon, "Boswell's Control of Aesthetic Distance," in *Twentieth-Century Interpretations*, pp. 51–65.

22 "Did you once see Johnson plain?," *New Questions, New Answers*, p. 77.

23 See Philip Davis, *In Mind of Johnson: A Study of Johnson the Rambler* (Athens: Georgia University Press, 1989), pp. 104–19.

24 Siebenschuh, *Fictional Techniques*, p. 68.

25 See Rader, "Literary Form in Factual Narrative," *New Questions, New Answers*, pp. 39–43; and Siebenschuh, *Fictional Techniques*, pp. 68–70.

26 "Life of Dryden," par. 329, *Lives of the English Poets*, I, 459.

27 "It will not easily be imagined how much Shakespeare excells in accommodating his sentiments to real life, but by comparing him with other authours..." ("Preface to Shakespeare," I, 63, also 64–5).

28 Note to the play, *Johnson on Shakespeare*, I, 472. In what follows I am indebted to Parker's *Johnson's Shakespeare*, pp. 47–51. Permission to quote from Parker granted by Oxford University Press.

29 Note to the play, *Johnson on Shakespeare*, I, 523.

30 See *Rambler* 72, II, 15.

31 *Diary and Letters of Madame D'Arblay*, ed. Charlotte Barrett, 4 vols. (London: George Bell, 1891), I, 41, 42–3.

32 *Dubin's Lives* (Harmondsworth: Penguin, 1979), p. 352.

33 S. T. Coleridge, *Biographia Literaria*, ed. J. Shawcross, 2 vols. (Oxford: Oxford University Press, 1907), II, 12–13. Coleridge actually quotes three stanzas from *Nosce Teipsum, The Poems of Sir John Davies*, ed. Robert Krueger (Oxford: Clarendon Press, 1975), "Of the Soule of Man, and the Immortalitie thereof," 537–48.

34 While in the Hebrides Boswell reflects:

I was elated by the thought of having been able to entice such a man to this remote part of the world. . . I compared myself to a dog who has got hold of a large piece of meat, and runs away with it to a corner, where he may devour it in peace, without any fear of others taking it from him. "In London, Reynolds, Beauclerk, and all of them, are contending who shall enjoy Dr. Johnson's conversation. We are feasting upon it, undisturbed, at Dunvegan." (*Life*, v, 215).

As Donna Heiland argues earlier in this book, it is central to the imaginative structure of the *Life* that Boswell is metonymically related to Johnson as parasite to host. It may also be said that the relation of the *Life* (1791) to the *Tour* (1785) is of a similar kind, the later work feeding off the earlier: in presenting Johnson's "conversation" (artistically fashioned by Boswell) more abundantly than the *Tour*, the *Life* aims to possess and consume Johnson, in much the way Boswell imagines himself doing in the passage above.

35 When parting from Paoli in Corsica Boswell says: "I dare not transcribe from my private notes the feelings which I had at this interview. I should perhaps appear too enthusiastick" (*Account of Corsica*, p. 351).

36 See *Corr: Life*, pp. 96, 111–12.

37 *Alfred Lord Tennyson: A Memoir By His Son*, 2 vols. (London: Macmillan, 1897), I, xi.

INDEX

Gramley Library
Salem College
Winston-Salem, NC 27108